# CAMBRIDGE STUDIES IN ENGLISH LEGAL HISTORY

## FUNDAMENTAL AUTHORITY IN LATE MEDIEVAL ENGLISH LAW

This book seeks to reconstruct basic ideas about the nature of law and its fundamental authority as found in the literature of late medieval legal theory and practice. These ideas are drawn from the Year Books, parliamentary statutes and ordinances, local customary law and the largely Thomist legal theory of Reginald Pecock and John Fortescue. The views of these theorists are set against those of their English and continental civilian and canonist predecessors and contemporaries. The period covered, broadly that of the fifteenth century, is one in which a basic tension emerges, in both legal theory and practice, between two sets of ideas.

From one perspective human law derives its authority from a divinely created morality: in legal theory, the specific concepts of natural law and justice. This surfaces in actual law when practitioners dispose of cases and problems by using conscience, divine law and reason. These concepts are persistently used to shape and justify law and legal decisions on both substantive and formal levels. The alternative outlook treats the human will, and not an abstract morality, as the force which shapes law. Popular consent and usage supply the authority for law and legal decisions. Late medieval legal theory supposes that humanly created rules are laws even when they depart from abstract ideas of right and wrong. In addition, legislation and judicial practice explicitly treated as against conscience or as producing mischief nevertheless retained the status of laws. It is this view which culminates in the classical positivist thesis of modern jurisprudence.

NORMAN DOE is a Lecturer in Law at the University of Wales College of Cardiff.

# CAMBRIDGE STUDIES
# IN ENGLISH LEGAL HISTORY

Edited by
J. H. BAKER
*Fellow of St Catharine's College, Cambridge*


*Recent series titles include*
The Law of Treason in England in the Later Middle Ages
J. G. BELLAMY
William Sheppard, Cromwell's Law Reformer
NANCY L. MATTHEWS
The English Judiciary in the age of Glanvill and Bracton *c.*1176–1239
RALPH V. TURNER
Pettyfoggers and Vipers of the Commonwealth
The 'Lower Branch' of the Legal Profession in Early Modern England
CHRISTOPHER W. BROOKS
Sir William Scott, Lord Stowell
Judge of the High Court of Admiralty, 1798–1828
HENRY J. BOURGUIGNON
Sir Henry Maine
A Study in Victorian Jurisprudence
R. C. J. COCKS
Roman Canon Law in Reformation England
R. H. HELMHOLZ

# FUNDAMENTAL AUTHORITY IN LATE MEDIEVAL ENGLISH LAW

NORMAN DOE
*Lecturer in Law*
*University of Wales College of Cardiff*

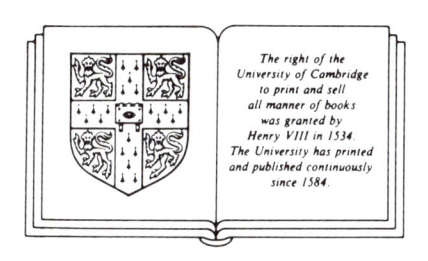

CAMBRIDGE UNIVERSITY PRESS

CAMBRIDGE
NEW YORK   PORT CHESTER
MELBOURNE   SYDNEY

Published by the Press Syndicate of the University of Cambridge
The Pitt Building, Trumpington Street, Cambridge CB2 1RP
40 West 20th Street, New York, NY 10011, USA
10 Stamford Road, Oakleigh, Melbourne 3166, Australia

© Cambridge University Press 1990

First published 1990

Printed in Great Britain by
Redwood Press Limited, Melksham, Wiltshire

*British Library cataloguing in publication data*
Doe, Norman
Fundamental authority in late medieval English law. –
(Cambridge studies in English legal history)
1. England. Law, history
I. Title
344.2′009

*Library of Congress cataloguing in publication data*
Doe, Norman.
Fundamental authority in late medieval English law / Norman Doe.
p. cm. – (Cambridge studies in English legal history)
Includes bibliographical references.
ISBN 0 521 38458 3
1. Law – Great Britain – History and criticism. I. Title.
II. Series.
KD612.D64 1990
349.42 – dc20
[344.2] 89–71312 CIP

ISBN 0 521 38458 3

For Heather, Rachel and Elizabeth

CONTENTS

| | | |
|---|---|---|
| *Preface* | | ix |
| *List of abbreviations* | | xi |
| *List of statutes and ordinances* | | xiv |
| *List of Year Book cases* | | xvii |
| | Introduction | 1 |
| 1 | Authority and consent: the populist thesis | 7 |
| 2 | Human law: the positivist thesis | 33 |
| 3 | Natural law: the superior moral law | 60 |
| 4 | *Iustitia, rigor iuris* and *aequitas* | 84 |
| 5 | Judicial decisions and the authority of reason | 108 |
| 6 | Conscience in the common law | 132 |
| 7 | Mischief and inconvenience | 155 |
| | Conclusion | 175 |
| | *Bibliography* | 180 |
| | *Index* | 189 |

# PREFACE

The materials considered in this book originally formed part of a doctoral thesis submitted to the University of Cambridge. I should like to express my thanks to my supervisors at Cambridge: to Professor S. F. C. Milsom, who has worked so hard in guiding me, and giving me invaluable assistance in the analysis and refinement of my materials, particularly the Year Books; and the late Professor Walter Ullmann, whose writings first stimulated my interest in medieval legal theory and who encouraged me to commence my studies at Cambridge. Thanks are also due to Professor J. H. Baker, Professor A. W. B. Simpson and Professor J. H. Burns for their important suggestions for improvement and painstaking scrutiny of the piece. I should like to record my gratitude to the Catherine and Lady Grace James Foundation, Aberystwyth, to the Anna Kroch Foundation, Manchester, and to the Master and Fellows of Magdalene College, Cambridge, for their generosity in providing financial support which enabled me to study and teach at Cambridge whilst carrying out the research for this work. I wish to give special acknowledgment to the staff of both the University Library and the Squire Law Library at Cambridge, for their constant and cheerful assistance, and to the staff at the Seeley Historical Library, Cambridge, the libraries of St John's and Trinity College, Cambridge, and the University of Wales College of Cardiff Humanities Library, for their help in making sources available.

It was Thomas G. Watkin who first introduced me to legal history at University College, Cardiff, and nurtured my interest from undergraduate days: I owe a particular debt to him for his encouragement and inspiration. I also owe a great deal, in clarifying and helping to formulate my thoughts, to countless conversations with many friends with expertise in a variety of disciplines, within and outside law – especially Richard Bartlett, Edward Curran, Donald Keir, John

Morison, Simon Leach, John Lodge and Paul Richardson. Special thanks I give to my brother Martin, also a lawyer, who typed up tirelessly the many drafts necessary in the early days of the work. Latterly, with word-processing, I have been given invaluable help by Alan Mayer, and, in organising footnotes, by Catrin Williams. I wish to thank, in addition, Professor J. H. Baker, the editor of the series Cambridge Studies in English Legal History, and the staff of the Cambridge University Press for their assistance and patience with the typescript.

Finally, I should like to thank my family – my mother and father (in giving his guidance with the French and Latin), from whom I first learnt the patience to persevere with studying, and for their influence upon me and constant support over the years; to my parents-in-law, always ready to show interest and encouragement; and, for her willingness to accept the medieval lawyers and their ideas into our home, my wife Heather who, trained in medicine and disposed to lucidity, has been of great help in reading the piece and suggesting ways of making the text more succinct. I accept full responsibility for any errors or misunderstanding in the book.

# ABBREVIATIONS

Complete citations are to be found in the bibliography.

| | |
|---|---|
| *AJLH* | *American Journal of Legal History* |
| Brooke, *GA*. | Robert Brooke, *Graunde Abridgement* (1573) |
| CB | Chief Baron of the Exchequer Chamber |
| *CH* | T. F. T. Plucknett, *Concise History of the Common Law* (5th edition, 1956) |
| CJCP | Chief Justice of the Common Pleas |
| CJKB | Chief Justice of the King's Bench |
| *CLJ* | *Cambridge Law Journal* |
| Co. Litt. | Sir Edward Coke, *The First Part of the Institutes of the Laws of England* (1628), a commentary on Littleton's *Tenures* |
| *Decretum* | Gratian, *Decretum* (or *A Concordance of Discordant Canons*) (*c*. 1140) |
| *De Laudibus* | Fortescue, *De Laudibus Legum Angliae* (1468–71) |
| *De Legibus* | Bracton, *De Legibus et Consuetudinibus Angliae* (*c*. 1220–40) |
| *De Natura* | Fortescue, *De Natura Legis Nature* (*c*. 1463) |
| *De Rep*. | Thomas Smith, *De Republica Anglorum* (1583) |
| *Dialogue* | Saint German, *Dialogue Between a Doctor of Divinity and a Student of the Common Law* (1528–31) |
| *DNB* | *Dictionary of National Biography* |
| *Donet* | Pecock, *The Donet* (*c*. 1443–9) |
| *DP* | Marsilius of Padua, *Defensor Pacis* (1324) |
| *EHR* | *English Historical Review* |
| *Faith* | Pecock, *Book of Faith* (1456) |

| | |
|---|---|
| Fifoot, *Sources* | C. H. S. Fifoot, *History and Sources of the Common Law: Tort and Contract* (sixth impression, 1969) |
| Fitzherbert, *GA* | Anthony Fitzherbert, *Le Graunde Abridgement* (1577) |
| *Folower* | Pecock, *Folower to the Donet* (c. 1453) |
| *Governance* | Fortescue, *The Governance of England* (c. 1471) |
| *HCLC* | A. W. B. Simpson, *A History of the Common Law of Contract* (1975) |
| *HFCL* | S. F. C. Milsom, *Historical Foundations of the Common Law* (2nd edition, 1981) |
| Holdsworth | W. S. Holdsworth, *A History of English Law* (1922–66) |
| *IELH* | J. H. Baker, *An Introduction to English Legal History* (2nd edition, 1979) |
| *Inst.* | Justinian's *Institutes* |
| JCP | Justice of the Common Pleas |
| JKB | Justice of the King's Bench |
| *JLH* | *Journal of Legal History* |
| LC | Lord Chancellor |
| *LEP* | Richard Hooker, *The Laws of Ecclesiastical Polity* (1594) |
| *LPMA* | W. Ullmann, *Law and Politics in the Middle Ages* (1975) |
| *LQR* | *Law Quarterly Review* |
| *MED* | *Middle English Dictionary* |
| *Mirror* | *The Mirror of Justices* (anonymous, thirteenth century) |
| *MPT* | R. W. and A. J. Carlyle, *A History of Mediaeval Political Theory in the West* (1903–36) |
| Oakley | F. Oakley, *The Political Thought of Pierre D'Ailly* (1964) |
| *OED* | *Oxford English Dictionary* |
| Pascoe | L. B. Pascoe, *Jean Gerson: Principles of Church Reform* (1973) |
| P&M | F. Pollock, and F. W. Maitland, *The History of English Law Before the Time of Edward I* (2nd edn. 1898, reissued 1968) |
| *PGP* | W. Ullmann, *Principles of Government and Politics in the Middle Ages* (1961) |

| | |
|---|---|
| Port, *Notebook* | Sir John Port, *Notebook* (1493–1535) |
| *Repressor* | Pecock, *The Repressor of Over Much Blaming of the Clergy* (1449–55) |
| *Reule* | Pecock, *The Reule of Crysten Religioun* (1443) |
| Sel. Soc. | Selden Society |
| Srjt | Serjeant-at-Law |
| Sigmund | P. E. Sigmund, *Nicholas of Cusa and Medieval Political Thought* (1963) |
| *Summa* | Aquinas, *Summa Theologiae* (1265–73) |
| *Tenures* | Littleton, *Tenures* (c. 1480) |
| *Works* | *The Works of Sir John Fortescue* (1869) |
| YB | Year Book |

# LIST OF STATUTES AND ORDINANCES

52 Hen. III, c.3 30 n.109
52 Hen. III, c.14 16 n.45
3 Ed. I (Westminster I), c.40 119 n.47
6 Ed. I (Gloucester), c.7 105–6
13 Ed. I (*Circumspecte Agatis*) 158 n.16
13 Ed. I (Westminster II), c.3 116, 164 n.47
13 Ed. I (Westminster II), c.14 58
13 Ed. I (Westminster II), c.24 106 n.105
25 Ed. I, c.1 14 n.39, 46 n.86
9 Ed. II, c.1 158 n.16
1 Ed. III, St. II, c.14 123 n.63
4 Ed. III, c.7 104 n.101
4 Ed. III, c.11 123 n.63
9 Ed. III, St. I, c.3 104
9 Ed. III, St. II, c.2 35 n.13
14 Ed. III, St. I, c.1 22, 41 n.48, 81
14 Ed. III, St. I, c.2 41 n.48
14 Ed. III, St. I, c.6 35 n.13
14 Ed. III, St. II, c.1 14
14 Ed. III, St. II, c.2 22 n.70, 81
20 Ed. III, c.1 137 n.26
20 Ed. III, c.6 123 n.63
27 Ed. III, St. II, c.17 67 n.37
34 Ed. III, c.7 124 n.65
36 Ed. III, St. I, c.6 35 n.13
38 Ed. III, St. I, c.12 124 n.65
42 Ed. III, c.3 46
45 Ed. III, c.2 156 n.3
1 Ric. II, c.9 55
1 Ric. II, c.12 29 n.102
1 Ric. II, c.13 148 n.74
8 Ric. II, c.2 40 n.40, 44 n.74
9 Ric. II, c.3 116
12 Ric. II, c.6 40 n.40
13 Ric. II, St. I, c.1 27 n.95
13 Ric. II, St. I, c.17 116 n.34, 164 n.47
14 Ric. II, c.2 44 n.74

15 Ric. II, c.2 35 n.13
16 Ric. II, c.5 10 n.15, 126
17 Ric. II, c.7 48
17 Ric. II, c.9 156 n.3
21 Ric. II, c.15 44 n.74, 46 n.84
21 Ric. II, c.18 44 n.74, 45
1 Hen. IV, c.1 89 n.28
1 Hen. IV, c.3 15 n.43, 45, 46 n.84, 56–7
1 Hen. IV, c.7 40 n.40, 48
1 Hen. IV, c.8 3 n.10, 157 n.5
1 Hen. IV, c.12 79 n.81, 111 n.16, 156 n.3
1 Hen. IV, c.14 169 n.85
1 Hen. IV, c.19 51 n.109
2 Hen. IV, c.1 22 n.70, 99 n.79
2 Hen. IV, c.9 157 n.6
2 Hen. IV, c.13 44 n.74, 46 n.84
2 Hen. IV, c.15 37, 67, 111 n.15
2 Hen. IV, c.16 56 n.125
2 Hen. IV, c.21 2 n.6, 48
4 Hen. IV, c.3 167 n.64, 172 n.100
4 Hen. IV, c.7 55
4 Hen. IV, c.11 67, 111, 156
4 Hen. IV, c.18 51 n.109
4 Hen. IV, c.22 27, 67 n.36, 95 n.56, 135 n.21
4 Hen. IV, c.25 31 n.114, 111 n.16
5 Hen. IV, c.5 68 n.42
5 Hen. IV, c.9 44 n.73
6 Hen. IV, c.1 42 n.60
6 Hen. IV, c.4 44 n.73
7 Hen. IV, c.4 29
7 Hen. IV, cc.8,17 157 n.6
7 Hen. IV, c.10 44 n.73
7 Hen. IV, c.14 40 n.40
7 Hen. IV, c.16 123 n.60
9 Hen. IV, cc.1–9 38 n.32
9 Hen. IV, c.6 44 n.73
11 Hen. IV, c.3 117 n.40

## List of Statutes and Ordinances

11 Hen. IV, c.4 40 n.40
11 Hen. IV, c.5 38 n.32
11 Hen. IV, c.8 44 n.74
11 Hen. IV, c.9 29 n.103
13 Hen. IV, c.2 40 n.40, 44 n.74
13 Hen. IV, c.3 40 n.40
1 Hen. V, c.3 123 n.64
1 Hen. V, c.5 40 n.40
1 Hen. V, c.6 38
1 Hen. V, c.9 40 n.40
2 Hen. V, c.7 68
2 Hen. V, St. I, c.1 68 n.42
2 Hen. V, St. I, c.2 31 n.114
2 Hen. V, St. I, c.6 38 n.32, 40 n.40
2 Hen. V, St. I, c.8 38 n.32
2 Hen. V, St. I, c.9 40 n.40
2 Hen. V, St. II, c.3 146
2 Hen. V, St. II, c.4 111 n.16
2 Hen. V, St. II, c.5 38 n.27
4 Hen. V, St. II, c.2 40 n.40, 111
4 Hen. V, St. II, c.3 111 n.16
4 Hen. V, St. II, c.7 117 n.40
9 Hen. V, St. I, c.1 45, 148 n.74
9 Hen. V, St. I, c.4 35 n.13, 40 n.40, 45 n.76
9 Hen. V, St. I, c.5 146 n.63
9 Hen. V, St. I, c.8 31, 40 n.40, 45 n.76
9 Hen. V, St. I, c.9 40 n.40, 45 n.76
9 Hen. V, St. I, c.11 99 n.79
9 Hen. V, St. II, c.3 67 n.37
1 Hen. VI, c.2 38, 39
1 Hen. VI, c.6 40 n.40, 111 n.15
2 Hen. VI, c.2 79 n.81
2 Hen. VI, c.6 35 n.13
2 Hen. VI, c.12 156
2 Hen. VI, c.15 89 n.28
2 Hen. VI, c.19 31
2 Hen. VI, c.21 31
3 Hen. VI, c.1 172 n.100
3 Hen. VI, c.3 31 n.114
3 Hen. VI, c.4 56 n.125
3 Hen. VI, c.5 89 n.28
4 Hen. VI, c.3 45 n.76
4 Hen. VI, c.5 48
6 Hen. VI, c.1 16 n.44, 148 n.74
8 Hen. VI, c.9 35 n.13, 89 n.28
8 Hen. VI, c.11 22 n.70
8 Hen. VI, c.12 68 n.42
8 Hen. VI, c.22 36 n.16
8 Hen. VI, c.24 36 n.16
8 Hen. VI, c.25 36 n.16
8 Hen. VI, c.27 31 n.114, 169 n.85
8 Hen. VI, c.29 147 n.67

9 Hen. VI, c.5 38 n.27
10 Hen. VI, c.5 44 n.74, 45
11 Hen. VI, c.1 146–7
11 Hen. VI, c.4 124 n.65
11 Hen. VI, c.6 117 n.40
11 Hen. VI, c.7 29 n.103, 111 n.15
11 Hen. VI, c.11 2 n.6, 48 n.96
11 Hen. VI, c.13 16 n.44
11 Hen. VI, c.14 40 n.40, 44 n.75
14 Hen. VI, c.4 111 n.16
15 Hen. VI, c.2 45
15 Hen. VI, c.4 172 n.100
15 Hen. VI, c.6 83 n.96
15 Hen. VI, c.7 148 n.77
18 Hen. VI, c.1 57 n.126, 138
18 Hen. VI, c.3 36 n.16
18 Hen. VI, c.4 36 n.16
18 Hen. VI, c.6 157 n.6
18 Hen. VI, c.11 36 n.16
18 Hen. VI, c.12 45
18 Hen. VI, c.13 167 n.66
18 Hen. VI, c.14 146 n.63
18 Hen. VI, c.18 111
18 Hen. VI, c.19 68 n.42, 167 n.66
20 Hen. VI, c.2 45 n.76, 46
20 Hen. VI, c.3 44 n.75, 56 n.125, 169 n.85
20 Hen. VI, c.6 45
20 Hen. VI, c.8 35 n.13
20 Hen. VI, c.9 31
23 Hen. VI, c.5 45
23 Hen. VI, c.9 142–3
27 Hen. VI, c.1 51 n.110
27 Hen. VI, c.5 67
27 Hen. VI, c.6 83 n.96
28 Hen. VI, c.1 44 n.75
28 Hen. VI, c.4 44 n.75, 148
31 Hen. VI, c.4 48 n.96
31 Hen. VI, c.6 44 n.73, 45 n.76, 46, 48 n.96
31 Hen. VI, c.9 2 n.6, 138
33 Hen. VI, c.1 68, 95 n.56, 111 n.16
33 Hen. VI, c.2 44 n.73, 46
33 Hen. VI, c.3 137
33 Hen. VI, c.6 148
33 Hen. VI, c.7 83
39 Hen. VI, c.1 44 n.73, 57, 139 n.31
1 Ed. IV, c.2 147 n.67
3 Ed. IV, c.1 51 n.110
4 Ed. IV, c.5 146 n.63
7 Ed. IV, c.1 111 n.16
12 Ed. IV, c.3 167 n.64
12 Ed. IV, c.9 146 n.63
17 Ed. IV, c.1 35 n.13

## List of Statutes and Ordinances

17 Ed. IV, c.2 45 n.76, 103, 150 n.84
17 Ed. IV, c.3 67 n.37
22 Ed. IV, c.3 40 n.40, 44 n.75
22 Ed. IV, c.4 51
1 Ric. III, c.1 58
1 Ric. III, c.2 69 n.44
1 Ric. III, c.4 138–9
1 Ric. III, c.6 45 n.76, 103, 150 n.84
1 Ric. III, c.9 51
1 Hen. VII, c.2 79 n.81
1 Hen. VII, c.7 167
1 Hen. VII, c.9 44 n.75, 95 n.56
3 Hen. VII, c.1 69, 167 n.66
3 Hen. VII, c.2 69
3 Hen. VII, c.5 68 n.41, 97
3 Hen. VII, c.6 69 n.44
3 Hen. VII, c.8 111 n.16
3 Hen. VII, c.9 48 n.96, 67 n.37
3 Hen. VII, c.10 117 n.40
3 Hen. VII, c.11 111
3 Hen. VII, c.12 68 n.41
3 Hen. VII, c.14 167 n.66
4 Hen. VII, c.8 103–4, 139 n.31
4 Hen. VII, c.9 137–8
4 Hen. VII, c.12 157
4 Hen. VII, c.16 146 n.63
4 Hen. VII, c.19 169 n.85
4 Hen. VII, c.21 111 n.16
7 Hen. VII, c.3 89 n.28
7 Hen. VII, c.10 111 n.15
7 Hen. VII, c.11 167 n.64
7 Hen. VII, c.12 99 n.79
7 Hen. VII, c.15 95 n.56, 139 n.31
7 Hen. VII, c.20 139 n.31
11 Hen. VII, c.1 46 n.86, 138
11 Hen. VII, cc.2,3 69 n.44
11 Hen. VII, c.7 111 n.16
11 Hen. VII, c.8 68 n.41, 97
11 Hen. VII, c.12 99 n.79
11 Hen. VII, c.18 111 n.16
11 Hen. VII, c.20 111 n.15
11 Hen. VII, c.24 124 n.65
11 Hen. VII, cc.25,26 40 n.40
11 Hen. VII, c.34 139 n.31
12 Hen. VII, c.6 56, 139 n.31
12 Hen. VII, c.7 68, 95 n.56, 157
3 Hen. VIII, c.12 104 n.99
3 Hen. VIII, c.23 90 n.33

# LIST OF YEAR BOOK CASES

H 7 Ed. III, 4, 7 145 n.57
M 17 Ed. III, 61, 65 3 n.10
H 21 Ed. III, 46, 65 3 n.10
T 21 Ed. III, 19, 4 3 n.10
P 24 Ed. III, 40, 22 3 n.10
P 39 Ed. III, f.7A 8 n.4, 23 n.73, 39
H 40 Ed. III, 17, 8 49 n.99
P 41 Ed. III, 10, 5 122 n.59
H 42 Ed. III, 4, 16 80 n.85
H 48 Ed. III, 1, 1 161 n.31
M 1 Hen. IV, 1, 1 147 n.68
M 1 Hen. IV, 5, 10 147 n.68
M 2 Hen. IV, 4, 14 89 n.28
M 2 Hen. IV, 11, 48 129 n.94
M 2 Hen. IV, 12, 49 129
M 2 Hen. IV, 12, 50 122–3
P 2 Hen. IV, 18, 6 2, 127
T 3 Hen. IV, 18, 15 118 n.43
M 4 Hen. IV, 4, 13 168 n.77
H 5 Hen. IV. 2, 6 159
H 6 Hen. IV, 3, 22 118
M 7 Hen. IV, 25, 3 170 n.89
M 7 Hen. IV, 31, 15 145
P 7 Hen. IV, 10, 1 100
P 7 Hen. IV, 41, 5 145 n.57
T 7 Hen. IV, 16, 4 114 n.26
T 7 Hen. IV, 16, 6 104 n.100, 105
M 8 Hen. IV, 12, 13 15 n.43, 57
M 8 Hen. IV, 16, 19 95 n.56, 170 n.92
M 10 Hen. IV, 6, 19 100–1
M 11 Hen. IV, 1, 1 158
M 11 Hen. IV, 7, 20 42 n.64, 57 n.128
M 11 Hen. IV, 16, 38 129
M 11 Hen. IV, 18, 43 125 n.74
M 11 Hen. IV, 31, 57 112
M 11 Hen. IV, 33, 61 100 n.84
M 11 Hen. IV, 37, 67 42 n.64, 57 n.128
H 11 Hen. IV, 40, 2 104 n.100
H 11 Hen. IV, 45, 20 104 n.100, 106 n.105

H 11 Hen. IV, 47, 21 50
H 11 Hen. IV, 50, 27 150
P 11 Hen. IV, 56, 2 104 n.101
T 11 Hen. IV, 86, 37 15 n.40
T 11 Hen. IV, 90, 46 95 n.56, 163, 165 n.58
M12 Hen. IV, 1, 3 104 n.100, 116 n.35
H 12 Hen. IV, 12, 3 81 n.91, 89
H 12 Hen. IV, 16, 9 114 n.26
P 12 Hen. IV, 19, 4 118 n.43
P 12 Hen. IV, 20, 5 104 n.100
T 12 Hen. IV, 26, 15 172 n.101
H 13 Hen. IV, 14, 11 14, 15, 16 n.44
M 14 Hen. IV, 2, 6 20, 21
H 14 Hen. IV, 14, 4 126
H 14 Hen. IV, 21, 27 124, 164, 170 n.92
H 14 Hen. IV, 27, 37 104 n.100
M 1 Hen. V, 11, 21 113
M 1 Hen. V, 11, 24 79 n.81
P 1 Hen. V, 4, 4 157 n.5
T 2 Hen. V, 8, 2 168 n.77
H 5 Hen. V, 6, 13 146 n.63
7 Hen. V, 5, 3 95 n.56, 101 n.87
H 8 Hen. V, 4, 16 100 n.83
H 8 Hen. V, 5, 21 89 n.28
H 8 Hen. V, 6, 26 165
M 9 Hen. V, 9, 5 165
M 9 Hen. V, 12, 13 114
P 9 Hen. V, 1, 2 167
M 2 Hen. VI, 1, 1 36 n.18, 172 n.98
T 2 Hen. VI, 14, 13 165
T 2 Hen. VI, 15, 15 119 n.47
M 3 Hen. VI, 14, 17 114, 130
M 3 Hen. VI, 14, 18 104–5
M 3 Hen. VI, 15, 20 168
M 3 Hen. VI, 18, 27 164–5, 171–2
H 3 Hen. VI, 26, 8 164–5, 171–2
P 3 Hen. VI, 43, 20 169 n.85, 171
T 3 Hen. VI, 51, 17 24 n.77

xviii  *List of Year Book Cases*

T 3 Hen. VI, 54, 25 24 n.77
M 4 Hen. VI, 2, 4 122 n.59
H 4 Hen. VI, 10, 4 168 n.77
H 4 Hen. VI, 13, 11 168
T 4 Hen. VI, 25, 4 95 n.56, 104 n.100, 105–6
T 4 Hen. VI, 26, 5 118 n.43
T 4 Hen. VI, 28, 12 90
T 4 Hen. VI, 31, 11 3 n.10, 23 n.76, 30, 167
M 7 Hen. VI, 5, 9 104 n.100, 105 n.103, 112
M 7 Hen. VI, 9, 15 170 n.92
M 7 Hen. VI, 12, 17 80 n.85, 89 n.28
M 7 Hen. VI, 14, 24 37 n.25, 100
P 7 Hen. VI, 28, 22 165, 166
P 7 Hen. VI, 31, 27 41 n.52, 79 n.81, 82 n.92
P 7 Hen. VI, 35, 39 17 n.47
M 8 Hen. VI, 3, 8 126 n.75
M 8 Hen. VI, 3, 9 41
M 8 Hen. VI, 4, 11; 11, 28 146 n.63
M 8 Hen. VI, 12, 30 158
M 8 Hen. VI, 35, 3 37 n.25
H 8 Hen. VI, 18, 6 28 n.96, 90 n.33
H 8 Hen. VI, 30, 26 160 n.25
H 8 Hen. VI, 26, 16 125 n.74, 172 n.98
M 9 Hen. VI, 30, 1 95 n.56, 169–70, 171 n.94
M 9 Hen. VI, 43, 21 79 n.81
M 9 Hen. VI, 44, 24 158 n.17
M 9 Hen VI, 44, 27 79 n.81, 80
M 9 Hen. VI, 50, 34 160
P 9 Hen. VI, 1, 3 169 n.85
P 9 Hen. VI, 2, 5 124
P 9 Hen. VI, 2, 6 157 n.5
M 10 Hen. VI, 7, 23 172 n.98
M 10 Hen. VI, 15, 51 105 n.103, 157 n.6
M 10 Hen. VI, 17, 58 161 n.33
P 11 Hen. VI, 27, 7 143 n.52, 159 n.18
P 11 Hen. VI, 42, 38 149
H 12 Hen. VI, 6, 5 165 n.58, 171 n.95
T 14 Hen. VI, 18, 56 165 n.58
T 14 Hen. VI, 19, 60 112 n.18
T 14 Hen. VI, 23, 67 171 n.94
M 18 Hen. VI, 20, 5 122 n.59
M 18 Hen. VI, 24, 9 113
P 18 Hen. VI, 5, 5 3 n.10, 36 n.16
P 18 Hen. VI, 6, 6 36, 123 n.64
M 19 Hen. VI, 3, 5 149
M 19 Hen. VI, 3, 6 160 n.25
M 19 Hen. VI, 7, 15 100

M 19 Hen. VI, 15, 36 37 n.25
M 19 Hen. VI, 25, 48 36 n.18, 95 n.56
M 19 Hen. VI, 39, 82 172–3
M 19 Hen. VI, 43, 89 160 n.28
M 19 Hen. VI, 44, 94 129 n.96
H 19 Hen. VI, 58, 23 160 n.28
P 19 Hen. VI, 62, 1 3 n.10, 15, 17, 27, 28, 57, 99
P 19 Hen. VI, 66, 10 167, 172 n.98
T 19 Hen. VI, 73, 2 36 n.18
M 20 Hen. VI, 5, 15 128 n.88
M 20 Hen. VI, 8, 17 19, 35
H 20 Hen. VI, 17, 8 158 n.15
P 20 Hen. VI, 23, 4 119 n.47
T 20 Hen. VI, 33, 3 29, 128 n.88
T 20 Hen. VI, 34, 4 2, 141–2
T 20 Hen. VI, 39, 9 89 n.28
M 21 Hen. VI, 13, 28 36, 74 n.63
M 21 Hen. VI, 14, 29 167
P 21 Hen. VI, 29, 9 30 n. 109
P 21 Hen. VI, 35, 2 151–2
T 21 Hen. VI, 56, 13 58, 171
T 21 Hen. VI, 57, 14 167 n.72, 172 n.100
M 22 Hen. VI, 4, 6 101 n.88
M 22 Hen. VI, 21, 38 42
M 22 Hen. VI, 28, 47 112 n.22
H 22 Hen. VI, 38, 8 127 n.83
H 22 Hen. VI, 39, 12 118–19, 164 n.52, 170 n.92
P 22 Hen. VI, 52, 20 157 n.6
P 22 Hen. VI, 52, 24 143 n.52, 159 n.18
P 22 Hen. VI, 53, 28 166 n.60
P 28 Hen. VI, 6, 3 172 n.98
T 28 Hen. VI, 12, 28 123
M 30 Hen. VI, 1, 6 168 n.84
M30 Hen. VI, 5, 15 29 n.104
M 31 Hen. VI, 8, 1 123 n.62
M 31 Hen. VI, 11, 6 117–18
M 31 Hen. VI, 11, 8 105 n.103, 157 n.6
M 32 Hen. VI, 10, 17 157
H 32 Hen. VI, 25, 13 168 n.77
H 32 Hen. VI, 28, 23 168
M 33 Hen. VI, 38, 17 116, 163–4, 167
M 33 Hen. VI, 45, 28 25 n.86, 95 n.56, 168 n.78
M 33 Hen. VI, 51, 37 165–6
H 33 Hen. VI, 2, 8 149
H 33 Hen. VI, 7, 23 23 n.76, 24, 25, 35, 150 n.88
P 33 Hen. VI, 17, 8 16 n.44, 57–58
M 34 Hen. VI, 3, 8 125 n.74
M 34 Hen. VI, 9, 20 119 n.47

## List of Year Book Cases

M 34 Hen. VI, 15, 28 79 n.81, 80 n.85, 82 n.92
M 34 Hen. VI, 22, 42 23, 42 n.63, 164, 168 n.77
P 34 Hen. VI, 36, 7 147
P 34 Hen. VI, 38, 9 140 n.34
M 35 Hen. VI, 11, 18 38 n.28, 149–150
M 35 Hen. VI, 14, 24 37 n.25
M 35 Hen. VI, 18, 27 157 n.5
M 35 Hen. VI, 24, 31 161 n.33
M 35 Hen. VI, 25, 33 28, 42 n.60, 74 n.63, 80, 157 n.9
M 35 Hen. VI, 39, 47 158 n.15
H 35 Hen. VI, 46, 11 159
H 35 Hen. VI, 52, 17 112 n.19
P 35 Hen. VI, 56, 2 15 n.40
T 35 Hen. VI, 60, 1 27 n.95, 28 n.99
36 Hen. VI, 7, 4 128 n.90
M 37 Hen. VI, 1, 1 171 n.94
M 37 Hen. VI, 1, 2 157 n.6
M 37 Hen. VI, 4, 6 95 n.56, 157 n.5
M 37 Hen. VI, 9, 19 167
P 37 Hen. VI, 17, 4 23 n.76, 41
M 38 Hen. VI, 2, 5 36 n.17, 100 n.83
M 38 Hen. VI, 11, 22 117
M 38 Hen. VI, 17, 43 104 n.100
P 38 Hen. VI, 30, 12 112 n.22
P 38 Hen. VI, 30, 13 42 n.64, 115 n.31
P 38 Hen. VI, 29, 12 151 n.89
M 39 Hen. VI, 12, 16 130, 160
M 39 Hen. VI, 16, 20 117
M 39 Hen. VI, 27, 38 30 n.106
M 39 Hen. VI, 27, 40 130, 160
H 39 Hen. VI, 38, 3 16 n.44, 35 n.14, 49 n.99
M 1 Ed. IV, 1, 5 157 n.5
M 1 Ed. IV, 2, 7 37 n.25, 164 n.52
M 1 Ed. IV, 5, 13 37 n.25, 41 n.48, 42 n.62
M 2 Ed. IV, 18, 13; 23, 21 28 n.98, 81 n.91, 89
M 2 Ed. IV, 27, 32 170
P 2 Ed. IV, 4, 8 24 n.77
M 3 Ed. IV, 8, 1 112 n.22
M 3 Ed. IV, 15, 10 24 n.78, 125 n.74, 158 n.17, 160
M 3 Ed. IV, 17, 12 24 n.78
M 3 Ed. IV, 19, 13 104 n.100
M 3 Ed. IV, 24, 18 24 n.77
M 3 Ed. IV, 24, 19 79 n.81
M 3 Ed. IV, 26, 20 24 n.77
H 3 Ed. IV, 28, 3 24 n.77
M 4 Ed. IV, 31, 12 24 n.77

M 4 Ed. IV, 38, 22 141
P 4 Ed. IV, 3, 4 35 n.13, 42 n.64, 103 n.94
P 4 Ed. IV, 8, 9 144 n.53
P 4 Ed. IV, 10, 13 24 n.78
P 4 Ed. IV, 12, 19 24 n.77
P 4 Ed. IV, 13, 20 24 n.77
P 4 Ed. IV, 13, 21 24 n.78
P 4 Ed. IV, 14, 25 161 n.33
P 4 Ed. IV, 16, 28; 19, 36 145–6
M 5 Ed. IV, 8, 23 41
M 5 Ed. IV, 86 24, 164
P 5 Ed. IV, 3, 26 158 n.17
T 5 Ed. IV, 4, 9 141
T 5 Ed. IV, 4, 10 143 n.52, 159 n.18
M 6 Ed. IV, 3, 7 158
M 6 Ed. IV, 4, 11 171 n.94
M 6 Ed. IV, 5, 14 147
M 6 Ed. IV, 5, 16 124 n.65
M 6 Ed. IV, 7, 18 121–2, 123
H 6 Ed. IV, 61, 6 122 n.59
M 7 Ed. IV, 18, 12 104 n.100
M 7 Ed. IV, 19, 16 30 n.109
M 7 Ed. IV, 20, 19 29 n.105
M 7 Ed. IV, 20, 23 41 n.55
H 7 Ed. IV, 29, 15 150 n.84
P 7 Ed. IV, 1, 3 167–8, 172 n.98
T 7 Ed. IV, 10, 1 24 n.77
M 8 Ed. IV, 9, 9; 20, 35 23, 35, 71, 95 n.56
M 8 Ed. IV, 17, 24 128
M 8 Ed. IV, 18, 30 19 n.57, 42, 48, 82
P 8 Ed. IV, 1, 1 71, 141 n.40, 151 n.89
T 8 Ed. IV, 5, 14 79 n.81
M 9 Ed. IV, 41, 26 144 n.53
P 9 Ed. IV, 2, 5 150 n.84
T 9 Ed. IV, 12, 4 140 n.34
T 9 Ed. IV, 14, 9 144 nn.53, 56
T 9 Ed. IV, 22, 24 112 n.21
T 9 Ed. IV, 27, 39 73 n.60
T 9 Ed. IV, 30, 45 104 n.100
P 10 Ed. IV, 9, 24 150 n.84
H 11 Ed. IV, 9, 1 161
H 11 Ed. IV, 10, 5 23 n.72
T 11 Ed. IV, 4, 8 29 n.105
T 11 Ed. IV, 6, 10 3 n.10, 36 n.16, 122
T 11 Ed. IV, 8, 13 95 n.56, 144 n.53
M 12 Ed. IV, 19, 25 24 n.77
P 12 Ed. IV, 1, 3; 8, 22 74 n.63, 82 n.92
P 12 Ed. IV, 9, 24 101 n.88
M 13 Ed. IV, 1, 3; 5, 14 125
P 13 Ed. IV, 8, 3 126 n.75

xix

P 13 Ed. IV, 9, 5 73 n.61
T 14 Ed. IV, 6, 8 144 n.53
H 15 Ed. IV, 16, 4 24 n.78, 165 n.54
P 16 Ed. IV, 2, 7 127 n.83
P 16 Ed. IV, 9, 10 119 n.47
M 17 Ed. IV, 5, 3 89 n.28
P 17 Ed. IV, 1, 2 112 n.22
T 17 Ed. IV, 3, 2 127 n.83
M 18 Ed. IV, 11, 4 144 n.53
M 18 Ed. IV, 16, 18 104 n.100, 106 n.105
T 18 Ed. IV, 8, 8 89 n.28
T 18 Ed. IV, 8, 11 101 n.88
T 18 Ed. IV, 9, 18 128 n.88
T 18 Ed. IV, 10, 25 112 n.22, 158 n.17
M 21 Ed. IV, 38, 5 115 n.31
M 21 Ed. IV, 53, 22 41 n.55
M 21 Ed. IV, 55, 28 16, 19 n.57, 41 n.55
M 21 Ed. IV, 63, 35 168 n.84
M 21 Ed. IV, 67, 50 22 n.70, 28 n.98, 41 n.48, 81
M 21 Ed. IV, 80, 27 30 n.109
H 21 Ed. IV, 16, 11 41 n.48
H 21 Ed. IV, 21, 2 140
H 21 Ed. IV, 74, 2 41 n.48
H 21 Ed. IV, 78, 14 160 n.28
P 21 Ed. IV, 22, 3 150 n.84
P 21 Ed. IV, 24, 10 144 n.53
P 21 Ed. IV, 24, 11 117 n.41
P 21 Ed. IV, 28, 23 80–1
M 22 Ed. IV, 22, 2 80 n.85
M 22 Ed. IV, 30, 11 21 n.63, 41 nn.48, 55
H 22 Ed. IV, 43, 4 81
P 22 Ed. IV, 2, 7 104 n.100
P 22 Ed. IV, 2, 8 152
P 22 Ed. IV, 6, 18 140 n.34
P 22 Ed. IV, 8, 24 20 n.60, 80–1
T 22 Ed. IV, 19, 45 147
T 22 Ed. IV, 19, 46 24 n.78, 115
T 1 Ed. V, 2, 3 147
T 1 Ed. V, 6, 12 37 n.25
M 2 Ric. III, 14, 39 151 n.89
M 2 Ric. III, 15, 42 81–2
M 1 Hen. VII, 2, 2 28 n.96
H 1 Hen. VII, 6, 3 73, 81 n.91
H 1 Hen. VII, 10, 10 10 n.15
P 1 Hen. VII, 14, 2 159 n.19
P 1 Hen. VII, 25, 18 152
M 2 Hen. VII, 4, 17 115–16
H 2 Hen. VII, 11, 9 127 n.83
P 2 Hen. VII, 15, 1 29 n.105, 37 n.25

M 3 Hen. VII, 12, 8 36 n.17
H 3 Hen. VII, 1, 4 38
H 3 Hen. VII, 19, 1 112 n.22
M 4 Hen. VII, 17, 3 101 n.88
M 4 Hen. VII, 18, 12 49 n.99
H 4 Hen. VII, 4, 8 72–3, 144 n.53
P 4 Hen. VII, 6, 2 101
P 4 Hen. VII, 8, 9 30
T 4 Hen. VII, 13, 12 143
M 5 Hen. VII, 2, 3, 24 n.78, 164 n.49
M 5 Hen. VII, 4, 10 29 n.105
M 5 Hen. VII, 9, 21 24 n.77, 168 n.84
H 5 Hen. VII, 10, 2 30, 125 n.74
H 5 Hen. VII, 11, 4 37 n.25
P 5 Hen. VII, 16, 8 116 n.35
P 5 Hen. VII, 27, 9 24 n.77
H 6 Hen. VII, 15, 9 119 n.47
P 6 Hen. VII, 3, 5 58
M 7 Hen. VII, 6, 9 104 n.100
M 7 Hen. VII, 16, 1 49 n.99
P 7 Hen. VII, 10, 2 72 n.58
T 7 Hen. VII, 14, 1 15
M 8 Hen. VII, 7, 4 104 n.100
P 8 Hen. VII, 11, 1 23 n.72
T 8 Hen. VII, 1, 1 42 n.60, 49 n.99
T 9 Hen. VII, 3, 4 23 n.72
H 10 Hen. VII, 17, 17 10 n.15
T 10 Hen. VII, 25, 2 104 nn.99, 100
T 10 Hen. VII, 25, 3 112 n.22
M 11 Hen. VII, 10, 33 24
M 11 Hen. VII, 11, 35 73–4
H 11 Hen. VII, 12, 3 48–9
H 11 Hen. VII, 15, 11 23 n.72
T 11 Hen. VII, 26, 10 15–16
P 12 Hen. VII, 15, 1 49 n.99
T 12 Hen. VII, 19, 1 16 n.44, 28–9, 103 n.94, 142, n.46
T 12 Hen. VII, 22, 2 30 n.106
M 13 Hen. VII, 2, 2 116 n.32
M 13 Hen. VII, 4, 3 28 n.99, 103 n.94
M 13 Hen. VII, 10, 10 73 n.61
M 13 Hen. VII, 11, 12 104 n.100
P 13 Hen. VII, 22, 9 112 n.19
T 13 Hen. VII, 26, 5 24
M 14 Hen. VII, 1, 4 128 n.92
M 14 Hen. VII, 5, 11 125 n.74
H 14 Hen. VII, 13, 2 104 nn.100, 101, 105 n.103
H 14 Hen. VII, 17, 7 36 n.17, 79 n.81, 103 n.94
T 14 Hen. VII, 29, 4 147 n.68
M 15 Hen. VII, 13, 1 147 n.68
M 16 Hen. VII, 2, 4 103 n.94

## List of Year Book Cases

M 16 Hen. VII, 2, 7 95 n.56
T 16 Hen. VII, 12, 5 79 n.81
M 20 Hen. VII, 2, 4 140
M 20 Hen. VII, 3, 8 112 n.21
M 20 Hen. VII, 4, 12 127
M 20 Hen. VII, 4, 14 23 n.76, 127 n.85, 140 n.34
M 20 Hen. VII, 5, 15 23 n.76
M 20 Hen. VII, 8, 18 126–7
M 20 Hen. VII, 10, 20 74 n.63
M 20 Hen. VII, 13, 23 3 n.10, 128
M 21 Hen. VII, 41, 66 23 n.76
H 21 Hen. VII, 1, 1 16 n.46, 46 n.86
H 21 Hen. VII, 13, 17 140 n.36
H 21 Hen. VII, 16, 28 142–3
H 21 Hen. VII, 18, 30 95 n.56, 142 n.46
T 21 Hen. VII, 27, 5 49
M 21 Hen. VII, 41, 66 127 n.82
P 21 Hen. VII, 22, 14 128

# INTRODUCTION

Today law is treated largely as a system of rules located principally in statute books and in reports of judicial decisions. The early common law, however, cannot be treated in the same terms. Though there were, of course, statutes and judicial decisions, the early common law cannot be understood entirely as an autonomous and identifiable system of substantive rules permitting this or prohibiting that. Contemporary scholars suggest, for example, that in the formative period of the common law (though there were procedures without writ) substantive rules existed only latently within claims that a litigant could put (in his count) before a court, within the writs (those instruments initiating suits in the royal courts) which facilitated these claims, and within the remedies which the writs embodied.[1] The settlement of individual disputes was based not upon the application of rules but upon making an acceptable claim by means of the correct writ: '[i]n the whole process the only substantive rules visibly at work are those implicit in the canon of acceptable claims'.[2] As the earliest tracts on the common law indicate, it was the writ system itself which operated as the focal point of legal practice and study. Legal literature expressed and accommodated a law of writs rather than a law of property or a law of contract.[3] The early medieval legal practitioner found the law not in an explicitly stated body of rules, based on legislation and judicial decisions, but in the *Register of Writs*: '[t]he common law writs came to be seen as somehow basic, almost like the

---

[1] Milsom, *HFCL*, pp. 4–5, 309. See, however, H. G. Richardson and G. O. Sayles, *Select Cases of Procedure Without Writ under Henry III*, 60 Sel. Soc. (London, 1941).

[2] *HFCL*, p. 39. The relationship between the absence of a substantive law and the non-consideration of facts by courts is discussed at ibid., pp. 38–9, 83–4, and S. F. C. Milsom, 'Law and fact in legal development', 17 *University of Toronto Law Journal* (1967) p. 1.

[3] Baker, *IELH*, pp. 49, 52; *HFCL*, p. 37.

Ten Commandments or the Twelve Tables, the data from which the law itself was derived'.[4]

In contrast, the medieval canon law can be conceived in terms of rules. In the church courts we do see judges applying to facts a body of legal rules (the *Corpus Iuris Canonici*) which (like its model, Roman Law) was found in written form.[5] Indeed, by the later medieval period, the secular law itself is more easily recognisable in the same terms, in our own terms, as a developing body of substantive rules. The treatment of particular harm by legislation of the fourteenth and fifteenth centuries certainly discloses the existence of substantive rules: that upon these facts this result ought to follow, and upon those facts that result. If a lord used or gave to squires and yeomen any livery, he would lose his livery and forfeit his fee; if an individual assaulted any lord or commoner attending parliament, he was to pay damages to the injured party with fine and ransom to the king; if a woman was forced to enter a contract against her will, then the contract would be void.[6] Similarly, at this time, we can see more clearly the royal judges dealing directly with instances of positive wrong-doing: the judicial provision of a remedy is the consequence of the formulation of an elementary idea of a rule. If A promised to convey land to B, who pre-paid to A the purchase price, and instead A conveyed to C, B was to be allowed his bill of deceit by way of remedy.[7] If D kept his fire negligently and P's property was damaged, P relied upon 'the custom of the realm' to recover for that damage.[8] When A brought an action on the case against an innkeeper for the loss of his goods through the innkeeper's default, again, to secure a remedy A would rely upon 'the custom of the realm' by which all innkeepers were bound to accommodate travellers and look after their goods.[9]

---

[4] *HFCL*, p. 36 (and p. 37); and E. de Haas and G. D. G. Hall, *Early Registers of Writs*, 87 Sel. Soc. (London 1970); F. W. Maitland, 'The history of the register of original writs', in *Collected Papers*, volume II, edited by H. A. L. Fisher (Cambridge, 1911) p. 110.

[5] H. J. Berman, *Law and Revolution: the Formation of the Western Legal Tradition* (Harvard, 1983), p. 224; for the influence of Roman Law on the canonists, ibid., pp. 144, 146, 149 and Ullmann, *LPMA*, pp. 125, 139. For canonist reporting of cases, see J. H. Baker, 'Famous English canon lawyers: William Bateman LL.D. (d. 1355), Bishop of Norwich', 3 *Ecclesiastical Law Journal* (1988) p. 3.

[6] See 2 Hen. IV, c. 21, 11 Hen. VI, c. 11 and 31 Hen. VI, c. 9.

[7] T 20 Hen. VI, 34, 4, *Doige's Case* (1442); for the opportunities afforded for discussions of law in pleading, such as on demurrer, see *HFCL*, pp. 45, 59, 73, 74, and *IELH*, pp. 67–71.

[8] P 2 Hen. IV, 18, 6; *IELH*, p. 339.   [9] See generally, *HCLC*, pp. 229f.

*Introduction* 3

Arrangements such as these, found in legislative and judicial decisions, are some of the first signs of a substantive law which treats harmful conduct directly. Indeed, though they also appear before the period, of course, the word 'law' and phrases such as 'against law', 'contrary to the common law' or 'according to law' are clearly and extensively used during the fifteenth century in the context of what conduct is allowed or disallowed.[10] The modern lawyer is able more comfortably to view the law of this period as a means of conscious social control,[11] for it is then that judges, legislators and theorists begin explicitly to regard law as a means of regulating wrongs and harms in society. Whereas the absence of theory about secular law as an entity in the early medieval period is not surprising, as there was little explicit substantive law, the presence of theory about *law* towards the end of the period is more to be expected. It is then that we meet the philosophical works of Pecock (1395?–1460?),[12] Fortescue (1394?–1476?),[13] Saint German (1460?–1540),[14] and the more practi-

---

[10] For instance, 1 Hen. IV, c. 8 (king's entry not given by law); P 18 Hen. VI, 5, 5 at 6 per Fulthorpe JCP ('a wrong done by the defendant against law', to be punished); P 19 Hen. VI, 62, 1 at 63 per Newton CJCP (for the king to disherit a man or put him to death is *encontre le ley*); T 11 Ed. IV, 6, 10, per Neele JCP (it is forbidden by law to sell bad food); for the idea that a course must be pursued 'according to law', see, for instance, T 4 Hen. VI, 31, 11 at 32 per Martin JCP, and M 20 Hen. VII, 13, 23, per Rede CJCP. For similar terms in the earlier Year Books, see, for example, M 17 Ed. III, 61, 65 (*disaccordant a la ley*); H 21 Ed. III, 46, 65 at 47 (law and usage); T 21 Ed. III, 19, 4 ('for by the law'); P 24 Ed. III, 40, 22 at 41 (the judges held something for law).

[11] Compare the views of Ullmann, *LPMA*, pp. 27f. and Milsom, *HFCL*, p. 81.

[12] Reginald Pecock, Bishop of St Asaph, 1444, Chichester, 1450, Welshman, educated at Oriel College, Oxford, elected Fellow, 1417. Comments extensively on secular law in his theological works: in *Reule*, he discusses the nature of God and divine law; *Donet* introduces basic elements of the Christian faith; its supplement, *Folower*, explores the virtues; *Faith* treats the nature of faith; in *Repressor* he refutes Lollardy. The works are in English. For his life, see V. H. Green, *Bishop Reginald Pecock: A Study in Ecclesiastical History and Thought* (Cambridge, 1945); E. F. Jacob, 'Reynold Pecock, Bishop of Chichester', 37 *Proceedings of the British Academy* (1951) p. 121; A. B. Ferguson, 'Reginald Pecock and the renaissance sense of history', 13 *Studies in the Renaissance* (1966) pp. 147–65. For his downfall, see B. Wilkinson, *The Later Middle Ages in England: 1216–1485* (London, 1969) pp. 332, 333.

[13] John Fortescue, Serjeant-at-Law, 1438, Chief Justice of the King's Bench, 1442–61; works, *De Natura, De Laudibus* and *Governance*. For a short comparison of the legal thought of Pecock and Fortescue, see N. Doe, 'Fifteenth-century concepts of law: Fortescue and Pecock', 10 *History of Political Thought* (1989) p. 257.

[14] Christopher Saint German: *Dialogue*. See J. A. Guy, *Christopher St. German on Chancery and Statute*, 6 Sel. Soc. Supplementary Series (London, 1985) for his *Little Treatise Concerning Writs of Subpoena* (1532?) and the *Little Treatise Called the New Addition* (1531).

cal work of Littleton (1422–81).[15] What can be discerned in these is the incipient treatment of law as a recognisable entity. Yet, though there are many novel aspects in their work, these theorists do not invent a concept of law peculiar to the indigenous common law. It is to existing civilian, canonist and Thomist theories of law that they turn. In medieval terms, their philosophy of law is thoroughly orthodox and largely European. Nor is it the case that legal theory walks side by side with the ideas of the practitioners. There are major dissonances, differences of emphasis, perspective and conclusion: theoretical statements are often far more simplistic and exaggerated than the more complex, mundane and precise statements of legal practice.

In an analysis of the emergent substantive law (as well as the procedural law) and the philosophical literature, the following chapters explore the basic components of practical and theoretical thinking about, and within, the secular law of (roughly) the fifteenth century. The work is an attempt to re-construct the late medieval legal theorist's and practitioner's conception of law in terms not of ideas about debt, trespass or *assumpsit*, categories containing sets or species of legal rules functioning as the means by which factual instances of wrong-doing are regulated, but in terms of fundamental ideas, ideas antecedent to or causative of the substantive law. In short, their conception of the nature and authority of law.

Two sets of fundamental ideas are examined. One set stresses the autonomy of law. Practitioners and theorists are beginning to think of law in our own terms, as an independent phenomenon resting on the human will, composed of precepts and prohibitions, whose purpose is purely mundane, to deal with ordinary occasions of dispute and harm. Law is not given by God, it is of human origin, caused and altered by human usage and enactment, it exists because people consent to it, and it has the earthly object of governing the affairs of society in the way that people choose. As such, law is seen as having little to do with morality. It is not a divinely created abstraction of right and wrong which shapes the law, but the will of people. With the human will as the basis and authority for law, there are indications in this period of what might be described as the 'positivist' thesis of law. Practitioners and theorists are beginning to employ the idea that humanly created rules are to be treated as law irrespective of their moral quality.

On the other hand, the same literature also reflects another set of

[15] Thomas Littleton, Serjeant-at-Law, 1453, Justice of the Common Pleas, 1466–81. His *Tenures* is dated *c.* 1480.

Introduction 5

fundamental ideas about law and its authority. These ideas stress the *connection* between law and abstract ideas of right and wrong, between law and morality.[16] Through the persistent usage of moral language, not only is human law viewed as subordinate to abstract right and wrong, but morality is being incorporated into the developing substantive law. Morality, of divine origin, was considered not merely as an ideal imperative standing outside human law. It is being absorbed overtly into actual law. The practice of employing moral justifications for legislative and judicial decisions, and legal argumentation in general, is an important characteristic of the Year Books and legislation. Time and time again, throughout the fifteenth century, the developing substantive law and the old implicit law contain explanations and justifications for their own existence and operation. Legislators and judges use extensively ideas such as divine law and words like *conscience* and *reason*, to dispose of problems and cases. These usages spell out a fundamental way of thinking about law and its authority. Law has a moral basis: its authority is morality. This surface language is important, for it states an assumption underlying the disposition of ordinary problems and cases by legislators and judges. Often, discussions in the Year Books are almost casuistic in form. The practitioners obviously have duties to their client, to get this litigant out of today's difficulty, to dispose of an individual case.[17] But, at the same time, their minds are not devoid of elementary ideas about the purpose and nature of law. Through the symbolic vocabulary of morality, the proper disposition of individual cases is effected by thinking of specific problems within broad categories of what is right and what is wrong.

The two sets of ideas oppose each other fundamentally. The one set asserts the view that the basis for law is the human will. The authority for law derives from consent: the usages and enactments of people shape law. This populist thesis paves the way for a positivist outlook: humanly created rules are to be treated as laws even when they offend morality. Law and morality are separated. The other set of ideas

[16] 'Morality' is a term of convenience employed throughout this work to signify a specific idea of abstract right and wrong: the requirements of *divine law*, *justice* and *conscience* are all treated as indications or aspects of 'morality'. Connected to this, though used in a narrower and more mundane sense of right and wrong, are ideas of *reason* and *mischief*.

[17] For a cautionary note see *HFCL*, p. 7: 'The historian ... misunderstands it all if he endows the lawyers who took part with vision on any comparable scale, or attributes to them any intention beyond getting today's client out of his difficulty.'

asserts that there is a moral basis for law. The authority for law is morality, originating in the divine will, and rules are accepted as laws only insofar as they conform to the requirements of abstract right and wrong. Law relies for its authority upon divinely created morality, not merely upon the human will.

With regard to the common law, in the fifteenth century we see traces of the persistent dialogue between law and morality at work in both theory and practice. Today's general rejection of moral argument in practical legal discussion might be perceived in contrast to the thinking of the late medieval practitioner and theorist. However, we can also begin to discern this same positivist sympathy at a time of a developing substantive law. As Professor Milsom has observed: 'The discussion about the relative importance in a legal system of certainty and abstract justice is unending: but it begins at a definite stage of development, namely when the law is first seen as a system of substantive rules prescribing results upon given states of fact.'[18] The common fifteenth-century practitioner's assertion that 'a mischief will be suffered sooner than an inconvenience' (two distinct ideas, one related to the treatment of abstract wrongs, the other to adherence to established practice and consistency) is not without significance. It is an explicit reference to, and is part of, an intrinsic tension in late medieval legal thought, a tension which points the way to, and eventually culminates in, the modern pre-eminence of the positivist outlook.

[18] Ibid., p. 94.

# 1

## AUTHORITY AND CONSENT: THE POPULIST THESIS

With the most notable exceptions of Bracton and Ockham, it is not until the fifteenth century that questions concerning the origin or source of law generate any sort of detailed discussion by theorists in England. Yet such questions had for a very long time provided the standard diet of discussion for many continental medieval civilians and canonists. In the works of Reginald Pecock, written between 1443 and 1456, and those of John Fortescue, written between 1463 and 1471, the idea that law derives its authority from the will of the community is considered for the first time in a manner comparable with that of the continental jurists. It is an account of the origin of law dominated by the populist idea of consent. It is also an account, however, influenced in part by feudal conceptions of law. For Pecock and Fortescue popular consent is the basis for law in the form of parliamentary legislation created by the king and the community together. Consent is also considered to be the basis of law in the practical sphere: statutes are consented to by the community of the realm and local customary law originates in the usage and consent of local communities. In these arrangements, in terms of what is authorised as law, the human will comes to the fore. With the common law – the custom of the realm – on the other hand, rather than general popular consent, it is the judicial will and usage that create law. This form of law-making does not appear in the theory of Pecock or Fortescue.

### CONSENT AND THE MAKING OF LEGISLATION

Fortescue distinguishes three sorts of government. First, government in which the ruler governs in accordance with laws which he himself makes. This is the *dominium regale*.¹ Second, government carried on by a ruler who acts according to laws created by the community: the *dominium politicum*.² Third, the *dominium politicum et regale*, government by which the king and the community together consent to the creation of law. This was his description of the contemporary English system of law-making by king and people in parliament.³ In his analysis of the *dominium politicum et regale*, which is simply a device used to explain a law-making arrangement, we see combined the two influences of feudal practice and populist theory. Consent, as the basis of legislation, is crucial. It is the common feature of both feudal practice and populist theory.

Fortescue's use of consent, however, was not confined to law-making. Before examining consent in his feudal-populist account of legislation, it must be stressed that those occupying the law-making institutions, the king and parliament, were treated as elected. In parliament 'the whole body of the realm according to the laws of England is represented',⁴ and the king, as legislator, is elected to the office of kingship (which itself arose naturally from society).⁵ The idea was common. Like the conciliarists Pierre D'Ailly (1350–1420), Jean Gerson (1363–1429) and Nicholas of Cusa (d. 1464), who each saw

---

[1] *De Natura* I, c. 16.  [2] Ibid., c. 26.
[3] *De Laudibus*, c. 13, pp. 31–3. General discussions of Fortescue can be found at: *IELH*, pp. 144, 163, n. 14; *CH*, pp. 278–9; *MPT* VI, pp. 142, 172; *LPMA*, pp. 300, 301; S. B. Chrimes, *English Constitutional Ideas in the Fifteenth Century* (Cambridge, 1936) p. 60; F. Gilbert, 'Fortescue's *dominium regale et politicum*', 2 *Medievalia et Humanistica* (1944) pp. 88–97; R. W. K. Hinton, 'English constitutional theories from Sir John Fortescue to Sir John Eliot', 75 *EHR* (1960) p. 410; J. L. Gillespie, 'Sir John Fortescue's concept of royal will', 23 *Nottingham Medieval Studies* (1979) p. 47; J. H. Burns, 'Fortescue and the political theory of *dominium*', 28 *Historical Journal* (1985) p. 777.
[4] *Works*, pp. 514–17: 'pleno corpore regni in parliamento illo et secundum iura Angliae representato'. The idea is also to be found in P 39 Ed. III, f.7A: 'le parliament represent le corps de tout le royalme'.
[5] *De Natura* I, cc. 18, 19. The more general and related Aristotelian idea of human society and its government institutions as arising naturally is considered in W. Ullmann, *Medieval Foundations of Renaissance Humanism* (London, 1977) pp. 91f. For Aquinas and the ideas that 'man is naturally a social and political animal' and 'many people cannot live a social life together unless someone is in charge to look after the common good', see *Summa*, 1a, 96, 4 (see also generally *MPT*, V, pp. 10–12 and below, n. 24). For related ideas in Nicholas of Cusa, see Sigmund, p. 134; for Gerson, see Pascoe pp. 25, 28. Pecock's view was that scripture (and natural law) approved princehood: *Repressor*, II, p. 429.

Authority and consent: the populist thesis 9

popular consent as the source of secular authority,[6] Pecock envisaged the prince as 'chosen for himself and his heirs to be ruler'.[7] According to Fortescue, when there is no heir the lords and commons must elect a successor.[8] Indeed, the lords and commons elected (*elegerunt*) Stephen as king: he was 'by common consent of the kingdom elected'. Matilda had failed to admit her son as king because 'the lords, nobles and commonalty of England refused their votes to assent thereto'.[9] On Stephen's death it was 'by the common consent of the realm of England in open parliament' that Henry II was made king.[10] Moreover, Fortescue maintained that, during his own lifetime Henry VI was king of France 'with the assent and consent' of that realm.[11] There was, however, something of a tension in Fortescue. His work also expresses the view that the king was appointed

[6] Generally *MPT*, V, pp. 86f.; *LPMA*, pp. 140, 243, n. 1, 277, 289, n. 1; *PGP*, pp. 231–305. For D'Ailly, see Oakley, p. 63, n. 50: the people have a natural right 'which belongs to all those over whom any authority, either secular or ecclesiastical, is placed – that is, the right to elect their ruler'; for Gerson, see *MPT*, VI, p. 159, n. 2; and for Nicholas of Cusa, Sigmund, pp. 140, 144, n. 14. For John Major (1469–1550) see *Historia Majoris Britanniae* (1521), translated by A. Constable, Publications of the Scottish History Society, volume 10 (Edinburgh, 1892) p. 213; in a discussion of the authority of English kings, he concludes: 'And it is impossible to deny that a king held from his people his right to rule.'

[7] *Reule*, p. 338; nowhere, however, does Pecock identify the electing organ, yet, in relation to church government, at p. 318, he implies that the apostles could have been appointed 'by *eleccioun* thereto made *of the people*'; again, he argues that the popes 'in the church of Rome were heads to all the church of God, and that by election (*eleccioun*) and ordinance of men': *Repressor*, II, p. 439.

[8] *De Natura* II, c. 35. The idea that communities appoint one man to be king, is at *De Laudibus*, c. 13, p. 31: 'Quare populum se in regnum aliudve corpus politicum erigere volentem semper oportet unum preficere tocius corporis illius regitivum, quem per analogiam in regno a regendo, regem nominare solitum est': indeed, 'ex populo erumpit regnum'. *Governance*, p. 112, states the fiction that Brutus was chosen by the body politic to be king (the legend of Brutus was circulated widely: see also Port, *Notebook*, p. 135). See also, generally, the polemical tract *Defensio Iuris Domus Lancastriae*, *Works*, pp. 505f.: 'per dominos et communitatem regni cum casus hujusmodi contigerit, ante omnes alios a sanguine regis remotiores ad culmen regium erigatur'. For the political dimension of Fortescue's work, see P. E. Gill, 'Politics and propaganda in fifteenth-century England: the polemical writings of Sir John Fortescue', 46 *Speculum* (1971) p. 333.

[9] *Works*, p. 505; see also *De Titulo Comitis Marchiae*, p. 78; as to Stephen, Fortescue later retracts this: *Works*, p. 538.

[10] *Works*, p. 505: 'communi consensu procerum et communitatis regni Angliae ad instantiam et requisitionem ipsius Stephani, in publico parliamento ordinatum atque conclusum est quod Henricus ... fierat rex'.

[11] Ibid., pp. 513, 514: 'de assensu pariter et consensu majoris partis omnium principium et dominorum nec non procerum et communitatis totius regni Franciae'.

10  *Fundamental authority in late medieval English law*

by God. Certainly all power was from God: that was a common idea.[12] In addition, though, Fortescue perceived the king as 'hanging' from God (*ex deo pependit*).[13] Not only was Stephen popularly elected but also he was anointed as king.[14] Henry VI too was elected king yet at the same time 'God had set him most graciously on the throne', so that 'by holy unction [he was] ordained to be the Lord's Christ'.[15] The parallel with Bracton's notion of the king as *vicarius dei* is clear.[16] Unlike Ockham before him, for whom anointing was a purely human institution,[17] or Nicholas of Cusa, for whom authority existed only if the ruler's election was approved by God,[18] Fortescue does not attempt to reconcile these opposing ideas of authority.

### Feudal practice and populist theory

Feudalism arose as an essentially private arrangement of land tenure between lord and vassal. It possessed a consensual quality in which

---

[12] For Fortescue, *De Natura* I, c. 27; for Pecock, *Repressor*, II, p. 443. For Gerson, see Pascoe, p. 22; for D'Ailly, Oakley, p. 76, n. 5, and for Nicholas of Cusa, Sigmund, p. 148. For Aquinas, *Summa*, 1a, 2ae, 96, 4.

[13] *De Natura* II, c. 36; indeed, God chose Saul to be king: ibid., c. 11. For earlier theocratic views of kingship, see W. Ullmann, *Medieval Political Thought* (Harmondsworth, 1975) p. 31. Saint German wrote of 'the ordinance of God which has given power to princes to make laws': *Dialogue*, p. 262.

[14] *Works*, p. 505: 'Stephanus sic communi consensu regni electus unctus erat'; as to Henry IV and V, see p. 501; also p. 514, as to Henry V and VI: 'reges uncti et coronati regni Angliae per sexaginta et tres annos et amplium continuos communi consensu et assensu totius regni'. For Richard II resigning the crown to parliament, *MPT*, VI, pp. 71f. Legally, Henry VII was seen as king 'by authority of this present parliament': G. R. Elton, *The Tudor Constitution* (2nd edition, Cambridge, 1982) p. 4.

[15] *Works*, p. 84. Also p. 498 for the idea of English kings as established upon the consent of the people, approval of the church, possession, and acceptance by God. For his idea of the king as *persona mixta*, see ibid., p. 514. And William Lyndwood, *Provinciale* (1430), edited by J. V. Bullard and H. C. Bell (London, 1929) p. 126; see also H 10 Hen. VII, 17, 17 at 18 per Brian CJCP; for a hint of the theocratic idea by Hussey CJKB, see H 1 Hen. VII, 10, 10, and, for statute, 16 Ric. II, c. 5.

[16] *De Legibus et Consuetudinibus Angliae*, translated by S. E. Thorne, volume II (Harvard, 1968) p. 33; discussed by Ullmann, *Medieval Political Thought*, p. 152.

[17] A. S. McGrade, *The Political Thought of William of Ockham* (Cambridge, 1974) p. 86.

[18] Sigmund, p. 144, n. 14: 'all power ... rests potentially in the people, although, for the power to rule to be established, the form-giving radiance must be granted from above to set it into being'; and n. 15: 'rulership is from God through men and councils, by elective consent'.

## Authority and consent: the populist thesis 11

lord and vassal were bound together.[19] In his capacity as feudal lord, the king entered into contractual relations with his subjects, principally the tenants-in-chief, which in turn had implications for the king's governmental position. Whereas the theocratic aspect of kingship took the king outside the community (by stressing the divine origin of his authority), the feudal aspect brought the king into the community.[20] In consequence, according to the king's feudal role, it was not the king's *voluntas* alone that created law, but also the *consent* of the tenants-in-chief. The practice has been described in this way: '[f]or purposes of government and making of the law the feudal king had to proceed by consultation and agreement with the other parties in the feudal contract, for brevity's sake with the barons'.[21] It was from the starting point of baronial involvement in making legislation, the essence of feudal practice (whose focus was the joint effort of king and barons), that the gradual widening of participation was achieved during the thirteenth and fourteenth centuries to embrace the whole *communitas regni*.[22]

During the thirteenth century, Bracton's discussion of law-making is essentially an account of feudal government. Law obtains its force in England only when 'approved with the counsel and consent of the magnates and the general agreement of the *res publica*, the authority of the king or prince having first been added thereto'; nor could laws be changed or nullified without the consent of all those by whom they were created.[23] There is a definite similarity here with the populist theory of the continental jurists for whom the people's consent is the determining force in the creation of law. According to Marsilius of Padua (d. 1343?), in his *Defensor Pacis* (1324), law was created by the community of the citizens and its enforceable character is supplied

[19] See, for example, H. S. Maine, *Ancient Law* (1861), with an introduction by J. H. Morgan, (London, 1917, reprinted 1977) p. 214; F. L. Ganshof, *Qu'est-ce que La Féodalité?* (2nd edition, Brussels, 1944) p. 89. See, generally, S. F. C. Milsom, *The Legal Framework of English Feudalism* (Cambridge, 1976) p. 39.
[20] *PGP*, p. 151; *LPMA*, p. 215.
[21] *PGP*, pp. 150, 151.
[22] C. H. McIlwain, *The High Court of Parliament and Its Supremacy* (New Haven, Conn., 1934) pp. 9, 19–22; C. H. McIlwain, *Constitutionalism and the Changing World* (Cambridge, 1939) p. 248.
[23] *De Legibus*, II, pp. 19, 21. Grosseteste held a similar view: H. M. Cam, *Law-Finders and Law-Makers* (London, 1962) p. 137. The oath of kings was that they would keep the law consented to by the community: P. E. Schramm, *A History of the English Coronation* (Oxford, 1937) p. 206; for a cynical view see anon., *The Mirror of Justices*, edited by W. J. Whittaker and F. W. Maitland, 7 Sel. Soc. (London, 1893) p. 155.

simply by the will of the people as *legislator humanus*.[24] With the aid of Roman Law, Bartolus de Sassoferrato (d. 1357) saw explicit popular consent as the basis for written statute law. This was made by the will of the people acting through its general council or parliament which represented the entire community (*concilium totam civitatem repraesentat*).[25]

### Legal theory: the fusion of feudal practice and populist theory

Fortescue's *dominium politicum et regale* is a device used to describe the contemporary law-making arrangement: it simply represents the joint act of the king and community in making parliamentary statute. What he describes is, in effect, the product of actual past feudal practice. Whilst broadly expounding a form of developed feudal practice, Fortescue expresses law-making, creating legislation, largely in terms of populist theory. This he can do because of the similarities between feudal practice and populist theory converging around the idea of consent. Inherited forms of actual feudal practice, centred on the idea of consent, enable Fortescue to add a distinctly populist dimension to his exposition of law-making.

The *dominium politicum et regale*, Fortescue argues, is a system of government regulated by many, but the community cannot make laws alone without the authority of the king.[26] The *dominium politicum et regale* is rooted in the notion that the king cannot create (statutory) laws (nor impose taxes) on his subjects without the consent of the three estates of the realm. This lies at the heart of the feudal practice of government as stated by Bracton two centuries before. At the same time, the arrangement is infused with populist themes. Using

---

[24] *DP*, II, p. 45. In general terms Aquinas seems to favour a form of 'mixed' government (which he also implies is prescribed by divine law): 'Hence the best system in any state or kingdom is one in which one man, as specially qualified, rules over all, and under him are others governing as having special endowments, yet all will have a share inasmuch as those are elected from all, and also are elected by all. This is the best form of government, a mixture of monarchy, in that one man is at the head, of aristocracy, in that many rule as specially qualified, and democracy, in that the rulers can be chosen from the people and by them' (*Summa*, 1a, 2ae, 105, 1). Ockham tends to see 'popular consent as the normal original basis for legitimate secular authority', though with qualifications, for authority could at times be imposed on a people and he denies that a community could 'at its own discretion withdraw power from the government it has established': McGrade, *The Political Thought of William of Ockham*, pp. 103–7.
[25] See generally, *PGP*, pp. 283–5.   [26] *De Natura* I, c. 16.

Thomist ideas, Fortescue says that law created under the *dominium politicum*, 'political law', is established only with the consent of the people.[27] In any community the will of the people is the source of life, and this notion he applies to the *dominium politicum et regale*. Here, the king cannot change the law or deprive the people against their will,[28] nor can he take his subjects' goods or arrest them except according to the law of the land and before the ordinary judges.[29] Nor can the king impose taxes without the assent of the people 'expressed in his parliament', where the whole body of the realm is represented.[30] Fortescue actually sees statute as a species of law made by an elected king acting in conjunction with a legislature representative of the community: the bilateral legislative act, based on consent, is presented in large measure as populist, the by-product of developed feudal practice.

Fortescue's thesis, the conception of law-creation in terms of a joint effort between king and community, was anticipated by around twenty years in the work of Pecock. In Pecock's view secular law 'contains commandments and ordinances of *princes and of their commonalty together*, for to rule people in a peaceable and commodious civility'.[31] For Pecock, English judges were appointed by the

[27] Ibid., c. 26. For Aquinas' discussion of the two ideas of law as resting on the common agreement of the whole people and also of law as being ordained by the prince who has the care of the people, see *Summa*, 1a, 2ae, 90, 3; 97, 3; 2a, 2ae, 57, 2; see also *MPT*, V, pp. 68, 69. He favours, of course, a form of mixed government: above, n. 24.
[28] *De Laudibus*, c. 13, pp. 31–3: 'sic in corpore politico intencio populi primum vivens est'; '[e]t ut non potest caput corporis phisici nervos suos commutare, neque membris suis proprias vires et propria sanguinis alimenta denegare, nec rex qui caput corporis politici est, mutare potest leges corporis illius, nec eiusdem populi substancias proprias subtrahere reclamantibus eis aut invitis'.
[29] Ibid., c. 36, p. 89: 'Nec in placitum ipsi ducuntur, nisi coram iudicibus ordinariis, ubi illi per lege terre iuste tractantur; nec allocuti nec implacitati sunt de mobilibus aut possessionibus suis, vel arrettati de crimine aliquo qualitercunque magni et enormi, nisi secundum leges terre illius et coram iudicibus antedictis'.
[30] Ibid., c. 36, p. 87: 'Neque rex ibidem per se, aut ministros suos, tallagia, subsidia, aut quevis onera alia imponit legiis suis, aut leges eorum mutat, vel novas condit, sine concessione vel assensu tocius regni sui in parliamento suo expresso'.
[31] *Folower*, p. 53; and *Repressor*, II, p. 454: 'it is lawful for princes with their commonalty to make politic and civil laws and ordinances for the better rule of the people in temporal and civil government'. It is unclear to what extent Pecock embraced conciliarism and applied this idea to church government, though in his analysis of church law, again, consent was prominent: see N. Doe, 'Fifteenth-century concepts of law: Fortescue and Pecock', 10 *History of Political Thought* (1989) p. 257 at pp. 262–4. Lyndwood seems to reject conciliarism: F. W. Maitland, *Roman Canon Law in the Church of England* (London, 1898) pp. 15, n. 3, 16.

king 'to judge all causes after the law which he and his parliament make',[32] and it was the duty of princes to make laws serving the common profit 'with common assent of the people'.[33] In a statement which succinctly expresses Pecock's stance, he says simply that the people 'will and consent to the making of the laws'.[34] Moreover, all punishments must be fixed by laws 'made by the commonalty's assent'.[35] Indeed, argues Pecock, if the king was residing in Gascony and sent a letter to England exhorting the people to keep the law, then 'it ought not be said that this epistle grounded any of the laws or governances of England, for their ground is had ... before this epistle of the king ... by act and decree of the whole parliament of England which is the very ground to all the laws of England, as though the epistle of the king ... had not been written'.[36] When he discusses the king's subordination to law, Pecock explains that the king can take 'no tax or tallage or tribute from his people, otherwise than for the need or profit of the community, and not without asking for and receiving the commonalty's assent'. Nor can the king take 'any personal service of his people against their will further or more than his reasonable law, *previously made by the consent of his people*, fixes, limits or assigns'.[37]

### Legislation and the practitioners' idea of consent

In practice it was firmly established by the late medieval period that taxation could be imposed only with the consent of the community of the realm in parliament.[38] Legislation from 1340 asserts that the people ought not 'to make any aid, or to sustain charge, if it not be by the common assent of the prelates, earls, barons and other great men, and the commons of our said realm of England, *and that in the parliament*'.[39] In our period, the idea is illustrated in 1410 when it was held by Hill JCP that the king could not empower any person by letters patent to levy charges on others, 'for by the patent the office cannot commence to the burden of his people'. If the donee of the

---

[32] *Faith*, p. 281.  [33] *Reule*, p. 335.  [34] *Folower*, p. 217; also pp. 143, 216.
[35] *Reule*, p. 336.  [36] *Repressor*, I, pp. 21, 22.
[37] *Donet*, p. 76: 'noon taxe or talage or tribute of hise peple, withoute nede or profite of the comounte, and not withoute the comounte assent, asking and taking; not taking eny personal service of his peple agens her wil, ferthir or more than his lawe resonable, afore made bi consent of his peple, taxith, lymytith and assignith'.
[38] W. Stubbs, *The Constitutional History of England* (1874–8), abridged by J. Cornford (Chicago, 1979) pp. 286–90.
[39] 14 Ed. III, St. II, c. 1; see also 25 Ed. I, c. 1 (1297).

supposed power attempted to impose such a charge then 'this would be judged only a wrongful taking'. Gascoigne CJKB agreed: the king cannot 'charge his people outside the parliament'.[40] The idea was repeated by Serjeant Fortescue in 1441: the king cannot have a tenth or a fifteenth 'unless by grant of his people'.[41]

Turning to general enactments outside the field of taxation, the idea of consent is nowhere better expressed than in the wording of parliamentary statutes themselves. The standard formulae represent legislation as enacted 'by the assent' or 'with the consent' of the community of the realm.[42] As Serjeant Fineux said in 1492: 'For an act of parliament is nothing except *judicium*, and an act is a judgment; and the king, lords and commonalty are required to make this judgment, and none of them can be left out.'[43] In 1496 Vavasour JCP repeated the idea: 'If an act of parliament be of such manner that by the assent of the king, and the lords spiritual and temporal, and of the commons [it] is ordained and enacted, this is a good act of parliament.' Whereas tripartite consent, from king, lords and commons, confers validity upon a statute, 'this is not taken [to be an] act, if the king, and the lords and the commons do not make the act', says Vavasour. However, it is not entirely certain whether Vavasour considers that it is *actual* consent that confers validity or whether a mere reference to consent on the face of the statute is sufficient. At one point Vavasour implies the modern constitutional idea that the appearance of validity

[40] H 13 Hen. IV, 14, 11 at 16A for Gascoigne; for Hill, ibid., at 14B (for the rest of the case see T 11 Hen. IV, 86, 37). However, at 14B Gascoigne discusses circumstances when the king alone can charge if this profits the common people; also, per Littleton, P 35 Hen. VI, 56, 2 at 57: a grant by parliament is stronger than one by the king alone.
[41] P 19 Hen. VI, 62, 1 at 62A: 'issint icy le Roy n'ad aucun cause d'aver X ou XV, sinon per grant de son people'.
[42] See the preambles. Typical is 4 Hen. IV: 'Our Lord the King *by the assent* of the Lords spiritual and temporal, and at the special instance and request of the Commons ... has ordained and established certain statutes and ordinances by the manner as follows'; sometimes legislation is created 'by advice and assent': see, for example, 5 Hen. IV, preamble, or 23 Hen. VI: 'the same our Lord the King, *by the advice and assent* of the Lords spiritual and temporal, and the Commons being in the said parliament...'
[43] T 7 Hen. VII, 14, 1 at 15; Brooke, *GA*, 'Parliament', 76: 'Car un Act de Parliament n'est forsque *Judicium*, et un Act come un jugement; et le Roy, Seigniors et Communalty requir' a faire cest Jugement, et nul d'eux poit estre enterlesse.' The idea of a statute as a judgment was not new: M 8 Hen. IV, 12, 13 at 13A per Srjt Tirwit; 1 Hen. IV, c. 3; for the idea of parliament as the 'highest court', see P 19 Hen. VI, 62, 1, at 63A per Fray CB; generally, A. Harding, *The Law Courts of Medieval England* (London, 1973) pp. 80–2. The modern idea of the appearance of validity is expressed, for example, in *Manuel* v. *AG* [1983] 1 Ch. 77.

suffices: 'but because it says that it was ordained by their assent, it is understood that they made the act'.[44] Provided that the enactment before the court recites that tripartite consent has been given, the judges will not question the statute.

Fortescue's idea that law is created by a legislature, parliament, which represents the community of the realm, is rarely found in the Year Books. But it does appear in a case of 1480. In this an individual was considered to be discharged from a jury by virtue of a royal grant exempting the citizens of Norwich from jury service outside the city.[45] Whilst discussing the general confirmation of franchises and liberties by legislation, Neele JCP said that all acts of parliament 'must be known to every man in the realm, for every man has his attorney in parliament, namely the knights of the shire for the county, and the burgesses of the parliament for the cities and boroughs'. Thomas Smith, in the following century, echoed an observation of Vavasour from 1506 that 'everyone of England is party to the act of parliament'; for Smith, and the idea was certainly an old one, 'every English man is understood to be there present ... [a]nd the consent of parliament is taken to be every man's consent'.[46]

[44] T 11 Hen. VII, 26, 10 at 27; see also: P 33 Hen. VI, 17, 8; T 12 Hen. VII, 19, 1 at 20, per Srjt Mordant. However, it is important to note the apparent scope for the unilateral alteration of legislation by the royal will. See 6 Hen. VI, c. 1: 'And this ordinance shall endure as long as shall please our Lord the King.' Again, 11 Hen. VI, c. 13, empowers the king to modify the measure whenever it pleased him, by the advice of his council, or when it would profit himself and the realm. See H. G. Richardson and G. O. Sayles, 'The early statutes', 50 *LQR* (1934) p. 540 at p. 549 for thirteenth-century examples of the king varying, delaying and abrogating statutes. For analogous judicial statements, H 39 Hen. VI, 38, 3 at 40, per Moile JCP; H 13 Hen. IV, 14, 11, at 14B, per Gascoigne CJKB (for unilateral royal taxation); for the idea that the law 'lay in the mouth' of Richard II, see *MPT*, VI, p. 72. For Fortescue on the *voluntas* of the prince as the basis of the *ius regis*, see *De Natura* I, c. 16. The prince's *voluntas* was fundamental to theocratic ideas of government: *PGP*, pp. 119, 123, 126, 150, 154, 156, 157f.

[45] M 21 Ed. IV, 55, 28 at 59; Brooke, *GA*, 'Corporations', 63: 'chescun act de parlement covient estre entendu general, et covient d'estre conu a chescun home deins le realme, car il est fait per tout le realme, car chescun home ad son attorney en parliament ... (etc)'. For restrictions on the purchase of charters of exemption, see 52 Hen. III, c. 14.

[46] For Smith see J. W. Allen, *A History of Political Thought in the Sixteenth Century* (3rd edition, London, 1951) p. 264; for Vavasour, H 21 Hen. VII, 1, 1 at 4: 'car chescun de Angl' est party al' Act de Parlement'; see also at 1 Srjt Butler: a statute is something 'a quel chescun in Angleterre est prive, et sera lye per ceo [and will be bound by this]'. The idea is an old one: M. S. Arnold, 'Statutes as judgments: the natural law theory of parliamentary activity in medieval England', 126 *University of Pennsylvania Law Review* (1977) pp. 329–43.

## Justifications for the idea of consent in legislation

As the idea of a representative legislature does not appear too frequently in the Year Books, so too the practitioners are rarely seen justifying the requirement of consent. A basic justification was proposed by Newton CJCP, however, in a case of 1441. The facts of the case were these. Henry IV had granted a rector and his successors exemption from tenths awarded to the king by the clergy. When a tenth was awarded to Henry VI, in order to avoid payment the rector relied on the letters patent of Henry IV. Though the case was adjourned, Newton CJCP considered taxation and exemptions in general terms. Because the rector was a member of the clergy who awarded in parliament the tenth to the king, Newton argued that he would be estopped from denying liability to pay: '[i]t seems that he will be estopped, as has been said, by the grant made afterwards by him *as one of the parliament*'. Whereas the king could disherit a man, says Newton, and put him to death, if parliament did not exist, 'why then will the king by his parliament not estop the rector from having the benefit of [the exemption from] the grant by another parliament, which wills that everyone will be charged for the tenth or fifteenth *to which he himself is party in law?*'[47] Hody CJKB added that if an individual member wished to say in parliament that he was not willing to agree to a particular grant, 'this will be of no value, because the grant is quite effectual if the greater part agree to this'.[48]

Implicit in Newton's statement is the idea that once a measure is approved, then it binds those who consent to it. Consent obliges them to comply with it. This is similar to the justification employed in the theory of Pecock. According to Pecock, the people ought to consent to the making of law because that deprives them of an excuse to disobey. Individuals are bound by laws, he says, 'if the [same] men which should be bound by the laws will and consent to the making of the

---

[47] P 19 Hen. VI, 62, 1 at 63A: 'Me semble que il sera estoppe come ad este bien dit per le grant enapres per luy fait come un del Parlement: par le Roy peut disheriter un homme, et luy mettre a mort, que est encontre le Ley, si le Parlement ne fuit: purque donc n'estoppera le Roy per son Parlement le Rector a aver benefice de cest grant per autre Parlement, que veut, que chaqun [homme] sera charge del X ou XV a quel il meme est party en Ley?'; Brooke, *GA*, 'Grants' 40, 'Estoppel', 183. See also Newton at P 7 Hen. VI, 35, 39 for the view that those in ancient demesne cannot be impleaded by actions given under statute for they are not parties to the making of the statute.
[48] P 19 Hen. VI, 62, 1 at 63 B.

18    *Fundamental authority in late medieval English law*

laws'. Pecock explains in this way: '[w]hen a law is justly made by consent of all people or the greater part of the people, and used and continued by the greater part of the people as for a law, each person of this people is bound by reason and the law of nature to keep it'.[49] Moreover, 'each person of the same people renounces and foresakes all right belonging to him which is contrary to the execution of this law'.[50] Not least, also, for its reference to majoritarianism, this is, arguably, one of the most significant and mature ideas in late medieval English jurisprudence. Like Newton, Pecock implies that consent is justified for reasons of obedience: what is approved by the people binds the people.

This is an interesting idea. It might be compared, by way of analogy, with the justification for consent employed commonly in continental medieval jurisprudence: the Roman Law *quod omnes tangit* principle.[51] According to this, what touches all must be approved by all. Nicholas of Cusa, for example, says that 'legislation ought to be adopted by all or a majority of those who are bound by it ... for what touches all ought to be approved by all'.[52] At this point, we can see a point of contact with Pecock, for Nicholas then argues that no-one can be 'excused from obedience to a law when each one has imposed it upon himself'.[53] By way of comparison, Fortescue justifies consent as the basis for law because of the potential for tyranny which attaches to purely 'regal' government. With the *dominium regale* law

[49] *Folower*, pp. 142: 'whanne a lawe is iustli maad bi consent of al peple or of the more parti of the peple, and usid and contynued bi the more part of the peple as for a lawe, ech persoun of thilk peple is bounden bi resoun and in lawe of kynde to kepe it'; ibid., p. 217: 'and that for as mych as men ben not bounde bi lawis maad among hem and of men but if tho men whiche schulde be bounde bi tho lawis wille and consent into the makyng of tho lawis, and that immediatli and expresseli, or into the sufficient antecedent thereto, and that bi hem silf or bi her sufficient procutoures or attorneyes'; see too *Reule*, pp. 322–8 for a similar idea in relation to church law.
[50] *Folower*, p. 142. The majority principle, however, though important, was not new: it appears in the earlier canon law and in Nicholas of Cusa, see *LPMA*, pp. 155, 156, 303. For Marsilius and the *valentior pars* of the citizens as making law, see *DP*, II, p. 51. Indeed, in England, writs of election from the time of Henry VI state that members elected to parliament were to be held as elected 'qui habuerint majorem numerum ipsorum, qui quadraginta solidos per annum et ultra expendere possunt ...': see L. Riess, *The History of the English Electoral Law in the Middle Ages*, translated by K. L. Wood-Legh (New York, 1973) p. 82. The idea also operates in the sphere of the courts in relation to juries and their verdicts: see ibid., p. 82, n. 5.
[51] G. Post, *Studies in Medieval Legal Thought: Public Law and the State, 1100–1322* (Princeton, 1964) p. 163. The idea in Ockham can be found in McGrade, *The Political Thought of William of Ockham*, p. 107.
[52] Sigmund, p. 151, n. 29.   [53] Ibid.

is made in accordance with the (Roman Law) maxim *quod principi placuit legis vigorem habet*. Under this scheme of government, Fortescue fears that this law is as often bad as it is good.[54] However, though there are no clear allusions to *quod omnes tangit* in his legal theory, as a serjeant in the Exchequer Chamber in 1440 Fortescue did argue that 'the territory of Ireland is separate from the kingdom of England, for if a tenth or fifteenth be granted here, it shall not bind the people of Ireland unless they will to approve of this in their own parliament, even though the king under his great seal send the same statute to Ireland'.[55] It must be noted, of course, that *quod omnes tangit* might easily have been accommodated in Fortescue's feudally prepared populist idea of making legislation, particularly bearing in mind the contractual nature of the earlier feudal relationship.[56]

## CONSENT AND CUSTOMARY LAW

For Pecock and Fortescue law is created, it exists, because people will and consent to the making of law (to use Pecock's expression). Their use of consent, however, is restricted simply to *legislation*, parliamentary law. These theorists do not relate consent to *custom*, either local custom or national custom, the common law. Indeed, unlike the practitioners, and Littleton and Saint German,[57] both Pecock and Fortescue fail to distinguish between local and national custom. Their failure to visualise consent as the basis for customary law can be contrasted not only with the practitioners, but also with European jurists. Within the framework of Roman Law, Bartolus, for instance, maintained that as explicit popular consent supplied the authority for written statute law, so tacit popular consent produced unwritten customary law. Usage, says Bartolus, was the *causa remota* of custom, and tacit popular consent its *causa proxima*: 'This [custom] differs from statute, because statute is introduced by the express consent of the people, this [custom] tacitly.'[58]

[54] *De Natura* I, c. 28; to justify the *dominium politicum et regale*, Fortescue also uses the idea that government is wiser when carried on by many: ibid., c. 23. This idea is also used by Pecock: *Repressor*, II, p. 370.
[55] M 20 Hen. VI, 8, 17.
[56] Ullmann, *Medieval Political Thought*, p. 153.
[57] See, for example, M 8 Ed. IV, 18, 30, at 19 per Littleton, JCP, and M 21 Ed. IV, 55, 28 at 57 per Catesby JCP; *Tenures*, Bk. I, c. 9, s. 77; *Dialogue*, pp. 45, 71. Pecock does say, however, that 'the lawe of the kyng of englond, what is iugid bi iugis... thei callen her comoun lawe': *Folower*, p. 143.
[58] See W. Ullmann, 'Bartolus on customary law', 52 *Juridical Review*, (1940) p. 265 at pp. 269, 270.

## Consent and local customary law

The idea of consent was fundamental to late medieval local borough customs codified and collected in custumals. The mayor and commonalty of a town or city, as the custumals state, would 'concede', 'ordain', 'will' or 'award' a particular custom.[59] The custumals usually describe customs consented to as 'usage' or 'law',[60] and frequently the practices approved are expressed as 'used' by the commonalty.[61] Customs are also treated as issuing from the community itself. Terms such as 'our use', 'the custom among us', 'the law of the citizens', or of the community as 'having customs', constantly appear.[62] Simply, local custom enured or attached to a community. Hill JCP in a case of 1412 had spoken of 'gavelkind and other customs *queux trenchent a*

---

[59] For extracts from the texts of the custumals see *Borough Customs*, edited by M. Bateson, 18 and 21 Sel. Soc. (London, 1904 and 1906); 18 Sel. Soc. (London, 1904) p. 23, a custumal of Llantrisant, 1346, recites: 'Concessimus eciam quod nullus burgensibus nostris predictis capi nec imprisonari ...'; ibid., p. 149, Ipswich, from 1291: 'Item, ordine est par la dite comunalte ...'; ibid., p. 113, Bury, c. 15, 1327: 'E ensement nous voloms e grantoms qe ...'; ibid., p. 245, London, thirteenth-century: 'Ordinatum per discretiores viros civitatis'; ibid., p. 302, Reading, 1290: 'Consideratum est per totam communitatem burgi Radyng ...'; for the idea of consent in relation to village customs, see W. O. Ault, 'Village by-laws by common consent', 29 *Speculum* (1954) p. 378.

[60] 18 Sel. Soc. (1904) p. 135, London, 1305: 'secundum usus civitatis'; ibid., p. 304, Exeter, Court Roll, No. 18, 1321–2: 'Whereas the customs [*consuetudines*] hitherto used and approved in this city as in many other cities are to be held for law [*pro lege habeantur*]'; ibid., p. 145, Nottingham, 1395: 'Et dicunt quod usus et consuetudo ... de Notyngham, et de antiquo tempore ...'; ibid., p. 156, London, 1419: 'ils serrount rewles solonc les usages de la citee'; ibid., pp. 264, 265, Hereford, cc. 84–6: 'per legem et consuetudinem civitatis temporibus retroactis usitatam'. See also P 22 Ed. IV, 8, 24 per Catesby JCP, who says of a custom that even 'if it is lawful it is no good if it has not been used': for this translation see J. H. Baker and S. F. C. Milsom, *Sources of English Legal History: Private Law to 1750* (London, 1986) p. 315.

[61] 18 Sel. Soc. (London, 1904) p. 78, Ipswich, c. 73, 1291: 'Item use est en l'avauntdite vyle qe ...'; ibid., p. 57, Lydd, c. 20, 1476: 'Also it is used if anyone is found cutting purses or picking a purse' they shall make a fine to the town and swear never to come there again; ibid., p. 264, Hereford, cc. 84–6, 1486: 'And he [the bailiff] being ignorant how and by what process he ought to proceed, asked of his fellow citizens how to proceed by the law and custom of the city used in time past [*per legem et consuetudinem civitatis temporibus retroactis usitatem*].'

[62] Ibid., p. 190, Hereford, c. 36, 1486: 'De debitis nostris utimur quod ...'; ibid., p. 118, Hereford, c. 74, 1486: 'Item utimur inter nos quod ...'; ibid., p. 222, Waterford, c. 12, c. 1300: 'the law of the citizens and burgesses [*si com lei est chitesein et de burgeois*]'; ibid., p. 62, Kilkenny, c. 31: 'Item dicti superior et communitas ville predicte tales libertates habent et consuetudines.'

*un cominaltie et a un people*'.⁶³ Whereas Fortescue's *dominium politicum et regale* has a very strong populist aspect, but is not entirely populist in the sense that it also involves the royal will in the creation of law (though, at the same time, it must be remembered that he saw the king as elected), these are thoroughly populist ideas in the custumals, and they are rooted in the view that customs were 'assented to' or 'agreed' or 'approved' by local communities.⁶⁴

Consent appears in custumals well before the fifteenth century. An Ipswich custumal of 1291 recites that the borough records were taken by a deceitful clerk and to cure the uncertainty 'the commonalty of the aforesaid town ... of one will and one assent ordained that the laws and usages of the same town ... shall be openly put in Domesday and ensealed with the common seal of the town'.⁶⁵ A Northampton custumal of 1341 explains how 'the said mayor and community have agreed that in a plea of debt or trespass in which defamation is involved, the plaintiff shall have only one essoin after law has been waged [by the defendant]'.⁶⁶ In 1379, a custumal of London provided that executors ought to answer for the debts of their testators, arising with or without specialty, in the royal courts. It says how 'it was attested [*attestatum*] by the whole common council that from the time whereof memory runs not to the contrary this was the custom approved [*consuetudo approbata*] in the city of London'.⁶⁷ Similarly, in 1389, a custumal of Colchester recites that 'it was ordained by the consent [*assensum*] of the said twenty-four men of the council of the town' that on the day a

---

[63] M 14 Hen. IV, 2, 6, at 9 B: for *trenchent*, from *trencher a*, see J. H. Baker, *Manual of Law French* (Avebury, 1979), 'to enure'; see also Co. Litt., 209b ('because the money at the beginning trenched to the feoffee in manner as a duty'); generally, see also Pigot, M 22 Ed. IV, 30, 11: 'mayor and commonalty of London to certify their custom'.

[64] 18 Sel. Soc. (London, 1904) p. 256, Cork, c. 9, c. 1339: 'En primes est assentu qe cele auncien usage soit tins [be held]'; ibid., p. 181, Norwich, c. 27, before 1340: 'and make law according to the laws and ancient customs of this city used and approved here of old [*secundum leges et antiquas consuetudines illius civitatis ab antiquo usitatas et probatas in eadem*]'; ibid., p. 89, Bristol II, c. 21, 1344: 'Item ordinatum est et concordatum quod ...'; ibid., p. 184, London, 1356: 'Item ordeignez est et assentuz, qe ...'; ibid., p. 239, Kilkenny, 1543: 'it is therefore established and enacted by the whole assent and consent of the said sovereign, burgesses, and commons ...'.

[65] Holdsworth, II, p. 374, n. 7.

[66] 18 Sel. Soc. (London, 1904) p. 153, Northampton III, c. 58, 1341: 'E aussint le dit maire e la commune sont assentuz ...'.

[67] Ibid., pp. 210, 211, London, 1379; see also *HFCL*, p. 257, n. 1 (the testators were to swear to the best of their knowledge: compare exclusion of wager here at common law).

plea is brought against a burgess, he shall be allowed, if he chooses, one essoin and no more before his appearance.[68]

From 1486, a custumal of Hereford explained how 'by the custom of the city', before the time of William the Conqueror, individuals violent towards the bailiff should have their striking member cut off. It also describes how, in William's reign, a priest (sent to the city as the king's representative) struck the bailiff whilst forcibly taking the daughter of a certain citizen. The text continues: 'Therefore, the said William sent by letter praying that the penalty and custom should be remitted during his time, and especially on this occasion. And this was then granted [*concedebatur*] by the citizens, and in our time we have not seen such things happen.'[69]

Moreover, the idea of consent as the basis for local custom can be viewed in a wider context. Occasionally the community of the realm, by means of parliamentary legislation, would consent and approve local customs. By a statute of 1339, for instance, the community of the realm in parliament agreed that 'the city of London and all other cities and boroughs of the realm of England [shall] have all their franchises and usages, which they have reasonably had and used in time past'.[70]

### Common law and judicial consent: usage and precedent

Nowhere in the theory of Pecock and Fortescue or in the Year Books can be found statements which regard the consent of the community as the basis for national custom, the common law. Instead, alongside a developing notion of precedent, forensic and judicial usage and learning are treated as the basis of the common law. Indeed, rather than popular consent, the idea of judicial consent is sometimes used to express the source of the common law.

As the mechanics of law-suits and pleading often obstructed explicit discussion of law at a time when facts were hidden by the general denial, the occasions upon which judges recognised the legislative nature of their own decisions are few.[71] However, as more law came to

---

[68] 18 Sel. Soc. (London, 1904) pp. 155, 156.
[69] 21 Sel. Soc. (London, 1906) p. 25, Hereford, c. 70.
[70] 14 Ed. III, St. I, c. 1; see also, 14 Ed. III, St. II, c. 2: 'custumes resonablement grantez per nous et per noz auncestres a la citee de loundres, et autres citees, burghes et bones villes de nostre dit roialme dengleterre'; 2 Hen. IV, c. 1; 8 Hen. VI, c. 11. For the confirmation of London customs, M 21 Ed. IV, 67, 50 per Brian CJCP.
[71] *HFCL*, pp. 44–8, 59, 73, 74; *IELH*, pp. 69, 70, 171, 172.

Authority and consent: the populist thesis 23

be discussed upon demurrer or a special verdict, for example, so we see more instances in which decisions and statements of law are treated as precedents for the future. In 1305 Hengham asked counsel to 'leave off your noise and deliver yourself from this account; and afterwards go to the chancery and purchase a writ of deceit; and consider this from now on as a general rule [*e ceste reulle tiegnez desormes generale*]'.[72] In 1310 Bereford CJCP explained that by a decision on an avowry 'we shall make a law [*nous froms une lei*] throughout all the land'.[73] In 1313, when it was decided that a successor to a prior could make the law waged by his predecessor, Stanton JCP said: 'if judgment had been given against the claimant on this point he would have been without recovery for all time; and that you may safely put in your books for law [*ley*]'.[74]

From the fifteenth century also, there are statements which indicate that judicial usage was treated as creating the common law. In 1455 P brought debt on a bond against the executors of T who plead *non est factum*. The issue is found against them and the court decides that P can proceed against the executors' goods and not simply the testator's.[75] In the course of discussion, Fortescue CJKB said: 'If this judgment were to be given for the first time, in my opinion no judges would wish the plaintiff to recover goods belonging to the executors themselves. But because that is the law now, *and usage makes the law without other reason* [*et l'usage fait ley sans autre reason*], etc. [P was to recover].' Indeed, the idea that the common law was in the keeping of, or within the control of, the judges was implicit in several stock phrases: the judges speak of the common law as 'our law' [*nostre ley*], or of themselves as 'holding [something] for law', and in 1468 Yelverton JKB speaks of the court as 'laying down a positive law'.[76] Some-

[72] YB 33 and 35 Ed. I (RS) 4; for the 'common erudition' of lawyers as law, see *IELH*, p. 172: from the fifteenth century see for instance H 11 Ed. IV, 10, 5 per Catesby; P 8 Hen. VII, 11, 1, per Hussey CJKB; T 9 Hen. VII, 3, 4 at 4 per Brian, CJCP; H 11 Hen. VII, 15, 11, per Srjt Keble.
[73] YB 3 and 4 Ed. II (22 Sel. Soc., London, 1907) p. 161 (*Venour* v. *Blund*, which begins at p. 157); P 39 Ed. III, f.7 per Thorpe CJCP: 'commandons que vous allowes cela pur statut'.
[74] YB 6 and 7 Ed. II (36 Sel. Soc., London, 1918) p. 178: the case is *Midhope* v. *Prior of Kirkham*, which begins at p. 172.
[75] M 34 Hen. VI, 22, 42 (Fortescue is at 24A); for misappropriation to personal representatives of their testator's goods, exposing their own to execution, see S. F. C. Milsom, 'The sale of goods in the fifteenth century', 77 *LQR* (1961) p. 257 at p. 278, n. 42.
[76] M 8 Ed. IV, 9, 9 at 12; 'nous ferromus un positive ley sur cel point'; for 'our law', see T 4 Hen. VI, 31, 11 at 32 per Martin JCP; H 33 Hen. VI, 7, 23 at 9 per Ashton JCP; M 20 Hen. VII, 4, 14 at 5 per Hody CB; for the judges as 'holding' something for law, see M 20 Hen. VII, 5, 15; M 21 Hen. VII, 41, 66 per Fineux CJKB; for Moile JCP describing the usage of Common Pleas as *ley*, see P 37 Hen. VI, 17, 4.

times, the judges overtly employ the idea that a rule exists or a result is reached because they 'assent' to it.[77]

Though usually it was used in the technical sense of meaning a judgment entered on the roll, often a decision would be treated as a *precedent* for the future: and judges frequently based decisions on the law 'in our books'.[78] Toward the end of the fifteenth century Hussey CJKB stated that: 'Our decision in this case will be shown hereafter as a precedent [*pur un precedent*]';[79] and at about the same time, whilst addressing the judges in a case of *quare clausum fregit*, Serjeant Fineux concluded that: 'I apprehend that your decision in this case will be a precedent [*un precedent*] in similar cases on the statute from this day henceforth, and although the law [*le ley*] was against your opinion, yet it is not error for us to grant aid, even though aid did not lie.'[80] From time to time, we see the judges refusing to allow a particular result because to do so would offend the established practices of the past. For example, in 1464 P sued debt on a bond and D confessed the debt but pleaded a release. A date was set for D's plea to be tried but D defaulted and P prayed judgment. Judgment was given for P since, as Danby JCP said, 'diverse precedents as is said are in the court ... and therefore [this] must be done according to the precedents'.[81] Perhaps one of the clearest examples of the idea of the common law as being based on usage can be found in a case of 1455.

D brought *praecipe quod reddat* against T. At the return of the *capias* T appeared, ready to aver that he had not been summoned

[77] For assent: M 3 Ed. IV, 24, 18; H 3 Ed. IV, 28, 3. For agreement (that something is good law): M 3 Ed. IV, 26, 20; M 4 Ed. IV, 31, 12; M 12 Ed. IV, 19, 25 at 21B; M 5 Hen. VII, 9, 21; P 5 Hen. VII, 27, 9. For the judges 'ruling' the law: T 3 Hen. VI, 51, 17 at 51B per Babington CJCP. For the opinion of the court: T 3 Hen. VI, 54, 25; P 2 Ed. IV, 4, 8. 'Held' by the court: P 4 Ed. IV, 13, 20; T 7 Ed. IV, 10, 1. The judges 'will according to the better opinion': P 4 Ed. IV, 12, 19.

[78] See generally, T. E. Lewis, 'The history of judicial precedent' (1930–2) 46 *LQR* pp. 207–24, 341–60; 47 *LQR* pp. 411–27; 48 *LQR* pp. 230–47; C. K. Allen, *Law in the Making* (7th ed, Oxford, 1964) pp. 199–202. For the Year Books: M 3 Ed. IV, 15, 10 and 16 per Choke JCP; H 15 Ed, IV, 16, 4 at 17 per Neele JCP; T 22 Ed. IV, 19, 46 at 20 per Hussey CJKB; M 5 Hen. VII, 2, 3 per Hussey CJKB. For cases put to the court: M 3 Ed. IV, 17, 12 at 19, and for something adjudged before, P 4 Ed. IV, 10, 13. For the 'remembrance' of the judges, P 4 Ed. IV, 13, 21.

[79] M 11 Hen. VII, 10, 33: the case is post-dated; Hussey died in 1495.

[80] T 13 Hen. VII, 26, 5 at 27; the dating of this case in the YB as 1498 is incorrect: Fineux addresses the court here as a Serjeant whereas he succeeded Hussey as CJKB in 1495.

[81] M 5 Ed. IV, 86 (no plaint number) at 87: 'uncore pur ce que divers precedents come est dit sont en le court icy ... et pur ce il covient estre fait accordant as precedents'; Brooke, *GA*, 'Default and Appearance', 68.

'according to the law of the land'. When T sought to have the matter settled by jury, D demurred and the question was whether, in principle, T was entitled to have a jury try the matter. D attempts to persuade the court that T should wage his law on the question of the summons, whilst T argues that trial by jury is permissible.[82] According to the established rule (as described, for instance, by Bracton)[83] when denying summons, as here, the defendant would wage his law. The judges are divided. In addition to exploiting policy arguments about the potential delays involved in trial by jury, both Moile and Ashton JJCP favour the established rule and decide that trial will be by wager of law, for, as Moile explains, 'we rule the law according to ancient usage [*course*]'. Ashton says: 'For where it has been used [*este use*] always to wage his law, and no other way, then this proves in a way a positive law; for all our law is guided by usage [*use*] or by statute.' As to the matter in hand, he continues: 'for it has been used that none must wage his law in trespass, and in debt the contrary: thus we must adjudge according to the usage [*use*], and in a writ of deceit [it] will be tried by examination [wager of law] and not by the country [jury]'. His conclusion, therefore, is that 'in this case it has been used to wage his law, and not otherwise, wherefore to change the ancient usage [*use*] will be strange'.[84] With this contention Danvers and Danby JJCP and Prisot CJCP disagree. They decide that, in principle, trial by jury is permissible to settle the matter of the summons. Danby and Prisot argue that, because the matter lay in the knowledge of the country [*pais*], it and all such things should be triable by jury.[85] In the course of his decision Prisot says: 'And where Ashton says, that [it] is a positive law, etc., this is not so: for it cannot be a positive, but such that was adjudged or made by statute: and this has not been.' For Ashton both common law, based on usage, and statute constituted positive law; for Prisot only that which was contained in statute (which was, of course, treated as a judgment of parliament)[86] was truly 'positive' law. The case was adjourned.

---

[82] For examples of litigants not wishing to wage, see *HCLC*, p. 139.
[83] *De Legibus* IV, pp. 64, 151.
[84] H 33 Hen. VI, 7, 23 at 9; by this time it was common for the defendant in debt to choose jury trial if he so wished: on this matter generally, see *HCLC*, pp. 137–44; for the denial of wager in trespass, see *HFCL*, p. 293.
[85] The case was adjourned, but Brooke gives this as *optima opinio*: Brooke, *GA*, 'Trials', 3; 'Ley Gager', 9.
[86] See above n. 43. See also M 33 Hen. VI, 45, 28 per Prisot: 'jeo entende que l'auncien cours fuit que...'

As compared with parliamentary legislation and local customary law, whose authority is derived predominantly from the consent of the community at large, the judges do not employ the idea that the basis for the common law is the consent of the community: judicial consent alone shapes the common law. Neither do Pecock or Fortescue consider that the custom of the realm, the common law, was founded upon popular consent. Nor do they relate consent to local custom, as was the case in practice. Their statements about consent are narrow, applicable only to parliamentary legislation. Yet the connection between consent and the common law was made occasionally. The author of *The Mirror of Justices* in the late thirteenth century wrote of national custom that 'because it is given to all in common it is called common law. And for that there is no other law than this, it exists as one from of old, and in general councils or parliaments it is suffered to be observed.'[87] The connection between consent and the common law is also to be found in Saint German, who argues that the custom of the realm is consented to by the community of the realm: 'The third ground of the law of England stands upon diverse general customs of old time used through all the realm: which have been *accepted and approved* by our sovereign lord the king and his progenitors *and all their subjects.*'[88]

### THE SUPREMACY OF LAW

Central to the concept of authority based on consent is the notion of the authority *of* the law itself: the idea that the makers of law are subject to the law that they make. The legal thought of this period advances the idea that both the king and the community are subordinate to consensual law, and that individuals must pursue their entitlements or be punished only *according to law*.

### The king's subjection to law

Like their continental contemporaries (such as Pierre D'Ailly and Nicholas of Cusa),[89] our theorists propose the supremacy of law.

[87] 7 Sel. Soc. (London, 1893) p. 5. Edward II's coronation promise was 'to hold and keep the laws and rightful customs which the commonalty of the realm had chosen': T. F. T. Plucknett, *The Legislation of Edward I* (Oxford, 1949) p. 159.
[88] *Dialogue*, p. 45.    [89] *MPT*, VI, pp. 138, 141, and for Gerson, p. 140, n. 5.

Fortescue explains that the king can take away his subjects' goods only with a *lawful cause*.[90] Even in times of necessity, when he takes from his subjects, the king must make due satisfaction and pay a reasonable price.[91] In general terms, the king's subjects can be arrested and their goods taken only according to the law of the land and before the ordinary judges.[92] There is an obvious parallel here with Bracton's celebrated assertion that the king is under God and the law.[93] Whereas Fortescue implies the king's subjection to *all* forms of law, Pecock proposes the king's subjection merely to legislation. The king, he says, can take 'no tax or tallage or tribute from his people, otherwise than for [*withoute*] the need or profit of the commonalty, *and not without asking for and receiving the commonalty's assent*'. Neither must the king take 'any personal service of his people against their will *further or more than his reasonable law, previously made by the consent of his people*, fixes [*taxes*], limits or assigns'.[94]

The idea also appears from time to time in legislation and the Year Books. A statute of 1402, for example, provides in part that if the king presented to any benefice already occupied by an incumbent, the king's presentee shall not be received by the ordinary 'till the king has recovered his presentment *by process of the law* in his own court'. If any presentee of the king be received otherwise 'and the incumbent put out *without due process*', the incumbent can commence his suit within a year after the induction of the presentee to secure his remedy.[95] Similarly, in the course of discussion in the case of 1441 (about a rector's claimed exemption from taxation) Fray CB said: 'for the parliament is the court of the king, and the highest court he has, and the law [*le ley*] is the highest inheritance that the king has: *for by the*

[90] *Governance*, p. 139.
[91] *De Laudibus*, c. 36, p. 87: 'sed nichilominus ipse illud precium in manibus, vel ad diem per maiores officiarios domus sue limitandum, solvere per leges suas obnoxius est, quia nullius subditorum suorum bona iuxta leges illas ipse deripere potest sine satisfaccione debita pro eisdcm'. *De natura* I, c. 25 for occasions when the political king was to rule regally.
[92] *De Laudibus*, c. 36, p. 89: 'Nec in placitum ipsi ducuntur, nisi coram iudicibus ordinariis, ubi illi per lege terre iuste tractantur; nec allocuti nec implacitati sunt de mobilibus aut possessionibus suis, vel arrettati de crimine aliquo qualitercunque magni et enormi, nisi secundum leges terre illius et coram iudicibus antedictis'.
[93] *De Legibus*, II, p. 110; also, *Mirror*, 7 Sel. Soc. (London, 1893) p. 155: 'The first and sovereign abuse is that the king is beyond the law, whereas he ought to be subject to it, as is contained in his oath.'
[94] *Donet*, p. 76; above, n. 37.
[95] 4 Hen. IV, c. 22; see T 35 Hen. VI, 60, 1 at 62 for Moile on this statute (no ouster except by law); the statute confirms 13 Ric. II, St. I, c. 1.

*law he himself and all his subjects are ruled*, and without the law there would be no king and no inheritance'.[96]

However, occasionally the practitioners assert that the king is not subject to local custom and some forms of legislation. In 1456 the Exchequer Chamber heard how T acquired jewels belonging to the king and in return for a loan delivered the jewels to S as a pledge.[97] S, claiming he did not know they were the king's, argues that by a custom of London those to whom goods are given in pledge are permitted to retain them until repaid. Serjeant Hyndestone says the 'custom is against common right [*comen droit*] and in prejudice of those in whom the property resided, and therefore it cannot lie in custom'. He continues: 'and even if it could, still against the king it is of no value, *for the king is above the law* . . . if a man has the profits of a fair, even if the king passes through, still the king will not pay for his passage, *inasmuch as he is above the law*, and no man can have correction of him'. Serjeant Choke agrees, adding: 'even if the custom was good, still the king will not be bound by this'. Prisot CJCP too considers that 'the king will not be said to be bound to obey such custom'. Moile JCP, on the other hand, distinguishing between customs attaching to a locality and those attaching to a person, argues that the king will always be bound by the former but not by the latter.[98] A corresponding idea existed in relation to statute. The king was not bound by legislation when he was not expressly named in it.[99] In 1497 Serjeant Mordant observed that if legislation 'restrains the liberty of all people', the king will not be bound by it unless it makes explicit mention of him, as with the statute *Quia Emptores* 'all people are bound except the king'. However, when a statute is made which is

---

[96] P 19 Hen. VI, 62, 1 at 63A; for similar ideas see H 8 Hen. VI, 18, 6 at 19 per Cottesmore JCP (the king cannot grant if A owes B in debt that B shall never have his action), and M 1 Hen. VII, 2, 2.

[97] M 35 Hen. VI, 25, 33; for Hyndestone, 26A: 'car le Roy est desus la Ley'; Brooke, *GA*, 'Custom', 5; see also 41 Sel. Soc. (London, 1924) p. 74, per Bereford (for the idea of the king as above law).

[98] The distinction between personal and local custom is discussed well in W. G. Salmond, *Jurisprudence*, edited by P. J. FitzGerald (12th ed, London, 1966) pp. 203–4; compare, for example, the custom in M 2 Ed. IV, 23, 21 and M 21 Ed. IV, 67, 50.

[99] See, for instance, T 35 Hen. VI, 60, 1 at 62B for the orthodox view of Ashton and Moile; see also M 13 Hen. VII, 4, 3; for later examples, see *William* v. *Berkeley* (1561) Plowden, 239–40, and the *Case of Ecclesiastical Persons* (1601) 5 Coke's Reports 14b.

## Authority and consent: the populist thesis 29

beneficial to the king, even if he is not named in it, he can avail himself of it.[100]

The basic idea that official acts must be authorised by law before they are permissible, an idea akin to the modern *ultra vires* principle, also appears in the practical sphere. In the exercise of their powers, lesser officers of government must act according to law: official action must have a legal basis. A statute of 1405 describes how debtors condemned by *due process of law* are committed to prisons throughout the realm.[101] It explains that the keepers of these prisons 'of their own authority do let the said debtors go at large at their will'. It also states how, when sued in such cases by the creditors (as creditors were entitled to sue by statute),[102] the keepers purchased the king's protection, thereby delaying and deferring the creditors of their recovery. The legislation ordains, therefore, that protection was no longer available for the keepers' acts which, it recites, were done *in derogation of the common law*. The requirement of legal authority is clear. The arbitrary conduct of the keepers (acting 'of their own authority') in releasing debtors condemned by 'due process of law', is described as 'in derogation of law'. The basic form of the statute is repeated throughout the period.[103]

A development of this idea, in the form of a notion of ostensible authority, was used by Serjeant Markham in 1442. If a commission was directed to certain persons to enquire of *trespasses* in a county, and twelve jurors are sworn before the commissioners to enquire of *felonies*, and these then 'indict me of felony, *all this is without authority*'.[104] Yet the jurors would not be legally liable 'because they were compelled by process made by the commissioners to do this, *which is for them authority of the law [autorite del' ley]*'. Likewise, says Markham, if a court erroneously awards a writ to arrest a person and the sheriff executes that writ, the sheriff is not liable for false imprisonment, 'because he took him *by authority of the law*'.[105]

[100] T 12 Hen. VII, 19, 1 (for legal issues raised in the case see *CH*, p. 580 and n. 2).
[101] 7 Hen. IV, c. 4.
[102] 1 Ric. II, c. 12.
[103] 11 Hen. IV, c. 9; 11 Hen. VI, c. 7.
[104] T 20 Hen. VI, 33, 3; M 30 Hen. VI, 5, 15; Brooke, *GA*, 'Conspiracy', 1: the court seems to agree that acts will not prejudice a person when committed on command of a court.
[105] However, in P 2 Hen. VII, 15, 1 Brian CJCP said arrest was valid only when the person arresting knows the arrest is lawful; see also M 7 Ed. IV, 20, 19 (per Brian CJCP: more than mere suspicion is required), T 11 Ed. IV, 4, 8, and M 5 Hen. VII, 4, 10.

## Due process and the community

The vertical dimension of the supremacy of law and the idea of the authority of law is completed by an examination of the position of ordinary members of the community. In both the Year Books and the statutes we can discern the principle that individuals must pursue their claims *according to law* and must not suffer the burdens imposed by law – be punished for instance – except *according to law*. In the courts, the idea was used by Martin JCP in 1426. In a case of that year he stated the rule (which had altered by the latter part of the period) that a married woman could not appoint executors as she was incapable in law of holding property.[106] Thus, if a married woman appointed an executor, then that person did not in law have the capacity to sue for debts owed to the woman, 'for when an action is brought in our law, *it must be brought according to our law*'.[107] Indeed, it is not surprising to find Brian CJCP stating as a matter of general principle in 1489 that, concerning grants of land, 'every grant must be by custom, common law, or by statute'.[108] Similarly, in 1490, the whole court agreed that when a lord breaks the close of a tenant and distrains for services which are later found not to be due, the lord can be sued by his tenant: and 'he will be punished as a trespasser *ab initio*, for the aforesaid cause, namely where one has *authority by law*, he must pursue his authority *as the law wills*'.[109]

The analogous principle was that an individual was not to be deprived of his property or punished except according to law. The

---

[106] Holdsworth, III, p. 542, n. 7; *HCLC*, p. 546; but see M 39 Hen. VI, 27, 38; compare church law, Holdsworth, III, p. 542. For the position at the end of the period, see T 12 Hen. VII, 22, 2 at 24 per Fineux, CJKB, and Holdsworth, III, p. 544. Generally, of course, executors could sue for debts owed to the testator: *HCLC*, p. 82.

[107] T 4 Hen. VI, 31, 11 at 32: 'car quand un accion est port en nostre Ley, il covient estre port accordant a nostre Ley'.

[108] P 4 Hen. VII, 8, 9: 'chescun grant covient estre per custome, common ley, ou per statut'.

[109] H 5 Hen. VII, 10, 2 at 11: 'il sera puni come trespassor *ab initio*, per le cause avandit, s. ou on ad authorite per Ley, il covient pursuir son authorite come le Ley veut'. See also 52 Hen. III, c. 3 and *Tenures*, Bk. I, c. 9, s. 77. See too M 7 Ed. IV, 19, 16 per Danby CJCP (a lord has no right to eject a copyholder who has performed his services), and M 21 Ed. IV, 80, 27 per Brian CJCP (a lord who did so could be sued in trespass). In P 21 Hen. VI, 29, 9, a party is allowed to pursue and chastise trespassers only 'according to the law of the land'. Srjt Keble, in *Rollesley* v. *Toft* (1495), repeated the idea that 'everyone is bound by the common custom of the realm [chescun est tenuz par le comen custome de le realme]': Port, *Notebook*, p. 31.

fundamental principle, asserted in Magna Carta, of course, was repeated in legislation of 1441: 'no freeman shall be taken or imprisoned, or be disseised of his freehold, or liberties, or free customs, or be outlawed or exiled, or in any other way destroyed; nor will we pass upon him, nor condemn him, but by lawful judgment of his peers, *or by the law of the land*'.[110]

The idea is common. Enacted to penalise the fastening of nets across rivers because of the disturbance to vessels and the destructive effect on fish, legislation of 1423 prescribed that those who set these nets shall be 'duly thereof and *by course of law* convict', and shall forfeit one hundred shillings to the king each time 'so proved in default'.[111] Likewise, in the same year, parliament enacted that when any prisoner convicted of high treason escaped, 'that such escape shall be adjudged and declared treason, if such person be thereof duly attainted *according to the law of this land*'.[112] An interesting example comes from 1421. Many unknown clerks and scholars of the University of Oxford disseised others, hunted in various parks, threatening to kill their keepers, and released other clerks 'convict of felony *by due process of the law*'.[113] Consequently, parliament ordained 'that *due process* shall be made against such scholars [who are] wrongdoers, for their offences, *as the common law and also the statutes of this land require*, according to the case, till they come to answer, or else be outlawed'.[114]

CONCLUSION

There is considerable evidence to support the view that the legal practitioners of the fifteenth century, as well as the theorists Pecock and Fortescue (and later Saint German), treated the basis for law as the human will and consent. In practice, the underlying authority of legislation was conceived to be consent, the consent of the community of the realm and, of course, the consent of the king: together, their consent was the source of legislation. Moreover, it is repeated time

---

[110] 20 Hen. VI, c. 9. See K. Jurow, 'Untimely thoughts: a re-consideration of the origins of due process of law', *AJLH* (1975) p. 265, and C. H. McIlwain, 'Due process of law in *Magna Carta*', 14 *Columbia Law Review* (1914) p. 27.
[111] 2 Hen. VI, c. 19.    [112] 2 Hen. VI, c. 21.    [113] 9 Hen. V, St. I., c. 8.
[114] For other illustrations, see 4 Hen. IV, c. 25 (duly proved); 2 Hen. V, St. I, c. 2 (imprisonment according to law); 3 Hen. VI, c. 3 (duly attained or convicted by the law); 8 Hen. VI, c. 27.

and time again in custumals that the usages of a local community were assented to by that community: local custom was shaped simply by the will and consent of a community. Certainly, the theorists saw consent as the basis for legislation, and in this Pecock anticipates Fortescue by around twenty years. But they did not describe it as the basis for either local custom or the custom of the realm, the common law: their analysis is far less complicated than arrangements in the practical sphere. Instead, and this was the predominant opinion of the practitioners, the common law was founded on established practice and the usages of the courts: judicial usage and consent, rather than popular consent, made the common law (though occasionally, a fiction was employed, notably by Saint German, that the community of the realm had consented to the common law). In consequence, then, in late medieval legal thought, we can see the idea that law, to which the entire community is subject, is not conceived to be found or given by God, it is shaped merely by human usage and enactment.

# 2

# HUMAN LAW: THE POSITIVIST THESIS

The view of law described so far is voluntarist. The human will creates law, through consent and usage. With legislation, it is the consent of the king and community; with local custom, the consent and usage of local communities. In the case of the common law, it is the consent and usage of the royal judges. Both theorists and practitioners develop the voluntarist view by constructing a wholly mundane conception of *human* law, in which there are fundamental points of contact with aspects of classical positivism in modern jurisprudence. The theorists see law as a command, and, with the practitioners, they recognise the variability of law: law must vary in terms of place, person and time. Conceptions of the purpose of law are equally earth-bound. Though the idea of law as advancing virtue appears in legal theory, in practice law simply serves the common profit, existing to resolve ordinary occasions of dispute. The separation of law from morality is another aspect of their notion of human law, and it grows from the idea of law as originating in the human will. Since rules acquire the quality of law because they are willed as such, and because of incorporation in usage and enactment, so we can begin to see the treatment of rules as laws regardless of their moral standing: abhorrent rules are nevertheless law. These ideas, central to classical positivism, are made possible only through the adoption of a voluntarist and populist conception of law.

## THE SUBSTANCE OF LAW

In this section we shall attempt to re-construct late medieval ideas about the imperative, obligatory and coercive nature of law, and the classifications of law.

## Law: commands and prohibitions

Law was not given by God. It was *made* by people. Fortescue saw laws as being 'put forth [*editae*] by man', the king as being unable to impose taxes 'or change their laws [*leges*], *or make new ones* [*vel novas condit*], without the concession or consent of his whole realm expressed in his parliament'.[1] Indeed, Pecock actually employed the expression 'positive law' to refer to legislation as made by human acts (though in practice the expression was used to apply to both legislation and the common law).[2] Pecock uses the term often: 'by the prince and his commonalty ... is made such a positive law'; 'no positive statute of the king and of the land is made thereupon'; 'a law of man's making'; 'politic laws made by men'; the 'making of any positive new ordinance'.[3] Pecock's voluntarist outlook is summed up in the idea that the people 'will and consent to the making of the laws'.[4]

Pecock's 'positive law' consists of the 'commandments and ordinances of princes and of their commonalty together'.[5] These imperative positive laws have a function quite distinct from that of the divine moral law: 'politic man's laws are none other than men's ordinances and men's traditions ruling men for to do this or that, to which as by God's plain law those men were not before bound'.[6] Not only does Pecock see law as commanding and forbidding: it also facilitates.

[1] *De Natura* I, c. 5; *De Laudibus*, c. 36, p. 87; see also *De Natura* I, c. 16. Thomas Smith, a century later, explained that 'The parliament abrogates old law, makes new ones, gives orders for things past and for things hereafter to be followed': *De Republica Anglorum* (1583) edited by L. Alston (Cambridge, 1906) II, c. 1.

[2] See below, n. 15; for Stillington's use of 'positive law' as chancellor in 1468, see B. Wilkinson, *Constitutional History of England in the Fifteenth Century: 1399–1485* (London, 1964) p. 315.

[3] *Folower*, p. 143; *Repressor*, II, pp. 463, 464. D'Ailly also writes of laws 'humana et positiva': Oakley, p. 174. The term 'positive law' is not new in the fifteenth century: J. Gaudemet, 'Équité et droit chez Gratien et les premiers décrétistes', ch. 10, *La Formation du droit canonique médiéval* (London, 1980) p. 270 at p. 281, n. 53. For Aquinas' use of *ius positivum*, *Summa*, 2a, 2ae, 57, 2. Saint German also uses the term: *Dialogue*, pp. 31, 158.

[4] *Folower*, p. 143; also p. 217.

[5] Ibid., p. 53. For the idea of the human will and commands as the basis for law in classical positivism, see J. Bentham, *Of Laws in General*, edited by H. L. A. Hart (London, 1970) chs. 1 and 2; J. Austin, *Lectures on Jurisprudence*, edited by R. Campbell (London, 1880) Pt I, sec. I, ch. I; see also H. L. A. Hart, *The Concept of Law* (Oxford, 1961) pp. 97–107, and generally J. Raz, *The Concept of a Legal System* (Oxford, 1970).

[6] *Repressor*, II, p. 453. The same idea applied to church law: see *Donet*, p. 53: 'to do any deed commanded by some certain rule written and approved advisedly by the church'.

In relation to the endowment of the church, 'man's law grants and maintains such endowments fully'.[7] On the other hand, for Fortescue law was simply a sanction 'commanding what is virtuous and forbidding the contrary'.[8] These ideas are not unorthodox. This same formula, which Fortescue uses, is to be found in the great *Glossa Ordinaria* of Accursius (from about 1240), and Bracton, again two centuries before, relying on the civilian Azo (d.1220) and ideas from Roman Law, not only agreed that laws and customs sometimes command and sometimes forbid, but also considered that 'not all *ius* enjoins, since some permits'.[9] According to Aquinas, 'law is a kind of directive or measure for human activity through which a person is led to do something or hold back'.[10] For Marsilius law is a standard commanding, prohibiting and permitting, containing admonitions for voluntary human acts,[11] and for the contemporary D'Ailly it was 'a precept or prohibition from one's superior'.[12]

In the practical sphere, of course, legislation is treated as made (*fait*),[13] and in a case of 1440, it is described how the lords and commonalty of Ireland, when assembled in their parliament, 'will [*ils veulent*]' the establishment of law.[14] In 1455, in a case considered earlier, Prisot CJCP had said that 'positive law ... was adjudged and made by statute', and in 1468 Yelverton JKB had asserted that 'nous ferromus un positive ley'.[15] In practice, however, the idea of a command is less conspicuous. More visible is the idea of a prohibition,

[7] *Repressor*, II, p. 320.
[8] *De Laudibus*, c. 3, p. 9: 'lex est sanccio sancta iubens honesta et prohibiens contraria'.
[9] For Accursius, see *De Laudibus*, p. 147, where S. B. Chrimes acknowledges his debt to H. Kantorowicz for informing him that the maxim was in the Accursian gloss; for the influence of Accursius, see *LPMA*, pp. 88, 91, 101. For Bracton, who stated that 'lex ... significat sanctionem iustam, iubentem honesta, prohibentem contraria', see *De Legibus* II, pp. 21, 22, 24. For Azo, *Select Passages from the Works of Bracton and Azo*, edited by F. W. Maitland, 8 Sel. Soc. (London, 1894) p. 24. See also below, n. 103.
[10] *Summa*, 1a, 2ae, 90, 1; also 91, 3, and, for permissive law, 92, 2.
[11] *DP*, II, pp. 35–7, 44, 45, 180, 189.
[12] Oakley, p. 192; for Gerson, Pascoe, p. 64, and Saint German, who follows Gerson, *Dialogue*, p. 27.
[13] For instance: 9 Hen.V, St. I, c. 4, referring to 14 Ed. III, St. I, c. 6 (*le statuit fait*); 8 Hen. VI, c. 9, referring to 15 Ric. II, c. 2 (*les estatutz et ordinances faitz*); 20 Hen. VI, c. 8, referring to 36 Ed. III, St. I, c. 6 (*lestatut fait*); 17 Ed. IV, c. 1, referring to 9 Ed. III, St. II, c. 2 and 2 Hen. VI, c. 6 (*lez quell ordeignancez furent faitz*). Also P 4 Ed. IV, 3, 4 at 4A per Choke *et al.*: 'car chescun statute fait, covient estre prise solonque l'entent de ceux que ceo feceront'.
[14] M 20 Hen. VI, 8, 17 per Fortescue; see also H 39 Hen. VI, 38, 3 at 40 per Moile JCP.
[15] H 33 Hen. VI, 7, 23 at 9: 'positive ley ... fuit ajuge ou fait per statut'; M 8 Ed. IV, 9, 9 at 12.

when, in legislation, parliament would prohibit conduct or 'ordain' that a state of affairs shall exist, or when judges describe conduct or a result as 'forbidden by law' or as 'against law'. Neele JCP used the idea in 1471 when he explained how 'il est prohibite per le ley' to sell bad food.[16] From time to time, in fact, the word 'rule' is used to signify a requirement of law: in 1443, for example, when the court had to consider a reversioner's claim to be received (to challenge a grant fraudulently made by the life tenant), Serjeant Yelverton said 'il y [a] divers rules de ce en nos livres'.[17] An expression which also appears in the Year Books is 'maxim'. In 1440 Newton CJCP maintained that 'it is an ancient maxim in law, *quod volenti non fit injuria*, on which it follows that he who committed the wrong cannot punish the same wrong, for he is *particeps peccati*'.[18] In his *Tenures*, Littleton uses maxim and principle to denote rules of law. It is a maxim, he says, that 'inheritance may lineally descend but not ascend', as it is a maxim that 'he who has an estate but for a term of life shall neither do homage nor take homage'. And it is a principle that 'every land of fee simple may be charged with a rent in fee by one or another'.[19]

Within the concept of laws as commands and prohibitions, the theorists are able to accommodate easily the notion that law obliges, binds and coerces individuals. The idea is common in continental

[16] T 11 Ed. IV, 6, 10. For legislation: 8 Hen. VI, c. 22 (no-one to 'force, clack or beard' wools); 8 Hen. VI, c. 24 (aliens shall not compel payment in gold); 18 Hen. VI, c. 4 (no alien shall sell merchandises to other aliens); 18 Hen. VI, c. 11 (no person to become a justice of the peace unless of twenty pounds income per annum); 8 Hen. VI, c. 25 (mayor of the staple to remain in office for two years); 18 Hen. VI, c. 3 (butter and cheese *may* be exported without licence). For the phrase 'against law' see, for example, P 18 Hen. VI, 5, 5 at 6 per Fulthorpe (a wrong done by the defendant against law which must be punished).

[17] M 21 Hen. VI, 13, 28. Also M 38 Hen. VI, 2, 5 per Moile: 'nous fesons bon rule pur le mischief'; M 3 Hen. VII, 12, 8 per Hussey CJKB: '[d]ivers rules ont este faits de ceo'; H 14 Hen. VII, 17, 7 at 18 per Vavasour: 'il ad este rule devant or'. The idea of a rule had certainly made its mark in theory: for Pecock, see *Reule*, p. 301: the people 'fynden reulis and governauncis profitable and worthy to be ordeyned and stabilid and be kept as lawis'; *Repressor*, I, p. 106; for Saint German, *Dialogue*, p. 97: 'generall rewles of the lawe of man' and 'generall rewle of every posytyve lawe'; p. 158: 'the commandment and rules [*rewles*] of the law of man or of a positive law'.

[18] P 18 Hen. VI, 6,6 at 7. Also: M 2 Hen. VI, 1, 1 (wrongly cited as 9, 1 in YB) per Rolf (principle and maxim); M 19 Hen. VI, 25, 48 at 26 per Yelverton; T 19 Hen. VI, 73, 2 at 74 per Markham.

[19] *Tenures*, Bk. I, c. 1, s. 3; Bk. II, c. 1, s. 90; Bk. III, c. 11, s. 648. Fortescue's use of *maxim* is at *De Laudibus*, c. 8, p. 23, where he describes the 'universals' of English law as 'maxims'. For Saint German see *Dialogue*, p. 59. An excellent general discussion of the use of 'maxims' in the Year Books, and of the Roman Law idea of *regulae*, is to be found in P. Stein, *Regulae Iuris: From Juristic Rules to Legal Maxims* (Edinburgh, 1966), pp. 154, 155.

## Human law: the positivist thesis 37

jurisprudence. Gerson maintained that law is 'a sign established through the medium of human authority which indicates that a man is obliged to perform or abstain from a certain action'.[20] For Nicholas of Cusa 'the strength of law lies in coercion', since 'law without its force loses its binding power and its life. It does not merit to be called law any more than a corpse should be called a man'.[21] Similar ideas can be found in Fortescue. 'Constitutions bind subjects', he says, and laws are not so named *a legendo*, but *a ligando*, because they bind. For this reason 'law may be said to be the bond of right by which a man is constrained to do or suffer what is just'.[22] According to Pecock, 'bondage comes in by men's ordinances'. It is incorrect, he argues, to say that individuals should not be bound by human laws.[23] Again, as we have seen, positive laws are none other than human ordinances and traditions ruling men 'to do this or that, *to which as by God's plain law the men were not before bound*'.[24] The authority of human law as an autonomous force imposing obligations on individuals is clear. Yet, Pecock reiterates that 'men are *not* bound by laws made among them and of men, unless those men which should be bound by those laws will and consent unto the making of the laws'; this idea of law as binding and coercive in nature also frequently surfaces in the Year Books.[25]

Deterrence, used to oblige, bind and compel obedience to law, is often found in the practical sphere. For example, a statute enacted against the Lollards in 1400 provides that offenders, having been convicted, be burnt before the people in a high place 'that such punishment may strike fear to the minds of others'.[26] The idea that wrongful conduct was an 'evil example' to the public at large was also

[20] Pascoe, p. 64.
[21] Sigmund, pp. 206, 211. For Aquinas, see *Summa*, 1a, 2ae, 90, 1; 95, 1; 99, 1; and Marsilius, *DP*, II, p. 36.
[22] *De Natura* I, cc. 10, 30: 'Unde lex dici potest juris vinculum quo quis constringitur facere aut pati quod est justum'; see also *De Laudibus*, c. 36, p. 87 (for the king as obliged (*obnoxius*) by his laws to pay for goods taken in times of necessity). Saint German too argues that 'a positive law that is lawfully made bind[s] all that be subjects to that law': *Dialogue*, p. 158.
[23] *Repressor*, II, pp. 454, 494.
[24] Ibid., p. 453; for similar ideas, I, p. 218, II, p. 525; above, n. 6.
[25] *Folower*, p. 217. For law as 'coercing', 'binding' and 'compelling' in practice (the root verbs usually being *lier* and *coharter*), see M 7 Hen. VI, 14, 24 at 15 per Paston; M 8 Hen. VI, 35, 3 per Martin; M 19 Hen. VI, 15, 36; M 35 Hen. VI, 14, 24 at 25 per Prisot; M 1 Ed. IV, 2, 7 at 2 for 'cohercion de ley'; M 1 Ed. IV, 5, 13 per Littleton: 'car custome et usage lyeront et serront allowes en touts courts'; T 1 Ed. V, 6, 12 at 7 per Sulyard; P 2 Hen. VII, 15, 1 at 16 per Brian; H 5 Hen. VII, 11, 4 at 14A.
[26] 2 Hen. IV, c. 15. Deterrence appears in Fortescue: *De Laudibus*, c. 34, p. 95; and Pecock, *Reule*, p. 150.

used to justify legislation. A statute of 1413 ordained that no actions were to be brought by Welshmen in respect of injuries sustained in recent rebellions.[27] Those involved in the uprisings now brought suits for acts (retrospectively legalised) committed during the rebellions, 'to the great damage and destruction of the said faithful liege people, and *evil example in time to come*'. An interesting use of the idea appears in a case of 1488 when a child of less than nine confessed to the killing of another child. Fairfax JKB argued that it was once said by Fortescue that the reason why an individual is hanged for murder 'is for the example of other men [*est pur example des autres homes*], that they will avoid this'. He added that, if any infant or man who lacks discretion kills another, they will not be hanged, 'for no person of their discretion can take example of this'.[28]

### Promulgation

According to Thomist legal thought, to obtain the full status of law measures enacted must first be promulgated. Aquinas himself argued that 'to have binding force, which is an essential property of a law, it has to be applied to the people it is meant to direct . . . when their attention is drawn to it by the fact of promulgation'.[29] There is no exact equivalent to this, treating promulgation as a pre-condition to validity, in Fortescue.[30] Promulgation was, however, a feature of law in practice. The usual method of promulgating legislation after enactment was upon the king's writ by the sheriffs in the counties or by direct communication to the judges.[31] Much legislation refers to or provides for its own promulgation,[32] and sometimes it provides for the promulgation, not of new law, but of existing, old statutory law. Legislation of 1422 prescribed that all operative measures relating to purveyors and buyers be 'proclaimed in all counties through the realm

[27] 1 Hen. V, c. 6; see also 2 Hen. V, St. II, c. 5; 9 Hen. VI, c. 5.
[28] H 3 Hen. VII, 1,4; Brooke, *GA*, 'Corone', 132; the problem of infants was discussed in an earlier case, M 35 Hen. VI, 11, 18, translated by Baker and Milsom, *Sources of English Legal History*, p. 326.
[29] *Summa*, 1a, 2ae, 90, 4. For Gerson, see *MPT*, VI, p. 140.
[30] At one point, however, he explains that when custom is written and promulgated it obtains the nature of statute: *De Laudibus*, c. 15; for the idea that ignorance of the law does not excuse, see *De Natura* I, c. 46.
[31] For publication generally, see Holdsworth, II, p. 436; T. F. T. Plucknett, *The Legislation of Edward I* (Oxford, 1949) pp. 11, 12; H. G. Richardson and G. O. Sayles, 'The early statutes', 50 *LQR* (1934) p. 540 at pp. 544f.
[32] For example, 9 Hen. IV, cc. 1–9; 11 Hen. IV, c. 5; 2 Hen. V, St. I, cc. 6, 8.

by the king's commandment'. The legislation also provided for subsequent periodical promulgation serving, it seems, the additional purpose of reminding those to whom it was addressed.[33]

Whether a failure to promulgate would invalidate law is doubtful. Certainly it was conceded occasionally that promulgation *ought* to take place. The author of the *Mirror of Justices* advocates this, along with codification, in relation to the common law: 'it is an abuse that the law and usages of the realm with their occasions are not put in writing, so that they might be published and known to all'.[34] With Pecock, too, though human law is 'made and published',[35] promulgation is not a criterion of validity. Nevertheless, laws ought to be published, he says, to minimise confusion on the part of subjects, 'to point in the better and in the clearer manner to them what and how and when they should do this or that thing or deed'.[36]

In a case of 1366, Thorpe CJCP rejects the idea that failure to promulgate will affect the validity of legislation. In it, the king was proceeding against the bishop of Chichester under a statute of *praemunire*, and the defendant objected that the statute had not been proclaimed in the counties according to the usual practice. Thorpe replied: 'although proclamation was not made in the county, everyone is now bound to know what is done in parliament'. Thus, 'as soon as parliament has concluded a matter, the law holds that every person has knowledge of it, for the parliament represents the body of all the realm, *and so promulgation is unnecessary* [*il n'est requisite*] for the statute has already become effective'.[37]

## Species of law

There is a difference between the theorists' classifications of law and those of the practitioners. The theorists' are far more simplistic: they divide laws into parliamentary legislation and, a somewhat ill-defined species, custom. Pecock considered 'political men's laws to be none other than men's ordinances and men's traditions'; he also wrote of 'positive statutes'.[38] For Fortescue 'laws put forth by men are all either customs or statutes'.[39] Nowhere do the theorists describe

[33] 1 Hen. VI, c. 2.　　[34] 7 Sel. Soc. (London, 1893) p. 156.
[35] *Donet*, p. 63.
[36] *Repressor*, II, p. 454. For Marsilius, '[t]he law is better observed by every citizen which each one seems to have imposed upon himself': *DP*, II, p. 47.
[37] P 39 Ed. III, f. 7; see also *CH*, p. 328.
[38] *Repressor*, II, p. 453; *Folower*, p. 143.
[39] *De Natura* I, c. 5; and *De Laudibus*, c. 15, p. 37.

the forms or types of parliamentary legislation, though the practitioners constantly distinguish between *statutes*, usually enactments of a more permanent nature, and *ordinances*, usually temporary legislation.[40]

A curious feature of Fortescue's treatment of law is his use of *lex* and *ius*. Generally, in Roman Law, *lex* signified enacted law (statute), and *ius* denoted the whole body of law or sometimes unenacted law, 'what was recognised or "found" to be right in a particular case'.[41] Again, in the context of natural law, *ius* was used rather than *lex*: the *ius naturale*.[42] Like Bracton, Fortescue, on the other hand, uses the terms interchangeably. Sometimes he described statute as *ius*, sometimes custom as *lex*, sometimes natural law as *lex* and sometimes as *ius*; and occasionally *ius* is used to cover all human law.[43]

Now, the *lex statuti*, says Fortescue, is usually written when enacted, whereas custom is not enacted or written.[44] Though corresponding with Bracton,[45] this view differs from some continental jurists. Bartolus, for example, considered that reduction to writing did not change the nature of custom: custom was not necessarily unwritten.[46] Even so, Fortescue argues that 'customs ... after they have been reduced to writing ... are *changed [mutantur]* into a constitution or something in the nature of statutes'.[47] The prac-

---

[40] 11 Hen. IV, c. 4 speaks of the 'statute' 12 Ric. II, c. 6; similarly, 13 Hen. IV, c. 2 of 8 Ric. II, c. 2, and 7 Hen. IV, c. 14 of 1 Hen. IV, c. 7. However some statutes were temporary: 11 Hen. VI, c. 14. See also 'acts', 22 Ed. IV, c. 3; 11 Hen. VII, cc. 25, 26. For 'ordinances' see 1 Hen. V, c. 5; 2 Hen. V, St. I., c.6. For temporary ordinances, see 2 Hen. V, St. I., c.9; 4 Hen. V, St. II, c. 2; 9 Hen. V, St. I., cc. 4, 8, 9; 1 Hen. VI, c. 6. There was sometimes confusion in the use of these terms: for enactments described as both 'statutes' and 'ordinances': 7 Hen. IV, c. 14; 13 Hen. IV, c. 3; 1 Hen. V, c. 9. For other terms used in practice to describe legislation, see Allen, *Law in the Making*, p. 436.
[41] B. Nicholas, *An Introduction to Roman Law* (Oxford, 1982) p. 14; Stein, *Regulae Iuris: From Juristic Rules to Legal Maxims,* p. 4 and pp. 8, 9.
[42] Nicholas, *An Introduction to Roman Law*, p. 54.
[43] See *De Laudibus*, c. 15, p. 37; *De Natura* I, cc. 4, 21, 30; *Governance*, c. 2.
[44] *De Laudibus*, c. 18, p. 41 (statute); *De Natura* I, c. 30 (custom).
[45] *De Legibus* II, p. 22.
[46] W. Ullmann, 'Bartolus on customary law', 52 *Juridical Review* (1940) p. 265 at pp. 267, 268, 271.
[47] *De Laudibus*, c. 15, p. 37. He is out of step with practice: local borough customs were codified in custumals and yet were still described as 'customs'; above, ch. I, n. 60.

## Human law: the positivist thesis 41

titioners, on the other hand, still spoke of customary rules which had been confirmed by statute as *custom*.[48]

Whatever the effect of reduction to a written form, it is important to stress that customs possessed the status of law. This was the common medieval outlook, and it becomes crucial when we consider the problem of natural law.[49] Fortescue writes of *lex consuetudinis*, and human *law (ius)*, he says, is either statute or custom.[50] Custom is a form of law created by usage. It grows from repeated acts and length of time.[51] As Serjeant Rolf put it in 1429, *consuetudo* is from usage 'and usage and custom are equipollent, *quia unum sunt*'.[52] Of course, in the practical sphere, local customs were treated as law. Saint German's idea that 'particular' customs (that is, local customs) are taken *for law*,[53] was used in 1459 when Moile referred to the *usage* of the Common Pleas as *droit ley*.[54] In a Note from 1464 gavelkind and borough english were treated as *quasi-law*, and in 1481 Catesby spoke of the same two customs as *local ley*.[55] The idea was an old one. An Exeter custumal of 1321, for example, recited that 'the customs [*consuetudines*] hitherto used and approved in this city as in many other cities are to be held *for law [pro lege habeantur]*'.[56]

Unlike Littleton and Saint German, and of course the practitioners, neither Pecock nor Fortescue distinguished between local custom and national custom.[57] The idea that this was *law*, the

[48] For London (and other) customs confirmed by statute, see 14 Ed. III, St. I, cc. 1, 2; for such usages still described as 'custom' see M 1 Ed. IV, 5, 13 per Littleton; H 21 Ed. IV, 16, 11; H 21 Ed. IV, 74, 2; M 22 Ed. IV, 30, 11. For an interesting idea that customs not founded on *reason* are *male usage* and cannot therefore be treated as confirmed by statute, see Brian CJCP in M 21 Ed. IV, 67, 50.

[49] For the author of the *Mirror*, see 7 Sel. Soc. (London, 1893) p. 155: 'soulle Engleterre negedent use ses custumes e ses usages pur lei'; for Bracton, *De Legibus*, II, p. 21; for Aquinas, *Summa*, 1a, 2ae, 97, 3; for Bartolus, Ullmann, 'Bartolus on customary law', p. 265 at p. 267; for Wyclif, see W. E. Farr, *John Wyclif as Legal Reformer* (Leiden, 1974) p. 138.

[50] *De Natura* I, c. 30 (contrast the reluctance of D'Ailly to regard custom as law: Oakley, p. 175); *De Laudibus*, c. 15, p. 37.

[51] *De Natura* I, c. 10; and *De Laudibus*, c. 17, p. 39; for Saint German, see *Dialogue*, p. 45.

[52] M 8 Hen. VI, 3, 9 at 4 (for the rest of the case, P 7 Hen. VI, 31, 27).

[53] *Dialogue*, pp. 71, 75.

[54] P 37 Hen. VI, 17, 4.

[55] M 5 Ed. IV, 8, 23, and M 21 Ed. IV, 55, 28 at 57 for Catesby. See also generally: M 7 Ed. IV, 20, 23; M 21 Ed. IV, 53, 22 at 54 for Brian on 'by-laws'; M 22 Ed. IV, 30, 11 at 32.

[56] 18 Sel. Soc. (London, 1904) p. 304.

[57] *Tenures*, Bk. I, c. 9, s. 77; *Dialogue*, pp. 45, 71. Though Pecock did refer to the 'comoun lawe' of England; *Folower*, p. 143.

common law, was unquestioned. According to Littleton JCP in a case of 1468 'custom that runs throughout all the land is common law [*common ley*]': this included the rule that innkeepers would be charged for the goods of their lodgers if stolen (though in 1443 Serjeant Markham described this rule as 'un custome *et* un ley').[58] Again, for Saint German, 'general customs of old time used through all the realm which have been accepted and approved by our sovereign lord the king and his progenitors and all their subjects ... have obtained the strength of a law ... And these be the customs that properly be called the common law.'[59]

In the Year Books statute was usually considered to be superior to custom. It could destroy inferior local custom,[60] as could a decision of the common law judges.[61] And judicial confirmation of local custom might have binding force for the future.[62] Whereas usage made law in the sphere of the common law,[63] non-usage of a statute would not have the effect of repealing or destroying that statute: as was said in 1463, 'though this statute has not been put in use, that is immaterial, for there are many articles in the books of statute which have never been put in use, but that does not matter, for they are still law [*ley*] and can be executed for every man who is aggrieved contrary to them'.[64]

---

[58] For Littleton, M 8 Ed. IV, 18, 30 at 19 (Choke JCP speaks in the same way of custom relating to the negligent keeping of fires); for Markham, M 22 Hen. VI, 21, 38; for the *Mirror*, see 7 Sel. Soc. (1893) p. 5.
[59] *Dialogue*, pp. 46, 47.
[60] T 8 Hen. VII, 1, 1 at 4 per Brian CJCP: a man cannot prescribe against a statute, except in another statute. Saint German agreed, *Dialogue*, pp. 57, 163. See also Pecock, *Reule*, p. 332, and, for a custom of Rome, 6 Hen. IV, c. 1. For a contrary view, see Ullmann, 'Bartolus on customary law', pp. 280, 281. See too M 35 Hen. VI, 25, 33 at 29 per Prisot CJCP: if a custom conforms with reason then it is valid 'notwithstanding that it be not according to the common law'.
[61] When, that is, the judges appealed to *reason* or *comen droit*: see below, chapter 3.
[62] M 1 Ed. IV, 5, 13.
[63] M 34 Hen. VI, 22, 42 at 24A per Fortescue CJKB.
[64] P 4 Ed. IV, 3, 4 at 4A; see too M 11 Hen. IV, 7, 20 at 8B per Hankford J, and M 11 Hen. IV, 37, 67 at 39A per Thirning CJCP: 'uncore per que il fuit un statut fait, et ne fuit unques repeal, il est assets bon'; P 38 Hen. VI, 30, 13 (misnumbered as 12) per Fortescue: 'il n'ad este tenu ple en noz livres adevant'. However, non-use of law did cause its own problems: 3 Hen. VII, 'An acte agaynst murderers', refers to previous measures, 'which law by negligence is disused, and thereby great boldness is given to slayers and murderers'.

## THE VARIABILITY OF LAW

The set of ideas advancing an earthly view of human law, rooted in the notion of commands and prohibitions created by the human will, is developed in the concept that laws of different communities *differ* and that humanly created laws are forever subject to *change*. Bracton's observation that England has 'local customs varying from place to place', is reflected in the *Mirror of Justices*: 'these [customs] differ from place to place according to the different qualities of the folk of diverse regions and places'.[65] However, in the late medieval period, there are considerable imbalances between the practitioners' and the theorists' ideas about variability. The theorists focus exclusively upon variability in terms of both place and time. On the other hand, though they recognise the changeability of law, the practitioners also value certainty and permanence in law: fixed term and perpetual legislation is common in the practical sphere.

### The theorists and variability

A major achievement of Fortescue is his comparison of the law of England with the civil law or that of France. His broad conclusion was that 'the civil and English laws differ'.[66] The English jury system, for example, functions well because of the existence of closely knit communities, in which individuals are never far from the fact in dispute, whereas 'the land where [the civil law] rules *is the cause* [*causam esse*] of its not eliciting the truth in disputes by so good a procedure as the law of England'. In point of fact, 'the law of England is ... more suitable [*accommodaciorem*] for that realm than the civil law and we have no desire to change it for the civil law'.[67] He also considers that, as a characteristic of the *dominium regale*, the *ius regis* is changeable at the will of the prince:[68] generally, kings 'make in the world transitory laws'.[69] Similarly, under the *dominium politicum et regale*, legislation

[65] *De Legibus*, II, p. 19; 7 Sel. Soc. (London, 1893) p. 5. For the idea generally in medieval jurisprudence, see Aquinas, *Summa*, 1a, 2ae, 95, 3, and, for Marsilius, *DP*, II, p. 45.
[66] *De Laudibus*, c. 20, p. 43.
[67] Ibid., c. 30, p. 73; for Saint German, *Dialogue*, p. 17, and the canonist Lyndwood (d. 1446), in his *Provinciale* (1430), F. W. Maitland, *Roman Canon Law in the Church of England* (London, 1898) pp. 29, 30.
[68] *De Natura* I, c. 29.
[69] *Works*, p. 484. (For the authorship of this tract, the *Dialogue*, see M. S. Blayney, 'Sir John Fortescue and Alain Chartier's *Traité de l'espérance*', 58 *Modern Language Review* (1953) p. 385.)

is easily revised, when it no longer gives effect to the intention of the law-makers.[70]

For Pecock laws 'never stand for a long time under one rule, neither under one manner to be done, neither stand in all places likewise, or under like rule to be done'. The proposition that laws should not change, he says, is incorrect. It is one 'not considering that in length of time, full great transmutation and change is always made in and about the circumstances of politic governances'. This applies as much to ecclesiastical government as to secular government. Accordingly, says Pecock, no-one ever wrote in laws all the exceptions which might arise because of change, for 'a law is not good but by its circumstances, which are thus changeable and transmutable'.[71] Laws must be revised when they cease to be profitable to the people, and when they 'do prejudice to the higher and worthier laws'.[72]

### Fixed-term and perpetual legislation

Of course, in practice parliament made actual changes in its law. There are several instances of legislation providing for the repeal of earlier measures.[73] Yet these are surprisingly few. Rather, the tendency is for subsequent legislation to recite and confirm earlier legislation.[74] The phenomenon which finds no parallel in theory, however, is that of fixed-term and perpetual legislation. Frequently, parliament would deliberately prescribe the length of time for which legislation was to be in force. It did so by including statements to the effect that legislation was to last for a fixed period of years, and no more (*et nemy outre*),[75] 'until the next parliament', or, more significantly, to be

---

[70] *De Laudibus*, c. 18, p. 41; see also pp. 39, 41.
[71] *Repressor*, I, pp. 106, 107. For equivalent ideas in Aquinas, see *Summa*, 1a, 2ae, 97, 1, and Gerson, Pascoe, pp. 62, 63.
[72] *Reule*, pp. 335, 341.
[73] See, for instance: 6 Hen. IV, c. 4 repeals 5 Hen. IV, c. 9; 9 Hen. IV, c. 6 repeals 7 Hen. IV, c. 10; 33 Hen. VI, c. 2 repeals 31 Hen. VI, c. 6; 39 Hen. VI, c. 1 repeals all the legislation of 38 Hen. VI.
[74] See, for example: 2 Hen. IV, c. 13 confirms 21 Ric. II, c. 15; 11 Hen. IV, c. 8 confirms 14 Ric. II, c. 2; 13 Hen. IV, c. 2 confirms 8 Ric. II, c. 2; 10 Hen VI, c. 5 confirms 21 Ric. II, c. 18.
[75] 11 Hen. VI, c. 14; four years: 22 Ed. IV, c. 3; five years: 28 Hen. VI, c. 4; six years: 20 Hen. VI, c. 3; seven years: 28 Hen. VI, c. 1; twenty years: 1 Hen. VII, c. 9.

'effectual in law for ever [*perpetuelment* or *a tout jours adurer*]', to continue for all time.[76] There are many examples.

An interesting statute is from 1439. This recites legislation of 1421, which was created in the ninth year of Henry V to deal with false appeals and indictments.[77] It was questioned whether the act of 1421 had expired, as it provided for its own operation until the next parliament to be held when Henry V returned from France. However, there was no other parliament in Henry's reign, 'which statute by the death of the said late king, by opinion of some is expired, and by the opinion of some not expired'. Thus, in 1439 it was ordained that 'the said ordinance made in the said ninth year, and so by the death of [Henry V], as some think expired, and not otherwise repealed, shall be and abide an effectual and available statute and ordinance in law perpetually to endure [*perpetuelment adurer*]'.

Whereas here the legislators were in doubt as to whether the earlier act was still operative, in the next example the fixed-term clause was given its literal meaning. An act of 1441 recited an enactment of 1436 (dealing with the exportation of wool) which itself was to last until the next parliament.[78] The 1441 act provides, therefore, that the king 'forasmuch as this statute [of 1436] *is not now in its force* ... has ordained ... that the statute and ordinance aforesaid [of 1436], *now expired as afore is said*', shall endure until the next parliament or for ten years, whichever is the shorter period. Indeed, by legislation of 1444, the statute of 1436 was made perpetual: 'by the authority of the same parliament [it] shall be perpetual [*perpetuel*], and stand in its force *for ever hereafter* [*tout jours en apres*]'.[79]

Nevertheless, sometimes fixed-term and perpetual legislation is expressly repealed by parliament, in opposition, it would seem, to these duration clauses. A measure enacted in 1397, providing for the maintenance of beacons at Calais, was repealed two years later in 1399.[80] The 1399 act stated that the 1397 legislation was repealed for ever (*pur touz jours*). However, in 1422 parliament overrode the act of 1399, instead making perpetual the earlier enactment of 1397.[81]

---

[76] 9 Hen. V, St. I, cc. 4, 8, 9; 27 Hen. VI, c. 3 (until the next parliament); 4 Hen. VI, c. 3 (*a toutz jours adurer*); 10 Hen. VI, c. 5 makes 21 Ric. II, c. 18 perpetual (*pur toutz jours*); 31 Hen. VI, c. 6 makes 20 Hen. VI, c. 2 perpetual (*perpetuelment dendurer*), as does 1 Ric. III, c. 6 makes 17 Ed. IV, c. 2 *(perpetuelment apres dendurer)*.
[77] 18 Hen. VI, c. 12, reciting 9 Hen. V, St. I, c. 1.
[78] 20 Hen. VI, c. 6 reciting 15 Hen. VI, c. 2.    [79] 23 Hen. VI, c. 5.
[80] 1 Hen. IV, c. 3 repeals all of 21 Rich. II including, therefore, c. 18.
[81] 10 Hen. VI, c. 5.

Similarly, in 1441 an ordinance, prescribing that anyone outlawed in Lancashire shall forfeit no lands in other counties, was made to last for seven years.[82] Yet, in 1452 parliament ordained that the act of 1441 (the 'statute', as it was described) was to endure perpetually (*perpetuelment dendurer*).[83] But, in 1455 legislation was passed declaring that the statute of 1452 'shall be annulled, void and stand in no force'.[84]

Standard fixed-term and perpetual legislation has considerable constitutional significance. Two interpretations suggest themselves. First, it sheds doubt on whether the idea that 'parliament cannot bind its successors', generally accepted in current constitutional theory and practice,[85] was a view held by fifteenth-century practitioners. Fixed-term and perpetuity clauses *appear* to bind the competence of successive parliaments to alter law for the duration of the prescribed period: they imply that legislation must last for a fixed term or for ever. The enactments do not say, after all, that 'this legislation is to last forever, *unless it is repealed*'. This interpretation is not impossible. The statute 42 Edward III, c.3, for instance, enacted that any legislation created contrary to Magna Carta was void.[86] On the other hand, of course, on those occasions when fixed-term or perpetual legislation is repealed, this suggests that parliament did understand its own capacity to over-ride the apparently permanent enactments of its predecessors. Consequently, it might be that duration clauses merely manifest an outlook implying that legislation *ought* to possess a degree of permanence: it is to last, so to speak, until further notice. This idea of permanence can be found nowhere in Pecock or Fortescue. They concentrate exclusively upon the changeability of law.

---

[82] 20 Hen. VI, c. 2.   [83] 31 Hen. VI, c. 6.
[84] 33 Hen. VI, c. 2. See also 2 Hen. IV, c. 13 which confirms 21 Ric. II, c. 15, even though repealed by 1 Hen. IV, c. 3, which purported to have repealed *all* of 21 Ric. II *for ever*.
[85] See, for example, E. C. S. Wade and A. W. Bradley, *Constitutional and Administrative Law* (10th edition, London, 1985) p. 70.
[86] See too 25 Ed. I, c. 1 (1297): 'consuetudines et statuta vacua et nulla sint imperpetuum'; and 11 Hen. VII, c. 1, which prohibited conduct described as against *conscience* and *reason*: this statute was ordained to prevail over subsequent conflicting legislation. See also H 21 Hen. VII, 1, 1 at 2 per Kingsmill JCP and parliament's limited power in spiritual matters, and, by way of analogy, *Mirror*, 7 Sel. Soc. (London, 1893) p. 185.

## THE PURPOSE OF LAW

Though there are differences in emphasis, there is much common ground between the theorists' and the practitioners' ideas about the purpose of law. The usual understanding of law in the middle ages is a teleological one. Law has a purpose and an end. Aquinas recognises that precepts are directed to some end inasmuch as what is commanded to be done is necessary or expedient to the attainment of that end.[87] Like Gerson,[88] and the earlier tradition, Pecock and Fortescue adopt two levels of purpose in law: a mundane function, serving the common profit, and a higher function, the advancement of virtue. The former is commonly stressed by the practitioners, the latter appears from time to time only, and then mainly in legislation, not in the Year Books.

### The mundane function of law

Pecock expresses the view that laws exist simply 'for the better rule of the people in temporal and civil government, longing unto worldly peace and prosperity and worldly wealth'.[89] Laws are made to deal with those matters, relating to the common profit, which are within man's natural faculty to entertain and determine: they exist for the furtherance of the common profit of neighbours, for instance, 'to rule all [the prince's] liegemen in contracts and covenants about property in temporal goods'.[90] According to Fortescue (and the same idea was used much later by Fineux CJKB in a case of 1521), law binds society as the sinews bind the human body: 'the law indeed by which a group of men is made into a people, resembles the sinews of the physical body for, just as the body is held together by the sinews, so this body mystical is bound together and united into one by the law'.[91] 'Under this law, therefore, life is quiet and secure', he says. Members of the community can enjoy a minimal material happiness, taking pleasure in the fruits of their own efforts. Therefore, Fortescue claims that the English laws are suitable for the government of the realm, adapted *to*

---

[87] *Summa*, 1a, 2ae, 99, 1.   [88] Pascoe, p. 61.
[89] *Repressor*, II, p. 454; for Gerson, Pascoe, pp. 54, 64; for Nicholas of Cusa, Sigmund, p. 202.
[90] *Reule*, p. 335. See also ibid., pp. 301, 334.
[91] *De Laudibus*, c. 13, p. 31: 'Lex, vero, sub qua cetus hominum populus efficitur nervorum corporis phisici tenet racionem, quia sicut per nervos compago corporis solidatur, sic per legem, que a ligando dicitur, corpus huiusmodi misticum ligatur et servatur in unum.' For Fineux, see Port, *Notebook*, p. 125.

*the utility of that same realm* as the civil law is adapted to the good of the empire. Of course, the essential point of consensual laws is that they promote the interests of those who consent to their creation, 'so that they cannot be injurious to the people nor fail to secure their advantage'.[92]

Words commonly used to signify public utility as the justifying basis of legislation are *expediency* and *necessity*. The words appear on numerous occasions during the first half of the fifteenth century. As one of a series of measures dealing with general unlawfulness,[93] a statute of 1399 penalised lords (except the king) who used or gave to knights, squires and yeoman any livery.[94] In 1400 another act confirmed the earlier measure considering 'the same to be very expedient and necessary [*expedient et necessaire*]'.[95] According to legislation of 1425, reciting an earlier enactment, licence had been granted to all individuals to ship corn out of the realm to whatever place they chose, except to the enemies of the realm. It also explains how Richard II had willed that his council restrain this free passage 'when to them seemed needful for the profit of the realm [*besoignable pur profit du roialme*]'.[96] As such, it was commanded that the earlier measure be held in all points 'so that his council may restrain the said passage when to them shall seem for the profit of the realm'.

An equivalent expression employed by the judges towards the end of the period is *common weal*. In 1468 Danby CJCP allowed the justification of a trespass by fishermen who dried their nets upon land adjoining the sea because fishing was for the *commonwealth* and for the sustenance of the whole realm.[97] In 1496, Fineux CJKB decided that if A grants land to B on condition that B makes a bridge on the land, or makes a beacon there, or recruits people to guard the king's castles, then the grant is good because the donor has advantage of this 'because it is for the *common weal* of the realm': basically, for Fineux, as he observed in 1521, 'the king and the whole realm are a body politic, which is kept and ordered by the law [*garde et order par le*

---

[92] Ibid., c. 18, p. 41; see too ibid., pp. 37, 65, 88, 89, and *De Natura* II, c. 29 for the view that human law exists to put an end to litigation.
[93] Holdsworth, II, p. 452.
[94] 1 Hen IV, c. 7; as the enactment says, its purpose was to 'nourish love, peace, and quietness of all parts through the realm'.
[95] 2 Hen. IV, c. 21.
[96] 4 Hen. VI, c. 5, reciting 17 Ric. II, c. 7; see also 11 Hen. VI, c. 11; 31 Hen. VI, cc. 4, 6; 3 Hen. VII, c. 9.
[97] M 8 Ed. IV, 18, 30: Danby dissented, the majority deciding that the custom was unreasonable.

*ley*]'.⁹⁸ Likewise, in the celebrated *Tithe Case* of 1506, Kingsmill JCP maintained that where someone's goods are taken against his will, or where a house is demolished to safeguard others, 'these things are justifiable and lawful for the maintenance of the commonwealth'.⁹⁹

## Law and the advancement of virtue

The theorists also postulate a higher purpose for human law, one to which the practitioners rarely allude. Law exists to direct individuals to the exercise of the virtues, and the avoidance of vices. This is conventional in medieval jurisprudence.¹⁰⁰ Aquinas argues that law is made to direct human acts, and the extent to which law makes people good depends upon how far they contribute to virtue. Virtue, in part at least, is vital, he says, as a political community cannot flourish unless its citizens are virtuous. But 'not all the acts of virtue are commanded, nor all the acts of vice forbidden by an obligation set up by human law'.¹⁰¹ The majority has no high standard of virtue, and so law exists merely to avoid the graver vices, those which the average person can avoid: those which do harm to others and society in general.¹⁰²

Fortescue follows the general pattern set by Aquinas. The objective of every legislator is to dispose people to virtue. It is by means of law that this is accomplished. Fortescue's definition of law (also found in Accursius and Bracton), after all, was 'a sacred sanction commanding what is virtuous [*honesta*] and forbidding the contrary'.¹⁰³ He

---

⁹⁸ H 11 Hen. VII, 12, 3; Brooke, *GA*, 'Tenures' 109; for Fineux on law and order, Port, *Notebook*, p. 125.

⁹⁹ T 21 Hen. VII, 27, 5; Fifoot, *Sources*, p. 199; for other examples of the judicial usage of *common weal* and ideas of public utility in general, see H 40 Ed. III, 17, 8; H 39 Hen. VI, 38, 3; M 4 Hen. VII, 18, 12; M 7 Hen. VII, 16, 1 at 2; T 8 Hen. VII, 1, 1; P 12 Hen. VII, 15, 1 at 17B per Tremaile

¹⁰⁰ For the fourteenth-century Italian jurist Baldus de Ubaldis (1327–1400), see W. Ullmann, 'Baldus' conception of law', 58 *LQR* (1942) p. 386 at p. 392; for Wyclif, W. E. Farr, *John Wyclif as Legal Reformer*, p. 73; for Bracton, *De Legibus*, II, p. 25.

¹⁰¹ *Summa*, 1a, 2ae, 92, 1; 96, 3.

¹⁰² Ibid., 92, 2. According to Ockham 'law is made for the unjust, not the just': McGrade, *The Political Thought of William of Ockham*, p. 214.

¹⁰³ *De Laudibus*, c. 3, p. 9: 'lex est sanccio sancta iubens honesta et prohibiens contraria' (see also *De Natura* I, c. 44, and II, c. 35). For Accursius, Azo and Bracton, above, n. 9. *Honesta*, in Fortescue, is translated as virtuous; see S. E. Thorne's translation of Bracton (*De Legibus* II, p. 25): 'honeste vivere, alterum non leadere, ius suum unicuique tribuens' (the three precepts of *ius*: 'to live virtuously, to injure no-one, to give each man his right'); see also T. G. Watkin, '*Honeste vivere*', 5 *JLH* (1984) p. 117, for Thorne's as the preferred translation.

50    *Fundamental authority in late medieval English law*

illustrates this aspect of human law in a discussion of the illegitimate child. The civil law, he says, is inferior to English law for the way in which it legitimates children born before marriage. By this the parties 'are rendered all the more disposed to commit the sin, and thereby neglect the precepts not only of God but also of the church'. The civil law, therefore, 'contradicts the very nature of a good law, since law is a sacred sanction commanding what is virtuous [*honesta*] and forbidding the contrary; for this law does not forbid, but rather invites wavering minds to do vicious acts'.[104]

In contrast Pecock devotes little time to the connection of human law and virtue. This is the work of divine and natural law.[105] Yet, Pecock proposes that the king should live virtuously, exhort his people to observe the law and 'rehearse the points and governances, virtues and truths of the law to remind the judges and the people thereon'.[106] The judges too used virtue very rarely in the Year Books. Only on one occasion, in 1410, is it referred to and then in the negative sense that law will not penalise virtuous conduct. Two masters of a school in Gloucester sued trespass against D for founding a rival school. The plaintiffs claim to have suffered loss from competition as they were forced to lower fees. For different reasons, the judges decide that the plaintiffs' writ does not lie. Thirning CJCP sees it as a spiritual matter and Hankford JCP as *damnum absque injuria*. It is Hill JCP, however, who adds: '[a]nd if another person, who is as well learned in the faculty as the plaintiffs are, comes to teach the infants, this is a *virtuous* and charitable thing, and [needful] to the people, *and for that he cannot be punished in our law*, wherefore, etc.'[107]

Nor is virtue much used in legislation.[108] Only a handful of acts

---

[104] *De Laudibus*, c. 34, pp. 93, 95; for Saint German, *Dialogue*, p. 31: 'the intent of a maker of a law is to make people good and bring them to virtue'.
[105] Pecock does, however, consider in great depth the nature of virtuous acts: *Folower*, p. 45; for divine law and the virtues, see ibid., p. 82.
[106] *Reule*, p. 334; *Repressor*, I, pp. 21, 22; see *Donet*, p. 75, for the idea that human law exists to keep God's virtuous law.
[107] H 11 Hen. IV, 47, 21: 'c'est vertuous et charitable chose, et ease al people, pur que il ne puit estre puny per nostre ley': *ease* has been translated here as 'needful', and it appears as *besoignous* in MSS. (Baker and Milsom, *Sources of English Legal History*, p. 614, n. 9); see also, for the case, Brooke, *GA*, 'Action on the Case', 42; Fitzherbert, *GA*, 'Action on the Case', 28; and Holdsworth, VIII, p. 425.
[108] For 'virtue' and 'virtuous' in late medieval non-legal sources, see *OED*: then, as (broadly) today, the words signified 'acting with moral rectitude': 'Christ is more

Human law: the positivist thesis 51

contain ideas of virtue. For example, a statute of 1482 explains that the king's 'subjects within every part of the realm have virtuously [*vertousement*] occupied and used shooting with their bows, whereby under the protection of Almighty God, victorious acts have been done in defence of the realm'. The statute proceeds to encourage practising archery by fixing the price of longbows and penalising excessive sales.[109] Rather than an idea of moral virtue, it is civic virtue which this statute implies. More often, legislation is designed to eradicate vice. The usage of vice (which is almost as rare) appears in relation to problems of unemployment and the ensuing state of 'idleness'. As an instance, one objective of an act of 1483 was to prohibit foreign merchants from employing servants brought to England from their own countries instead of hiring English people. As to the consequence of this, it recites: 'whereby your [the king's] said subjects for lack of occupation fall to idleness and are thieves, beggars and vagabonds and people of vicious living [*gentzs de vicious vivre*], to the great trouble of your said highness and of all your said realm'.[110]

THE STATUS OF ABHORRENT LAW:
THE POSITIVIST THESIS

Both the populist outlook and the mundane view of law prepare the way for a separation of law and morality. As law is reliant for its authority, not upon morality, but upon the human will, varying from time to time, and as the basic purpose of law is to serve the common weal, so law becomes divorced from abstract morality. Law is autonomous. A rule acquires the nature and authority of law because it is

excellent and *vertuosor* than other creatures', *An Apology for Lollard Doctrines* (attributed to Wyclif) (*c*.1400), edited by J. H. Todd, Camden Society Publications (London, 1842) p. 91; 'How that ye shall keep your soul from vices and ill manners and virtuously to live', *Three Prose Versions of Secreta Secretorum* (1422), edited by R. Steele and T. Henderson, Early English Text Society, Extra Series, 74 (London, 1898).

[109] 22 Ed. IV, c. 4; see also 1 Hen. IV, c. 19 (for the ease and relief of the poor common people); 4 Hen, IV, c. 18 ('and they that be good and virtuous').

[110] 1 Ric. III, c. 9; see also 27 Hen. VI, c. 1 (for sin and evil life); 3 Ed. IV, c. 1 (vices which may by the pleasure of God be avoided); it was a time of frequent legislation directed against aliens: see Holdsworth, II, p. 471. For 'vice' and 'vicious' in contemporary non-legal sources, see *OED*: for example, 'Upon thieves and murderers . . . misproud men and vicious there shall be fires in judgment', *The Pylgremage of the Sowle* (from the French of G. de Guilleville) (*c*. 1400) (MS. Egerton 615) IV, xxxv, 85.

willed as such: it becomes law by an act of volition. One consequence of these ideas is a concept fundamental to the positivist thesis. Rules are attributed the status of law simply because they are willed and incorporated in the common law or in legislation. Rules are laws, if incorporated in cases or enactments, regardless of their actual moral quality. To put it in the language of the medieval jurists, a rule is law when it is 'used', when it is found 'in the books', and in statutes and ordinances, not because it conforms to morality. Abhorrent rules can still be law: they are not void.

### The positivist outlook and legal theory

The positivist aspects of Pecock's conception of law appear in his discussion of natural law (which will be described later). He considers that conduct obtains additional legality when it conforms to natural law and, thus, human laws approved by natural law are *lawful* 'in the proper way to call a thing lawful'.[111] However, human law too is needed to confer a complete lawfulness for 'whatever governance neither holy scripture, nor the judgment of reason, *nor man's just positive law forbids* is not unlawful'.(Elsewhere Pecock omits the word *just* and uses, simply, *the law of man.*)[112] Consequently, Pecock asserts that a humanly created rule which fails to agree with natural law, and thereby produces evil, is only to be considered as *unlawful* (offensive to natural law). It is not to be treated as void, as a nullity. Abhorrent rules are still laws, he argues: they are merely not worthy of being used as such. These laws, says Pecock, 'out of which come these said evils, are by right judgment of reason *unlawful, and not worthy to be had and used*'.[113] This certainly implies that bad rules are still laws, but it is not entirely clear what 'not worthy to be had and used' means. Certainly, in his discussion of the variability of law, he favours revision of laws by the legislator when these are no longer profitable to the people. Above all, however, the idea that laws are not 'to be had and used' raises the interesting question whether Pecock

[111] *Repressor*, I, p. 135.   [112] Ibid., I, pp. 161, 180, II, p. 372.
[113] Ibid., II, p. 432: 'out of whiche wallen the seid yvelis, ben bi right doom of resoun unleeful and not worthi to be had and usid'; also, I, pp. 227, 228; for a short discussion of the positivist thesis see N. Doe, 'The positivist thesis in fifteenth-century legal theory and practice', 11 *JLH* (1990) p. 31.

envisaged that subjects ought not to obey bad laws or, perhaps, that judges ought not to apply bad laws. On these points he is silent. In any event, Pecock might be contrasted with Aquinas, who thought that unjust laws 'ought not to be obeyed', and that such laws 'do not bind in conscience unless observance of them is required in order to avoid scandal or public disturbance'.[114]

The positivist views of Fortescue are more elaborately, though less succinctly, rehearsed. Fortescue is alert to the reality of wicked law. The *ius regis* declared by Samuel, he says, was evil, for it allowed the king to do to others what he would not have done to himself; nevertheless, it was still law.[115] He uses torture, allowed under the *ius regis* of France (for which the continental jurists provided theoretical justification)[116] as a contemporary illustration. 'The law of France, therefore, is not content to convict the accused in capital cases by witnesses ... but that law prefers the accused to be racked with torture until they themselves confess their guilt.' Indeed, 'the civil laws themselves extort the truth by similar tortures in criminal cases where sufficient witnesses are lacking and many realms do likewise'.[117]

Fortescue advances the positivist outlook in the proposition that 'when law is referred to the people, then to them *the law is always law even though it is sometimes good and sometimes bad*'. And under the *dominium regale*, when the *ius regis* is made according to the maxim *quod principi placuit legis vigorem habet*, 'the law itself is as often bad as good'.[118] It is from the prince's will that it acquires the *nomen legis*, though nothing could be more iniquitous than such a law. Moreover,

---

[114] *Summa*, 1a, 2ae, 96, 4; 2a, 2ae, 104, 6: 'Man is bound to obey secular rulers to the extent that the order of justice requires ... if they command things to be done which are unjust, their subjects are not obliged to obey them, except perhaps in certain special cases, when it is a matter of avoiding scandal or some public disturbance'; see A. P. d'Entreves, *Natural Law: An Introduction to Legal Philosophy* (2nd edition, London, 1970) p. 46; see also F. C. Copleston, *Aquinas* (Harmondsworth, 1955, reprinted 1970) p. 240.

[115] *De Natura* I, cc. 12, 17.

[116] See A. Esmein, *History of Continental Criminal Procedure*, translated by J. Simpson, volume V, The Continental Legal History Series (New York, 1968) pp. 79–113, esp. p. 112; see also Holdsworth, V, p. 170–6.

[117] *De Laudibus*, c. 22, pp. 47–51.

[118] *De Natura* I, c. 27: 'sed cum ad populum ius illud referatur lex semper illis est, quandoque vero bona quandoque vero mala'; c. 28:"lex ipsa tamen sepius mala est'.

the positivist idea is implied in the assertion that 'all decrees of the *ius regis* when in error *ought to be reformed* by the rules of natural law'. These erroneous laws must exist to be capable of being reformed. Fortescue applies the same view to law made under the *dominium politicum*: 'the rules of political law, the sanctions of customs and constitutions, *ought to be quashed* when they depart from the institutes of natural law'.[119] Fortescue's broad conclusion is that '*all laws decreed by man*, though they be not directly opposed to natural law, from which they start and in which they must of necessity share, do, nevertheless, undoubtedly, within certain limits, differ from that law; for they would not be other laws but the same law, if they did not in some respects differ therefrom': therefore, argues Fortescue, 'a law promulgated by man does not prove that natural law points the same way'.[120]

These statements by Fortescue, in which he attributes an autonomy to human law, and in which rules are treated *as laws* in spite of their badness, express a proposition fundamental to the modern positivist theory of law. Fortescue is able to advance these ideas principally because of his analysis of law as originating in the human will and consent. In terms of clarity, they appear to be rather more refined than equivalent ideas in Pecock. What is more, they reflect a standpoint which seems to be difficult to detect readily in any developed form in the work of other major medieval jurists. An extensive study is needed to explore thoroughly the incipient positivist thesis in medieval jurisprudence generally, especially civilian and canonist thought, if we are to identify the thesis in forms other than its implicit reflection in the recognition of the phenomenon 'unjust law'. It is an idea which is merely implicit, for example, in Aquinas, who not only recognised (as we have seen) the possibility of unjust laws but also considered that they do not bind in conscience and ought not to be obeyed; though this view is to be looked at as subject to his comments

---

[119] Ibid., c. 29: 'omnia etiam iuris regalis decreta cum erraverint docuimus legis naturae debere regulis reformari'; ibid.: 'sic et politicae legis normas et consuetudinum ac constitutionem sanctiones cassari debere probavimus, quoties a legis naturae dissesserint institutis'.

[120] *De Natura* II, c. 51: 'Unde leges omnes ab homine statutas, licet legi naturae, a qua profisciscuntur et quam participare eis necesse est, se directe non opponant, discrepare tamen eas a lege illa moderamine quodam non ambigitur, nam non aliae ipsae forent sed eadem lex, si non ab ea in aliquo variarentur'.

Human law: the positivist thesis 55

on natural law (which are considered later), in this context such laws must exist to be capable of being disobeyed by citizens.[121]

## Parliament's treatment of bad legislation

Elementary aspects of the positivist thesis surface, with regard to legislation, when parliament alters a single statute which is described in the amending statute as offensive or bad. On the following occasion, a later statute treats an earlier statute as law despite the fact that the earlier statute is considered to be (and is described as) bad (*mischievous*) and damaging: the preceding statute is still law; it is not void because of its badness. The basic idea is that the earlier measure is merely voidable: it is law which had to be altered by other law.

In the late fourteenth century, frequently disseisors would alienate to others collusively and reserve the profits of the land for themselves. Often the disseisee did not know the identity of those to whom disseisors alienated. By legislation of 1377 such alienations were void and a disseisee could recover against the person who actually took the profits of the land (usually the original disseisor) only if he proceeded within a year after the disseisin.[122] In 1402, as the time limit was considered insufficient, causing a mischief to disseised persons, legislation was enacted to extend it.[123] The legislation provides, therefore, 'the king thinking the said statute to be very mischievous and damaging to his people [*le dit estatut estre molt meschevous et damageous a son people*], because of the shortness of the time', that the action could be brought against the first disseisor who was taking the profits at any time during the life of the same disseisor. Here the measure was not

---

[121] For Aquinas, above, n. 114 and, for the idea as subject to the notion of natural law (when we find the view that unjust laws are void), below chapter 3, n. 79. See also, for implicit positivist ideas, Bracton, *De Legibus*, II, p. 24, for *ius* as a judgment which may sometimes be unjust. For Marsilius, see E. Lewis, 'The positivism of Marsiglio of Padua', 38 *Speculum* (1963) p. 541; compare, though, J. Quillet, *Le Défenseur de la paix* (Paris, 1968): see *DP*, II, p. 191: 'some things are lawful according to human law which are not lawful according to divine law'; and ibid., p. 36: 'unjust laws are not perfect'; but also see ibid., p. 191: '[h]owever, what is lawful and what is unlawful in an absolute sense must be viewed according to divine law rather than human law, when these disagree in their commands, prohibitions and permissions'.

[122] I Ric. II, c. 9; see A. W. B. Simpson, *An Introduction to the History of the Land Law* (2nd edn, Oxford, 1986) pp. 183, 184.

[123] 4 Hen. IV, c. 7; for a general discussion of this and other statutes dealing with similar subjects see Holdsworth, IV, p. 444.

treated as void because it was mischievous. The 1377 statute was still treated as possessing the quality of law and had to be specifically altered by the 1402 statute.

In this example a statute treats earlier parliamentary legislation as bad law and, consequently, alters it. On the following occasion legislation of 1497 treats an ordinance created by the merchants of London as valid law requiring amendment. Again the measure is not treated as automatically void even though it is described as offending (amongst other things) reason and conscience.[124] Certain merchants outside London complained that their freedom to sell and exchange goods abroad was being disturbed by merchants based in London. It is claimed that the latter had 'contrary to all law, reason, charity, right and conscience' made an ordinance that no Englishman should sell or buy any goods in various markets without having first made a fine to the London fellowship of merchants. Consequently, the statute restated the freedom and penalised any such fines exceeding ten marks, for the merchants' ordinance had resulted in other merchants having to sell their goods in London at lower prices. Rather than revoking the ordinance, the statute merely restricted its ambit. Here, a non-parliamentary ordinance, though contrary to conscience, was effective until it was expressly dealt with by parliamentary law.

Whereas in the last two examples a single legislative enactment (one parliamentary, the other non-parliamentary) is altered, the same positivist approach is adopted in the repeal of the entire legislative output of a parliament. In the following instances the legislators acknowledge the status of all a previous parliament's legislation as law and, more importantly, as bad law, not invalid (by virtue of its badness), but requiring further legislative enactment to destroy it.

An enactment of 1399 commands that all the measures created by the parliament of 1398 be repealed.[125] It explains in its own justification how the previous parliament had passed statutes, judgments, ordinaces and establishments erroneously and in destruction of many people in the realm. Thus, the king 'considering the great mischiefs [*tresgraundes meschiefs*] aforesaid, by the advice and assent of the lords spiritual and temporal and of all the commonalty of the realm ' adjudged enactments of the previous parliament to be of no force or

---

[124] 12 Hen. VII, c. 6; see also Holdsworth, IV, p. 323; for merchants as legislators see H. J. Berman, *Law and Revolution* (Harvard, 1983) pp. 340, 346–8.
[125] 1 Hen. IV, c. 3; see also 3 Hen. VI, c. 4 and, especially, 20 Hen. VI, c. 3 describing mischiefs ensuing from the operation of 2 Hen. IV, c. 16.

## Human law: the positivist thesis 57

value: its authority was 'reversed, revoked, avoided, undone, repealed and annulled for ever'.
The same idea is implicit in legislation of 1460. This explains how the parliament held in the previous year at Coventry was summoned by the king upon the instigation of certain evil-disposed persons to destroy various lords and others against whom they held malice.[126] It continues: 'by which sinister labour certain acts, statutes and ordinances, *against all good faith and conscience*, in the said parliament were made, finally to destroy the said lawful lords, estates and liege people and their various issues, as well innocents as other and their heirs for ever'. Indeed, the statute also explains that many members of the same parliament were present 'without due and free election, some of them without any election, against the course of the king's laws'. Therefore, all the acts, statutes and ordinances made by the authority of that parliament were reversed, annulled and of no force or effect. The statute clearly illustrates the idea that parliamentary legislation, created in opposition to conscience, is not void *ab initio* but simply voidable, and therefore valid and operative unless and until it is replaced by subsequent enactment.

### Judicial treatment of bad legislation

For legislators, then, bad legislation possesses the quality of law. It exists until amended or repealed by later legislation. The judges also treat bad statute as enforceable law despite its substantive badness: as Hody CJKB stated in 1441, the king by his parliament can disherit a man as can parliament defeat a statute made in another parliament.[127] The view seems to be based on an incipient idea of parliamentary sovereignty. In 1407 Serjeant Tirwit said: 'the ordinance of the parliament ... is a judgment given in parliament, that cannot be reversed or revoked in a lower court'.[128] Similarly, in a case from 1455, Fortescue CJKB stated the idea, very familiar in current constitutional thought, that the courts are far from willing to question readily any procedural defect in the enactment of legislation: 'this is

---
[126] 39 Hen. VI, c. 1; for the idea in the sphere of a private transaction, see 18 Hen. VI, c. 1.
[127] P 19 Hen. VI, 62, 1 at 63.
[128] M 8 Hen. IV, 12, 13 at 13A; also M 11 Hen. IV, 7, 20 at 8A per Hankford who, when speaking of a statute, said 'nostre poiar est restraint per authority de parliament'. And M 11 Hen. IV, 37, 67 at 39A per Thirning: 'uncore per que il fuit un statute fait, et ne fuit unques repeal, il est assets bon'.

58     Fundamental authority in late medieval English law

an act of parliament, and we will be well advised, before we nullify such act made in the parliament'.[129] The judicial acceptance of legislation, even when it is mischievous, can be found in a case of 1443. One of the provisions of the statute of Westminster II c.14 was that, in a writ of waste, if the defendant did not appear after summons, attachment and distress, the sheriff was to empanel a jury to enquire of the waste.[130] The process laid down in the statute permitted a decision against the defendant, if the enquiry was unfavourable to him, regardless of his absence by non-appearance. In our case the court recognised this, considering that such loss on default (in the defendant's absence) effectively constituted a mischief to the defendant. Nevertheless, Paston JCP explained that the process prescribed by the statute had to be applied even if there was a mischief caused by loss on default. He says: 'As to what you say of the mischief that can ensue; sir, we cannot take consideration of the mischief for now'. Paston continues: 'for when a statute is made although it be against law [that is, different from the common law] and *mischievous* [*encontre ley et mischevous*]; yet this will be held for law [*ley*] until it be repealed and annulled: and those who made the statute perhaps had consideration of the mischief'. Again, for Paston, mischievous legislation is not void, but valid until repealed.

The idea also appears in 1490 when it was explained how a statute of 1484 protected the purchaser of land granted to him by a beneficiary under a trust, thereby allowing the beneficiary to disrupt the trustee's obligation to hold the land for him 'in conscience'. It was said that 'in conscience' the land was to be held for the *cestuy que use*, but that the legislation, by effectively allowing him to alienate without having the legal estate, upset an obligation imposed on the trustees and arising in conscience.[131] With regard to the common law, the rejection of *conscience* arguments in favour of law, adherence to the idea of *rigor iuris*, and the idea that a 'mischief will be suffered rather than an inconvenience' are all aspects of the employment by late medieval

---

[129] P 33 Hen. VI, 17, 8 at 18 (the bill had been assented to by the commons in one form, and endorsed by the lords in another).
[130] T 21 Hen. VI, 56, 13; Fitzherbert, *GA*, 'Waste', 45; for a discussion of *distringas*, see J. C. Fox, 'Process of imprisonment at common law', 39 *LQR* (1923) p. 46.
[131] P 6 Hen. VII, 3, 5 (the YB reference is mistaken: it says '5' Hen. VII). For the statute, 1 Ric. III, c. 1, see Simpson, *History of the Land Law*, pp. 184, 185, *HFCL*, p. 215, and *IELH*, p. 213: the beneficiary now had the power to convey the legal estate. For the idea of an obligation arising in conscience under the trust, see *IELH*, p. 210.

practitioners of a positivist outlook. These we shall explore later, when considering the usage of *conscience, mischief* and *inconvenience*.

CONCLUSION

There seems to be some evidence, in legislation, in the Year Books and in legal theory, to suggest that there are several points of contact between late medieval jurisprudence and aspects of the 'modern' positivist thesis. The populist thesis, with its emphasis on the idea that law derives from an act of the human will, prepares the way for a set of propositions central to classical positivism. As consent is seen as the basis for parliamentary law and local custom, and as usage is the basis for the common law, so law is not dependent for its authority upon some divinely created morality, but simply on the independent exercise of the human will. The way is clear for a thoroughly mundane conception of *human* law. Laws are composed of commands and prohibitions. They differ according to changes in the human will: from time to time, from place to place. Yet, at the same time, the practitioners also valued permanence in law. It is a law whose fundamental purpose is merely to serve the common profit (though here there was something of a dissonance between theory and practice, as Fortescue in particular saw law as advancing virtue). Consequently, we begin to meet the concept that failure in a rule to conform to morality, or ideas of right and wrong, will not affect its status as law. Once a rule is incorporated in legislation (or, as we shall see, the common law) then it is to be treated as law irrespective of its moral standing: it is merely voidable and not void. In short, the result of the stress on law as issuing from the human will is the idea that humanly created rules are still laws even when they depart from abstract right and wrong.

# 3

# NATURAL LAW: THE SUPERIOR MORAL LAW

The concept of natural law is central in late medieval legal thought. It is a concept which, when placed alongside populist and positivist ideas, creates a basic tension in jurisprudence during this period. Whereas the mundane voluntarist idea of law concentrates upon the human will as the authority for human law, in their use of natural law, and the idea of divine law, the theorists and practitioners of the late medieval period postulate an additional and fundamentally different source of authority for law. The natural law outlook advances the view that law is not dependent for its authority solely upon human enactment or usage. Within the natural law view human law is also treated as originating in, and as deriving its authority from, the abstract notion of a divinely given morality. This has a profound effect upon the apparent autonomy of human law facilitated by the voluntarist thesis. From the natural law view, human law emerges as an inferior species of law, subordinate to the ethical imperative of natural law with which there must be agreement if it is to obtain a complete authority. According to natural law ideas, human law is not wholly autonomous, but relies for its authority on conformity with morality. In turn, this produces a wide conception of law. Law is not merely that set of commands and prohibitions consented to by the community, or the usages of judges, it is also that set of rules which corresponds to the extraneous formulations of divine morality represented in natural law.

## NATURAL LAW AND DIVINE LAW IN LEGAL THEORY

In their theoretical discussions, both Pecock and Fortescue propose sets of ideas about natural law which conform to the standard pattern of medieval jurisprudence. Natural law is seen as a system of precepts

Natural law: the superior moral law 61

and prohibitions created by God. The purpose of the rules of the divinely created natural law is to regulate human action in such a way as to produce conformity with the dictates of the divine will. These rules are accessible to humankind through the human reason, through revelation and through instinct.

### The relation of natural law to divine law

For Pecock and Fortescue the source of natural law is the divine will. It is created not by man but by God. As its source is the divine will so they treat natural law as a 'divine law', and often the terms are used interchangeably. This was common. The canonists of the twelfth and thirteenth centuries equated natural law and divine law fully: *ius naturale, id est, ius divinum*.[1] Aquinas also concentrated on the connection between natural law and divine law, from which we ascertain good and evil, and his ideas and those of the canonists greatly influenced Fortescue.[2] Adopting their ideas Fortescue considers that all things are subject to a divine plan, indicated in what he describes as the *eternal law*, which he also calls the *divine law*. When applied to human beings, this divine plan is expressed in natural law. Quoting directly from Aquinas' *Summa*, Fortescue reiterates that 'natural law is nothing else but the participation of the eternal law in a rational creature'. Accordingly, Fortescue says that natural law should not only be called *filia legis divinae*, but should carry the name of divine law: then follows the canon lawyers' conclusion, *sic ergo lex naturae lex divina est*.[3]

Pecock's analysis of natural law (the *lawe of kynde*) is entirely dominated by his use of *reason*. In a manner reminiscent of Aquinas, for whom there was a meeting of natural law and 'the light of natural

---

[1] W. Ullmann, *Medieval Papalism: The Political Theories of the Medieval Canonists* (London, 1949) p. 40; and B. Tierney, *'Natura id est Deus*: a case of juristic pantheism?', 24 *Journal of the History of Ideas* (1963) p. 307.
[2] *Summa*, 1a, 2ae, 71, 6; 91, 2; 94, 3; 97, 3; 100, 2; 3a, 84, 7; A. P. d'Entreves, *Natural Law: An Introduction to Legal Philosophy* (2nd edn, London, 1970) pp. 42–4. For a brief discussion of natural law in Fortescue, see E. F. Jacob, *Essays in the Conciliar Epoch* (3rd edition, Manchester, 1963) pp. 109–19: the precise relationship between natural law and human law is not discussed, nor the basic tension in Fortescue between natural law and positivist ideas.
[3] *De Natura* I, c. 42; and c. 5: 'ipsa nihil aliud est quam participatio legis eternae in rationali creatura'; for Aquinas, *Summa*, 1a, 2ae, 91, 2; and at 93, 1: 'the eternal law is nothing else than the plan of the divine wisdom considered as directing all the acts and motions' of creatures.

reason' and 'practical reason' (by which we discern good from evil),[4] Pecock argues that what the human reason requires itself constitutes natural law, and what natural law (as manifested in the human reason) requires is also required by divine law. Divine law and natural law, indicated by the dictates of human reason, coincide. It is the 'judgment of [man's] natural reason', he says, 'which is the moral law of nature and the moral law of God': in short, 'the common law of God [is] made of the law of nature'.[5] As the greater part of God's law to man is grounded in the law of nature, so then, whatever law the judgment of man's reason enjoins is commanded by the law of God.[6] The same view, basically, was proposed by D'Ailly. Divine law embraces all aspects of natural law, 'since such law comes from God, the founder of nature'.[7] In a sense later qualified by his remarks concerning man's access to each law, Gerson too contends that natural law and divine law are identical, for God the author of divine law is also the author of natural law.[8]

## The substance and purpose of natural law

From their equation of natural law and divine law it is clear that the theorists construct a theocratic conception of natural law. As with D'Ailly and Gerson, and in the Thomist tradition,[9] Pecock proposes

[4] *Summa*, 1a, 2ae, 91, 2: 'the light of natural reason by which we discern good from evil' is natural law; 94, 2: 'natural law commands extend to all doing or avoiding of things recognised by the practical reason of itself as being human goods'; at 1a, 2ae, 18, 5, 'when we speak of good and evil in human acts we take "reasonable" as our standard'.

[5] *Repressor*, I, p. 18, II, p. 504; and ibid., I, p. 6. Pecock often uses the expressions 'common law of kind' (ibid., II, p. 579), 'common law of Christ' (ibid., II, p. 462) and 'common law of Christianhood' (ibid., II, p. 463). The law of *kynde* also appears frequently in non-legal sources: *Mandeville's Travels* (fourteenth century) (translated from the French of Jean d'Outremeuse), edited by P. Hamelius, Early English Text Society, 153, volume I (London, 1919) p. 194 (see also p. 67).

[6] *Repressor*, I, pp. 18, 39, 40; at 189: '[w]hat ever governaunce doom of weel disposid resoun biddith, God biddith; and what ever governaunce doom of weel disposid resoun counseilith, allowith, or approveth, God the same governaunce counseilith, allowith, or approveth'.

[7] Oakley, p. 177, n. 19; for Nicholas of Cusa, see Sigmund, p. 143. For Saint German, *Dialogue*, p. 11, for eternal law, and p. 13 for natural law. For Richard Hooker, E. T. Davies, *The Political Ideas of Richard Hooker* (New York, reprint 1972) p. 44.

[8] Pascoe, p. 61. Natural law and divine law in the Italian jurist Baldus (1327–1400) are discussed in J. Canning, *The Political Thought of Baldus de Ubaldis* (Cambridge, 1987) pp. 76–9, 155–6, 182–3.

[9] For D'Ailly, see Oakley, p. 181, and Gerson, Pascoe, p. 60. Aquinas' view is at *Summa*, 1a, 2ae, 97, 3 (and 100, 2 for divine law enjoining virtue). For Saint German, citing Gerson, *Dialogue*, p. 13.

## Natural law: the superior moral law

that natural law is composed of commands requiring virtuous action and that it emanates from the divine will, not the human will: 'between us and God it is so that our will and consent is not required to run with God's will and consent that God made a law to bind us'.[10] Each 'positive law of God', says Pecock, is a 'voluntary and wilful assignment of God', containing everything which God *commands* to be done and all that God *counsels* to be done: 'however much God bids to be done or counsels or ordains to be done, so much is His law', and this 'is a law to us binding us'.[11] Because natural law and divine law are of the same essence, all that God commands, reason commands: 'since the law of God given to man is none other than God's commandments and God's counsels, it follows that the commandments and counsels of reason and of faith and the law of God are all one'.[12] The end of divine and natural law is to effect man's performance of the virtues towards God, himself and his neighbour, so that ultimately man may be led to salvation.[13] In the 'precepts and prohibitions' of divine law, every virtue is taught, and every vice prohibited.[14] Natural law is a divine statement of right and wrong and its rules are immutable.[15]

Similarly, Fortescue also treats natural law as immutable, as deriving from the divine will, and as consisting of rules (*regulae*), which, in turn, are composed of commands and prohibitions.[16] Chief amongst the precepts of natural law is the requirement that a person should do to others that which he would have done by others to himself.[17] Within

---

[10] *Folower*, p. 217: 'but bitwix us and god it is so that oure wil and consent is not requirid forto renne with goddis wil and consent that god make a lawe to bynde us'.
[11] *Repressor*, I, p. 18; also *Donet*, p. 202 (and pp. 183, 197). For Wyclif, see W. E. Farr, *John Wyclif as Legal Reformer* (Leiden, 1974) p. 43.
[12] *Donet*, pp. 15, 16: 'sithen the lawe of god govun to man is not ellis than goddis comaundementis and goddis counseilis; it folewith that the commaundementis and counseilis of resoun and of feith and the lawe of god ben al oon'; also p. 37, and *Repressor*, I, p. 189, II, pp. 505, 524.
[13] *Donet*, pp. 17, 72: for a fascinating discussion of the divinisation of natural and degenerate man through baptismal rebirth and membership of the 'a-natural' society of the church, and the effects of grace upon ideas of natural law, see W. Ullmann, *Medieval Foundations of Renaissance Humanism* (London, 1977) chapters 1, 4 and 5.
[14] *Donet*, pp. 179, 180.
[15] Ibid., p. 129. For the idea in Saint German, *Dialogue*, p. 15.
[16] *De Natura* I, cc. 5, 20, 38, for natural law as unchanging; also *De Laudibus*, c. 16. For Aquinas, *Summa*, 1a, 2ae, 97, 1 and the Italian jurists Baldus, Ullmann, 'Baldus' conception of law', p. 394, and Bartolus, Ullmann, 'Bartolus on customary law', p. 280, n. 5. Fortescue's idea of natural law as composed of rules, is at *De Natura* I, cc. 24, 29; also *De Laudibus*, c. 8, p. 23.
[17] *De Natura* I, c. 4 (Matt. 7:12).

this principle, not only is an individual commanded positively 'to do to another what he would have done to himself', but he is also forbidden 'to do to another what he would not have done to himself'.[18] For Fortescue, natural law has both a temporal and a spiritual function. Not only does it rule individuals in temporal things, governing conduct of individual to individual, but also, with the assistance of divine grace, through adherence to it individuals might attain eternal life.[19]

### The theory of human access to natural law

A problem which attracted considerable discussion in medieval thought concerned the way in which individuals were to recognise or identify the rules of natural law. Where and how was this superior divine morality to be found? Fortescue uses three means of access to natural law, three means which had already made their mark in earlier thought.[20] First, he considers that it is knowable through human instinct (an idea which was not readily acceptable to some notable canonists), since 'natural law is that which nature taught all animals'. It exists as something which 'is infused into and is innate in man so that it can by no means be separated from him'.[21] Second, Fortescue argues that the human reason can detect the rules of natural law: 'right reason [*ratio*] reveals the law of nature'.[22] Third, individuals ascertain

[18] Ibid. And *Governance*, c. 4: 'the law of nature wills in this case that the king should do to his subjects as he would have done to himself if he were a subject'.
[19] *De Natura* I, Introduction and c. 42; in relation to divine law this is thoroughly Thomist: *Summa*, 1a, 2ae, 98, 1; 2a, 2ae, 140, 1; for the earthbound purpose of natural law, ibid., 1a, 2ae, 91, 4. However, Aquinas' division of the rules of natural law into primary and secondary precepts is not used by Fortescue. The primary precepts ('that good should be done and pursued and evil avoided' – 94, 2) are general in nature and are applied in particular cases by the latter by means of human law and divine law; the secondary precepts are particular conclusions drawn from the primary precepts. Saint German does adopt Aquinas' division, *Dialogue*, p. 11.
[20] E. Levi, 'Natural law in Roman thought', 15 *Studia et Documenta Historiae et Iuris* (1949) p. 1 at pp. 2, 18; for Bracton, *De Legibus*, II, p. 26 (his emphasis seems to be on instinct), and Baldus, Ullmann, 'Baldus' conception of law', p. 394.
[21] *De Natura* I, c. 31: 'ius naturale est quod natura omnia animalia docuit'; see also ibid., c. 38. For the idea in Roman Law see *Inst.*, Bk. I, Tit. II. The role of instinct was questioned by, for example, Rufinus (a pupil of Gratian and writing around 1157): *MPT*, II, p. 104.
[22] *De Natura* I, cc. 31, 32: 'recta ratio nobis legem naturae revelat'. He explains that ordinary legal questions can be resolved by applying this law (ibid., c. 31), for neither human law nor its judges can pass by its mandates (ibid., c. 46). For Aquinas, *Summa*, 1a, 2ae, 91, 2; 94, 4.

natural law by examining scriptures 'for so say the canons when they speak of the *ius naturale* as that contained in the law and the gospels'.[23] Elsewhere Fortescue says that all the laws of the Old and New Testaments do not diminish natural law but rather approve it.[24] Fortescue's canonist idea that scripture 'contains' natural law differs from that of Wyclif (d. 1384) who argued that scripture *is* God's law, scripture manifests God's every ordinance.[25] Pecock's discussion of the location of, and access to, natural law, was devised to repudiate Wyclif. The idea that no ordinance is to be deemed a law of God unless it is grounded in scripture, Pecock argues, is wrong. Whatever knowledge scripture gives of divine law, so that same knowledge can be supplied by the human reason,[26] that power which enables man to judge between good and bad:[27] individuals 'cannot find one such law taught in holy scripture to be done, but that reason teaches it like well and like fully to be done'.[28] Even if scripture did not exist, he says, still people could discover natural and divine law by means of reason. Scripture is simply evidence of natural and divine law, 'it bears witness to them as grounded *somewhere else* in the law of nature or in the judgment of man's reason'.[29] The essence of his argument is that 'the greater deal and part of God's whole law to man on earth ... is grounded sufficiently out of holy scripture in the inward book of the law of nature and of moral philosophy and not in the book of holy scripture called the Old and the New Testament'.[30]

[23] *De Natura* I, c. 4: 'Et legem quam sic declarivit Dominus et custodire precepit legem esse naturae expresse declarant Canones (I Di. C. I) sic dicentes. Jus naturale est quod in lege et Evangelia continetur, quo quisque jubetur alio facere quod sibi vult fieri, et prohibetur inferre quod sibi nolit fieri'; also c. 5. For Gratian, E. Lewis, *Medieval Political Ideas*, 2 volumes (New York, 1954) I, p. 32. Contrast Marsilius, who says the NT only contains divine law (*DP*, I, p. 153).
[24] *De Natura* I, c. 5.
[25] W. E. Farr, *John Wyclif as Legal Reformer*, p. 43.
[26] *Repressor*, I, pp. 6, 11.
[27] *Donet*, p. 12: 'resoun is a power, with whiche power mowe be knowe unbodili thingis, goostli or spiritual thingis ... And also with which power may be dryve oute and founden in arguyng and concluding what is trewe, what is fals, what is good, and what is bad, and what is more good, and what is more bad.' *Folower*, p. 84: 'the doom of resoun is oon of the principal groundis and causis of moralte'. For Aquinas, *Summa*, 1a, 79, 11.
[28] *Repressor*, I, p. 12: 'for thou canst not fynde oon such governaunce taught in Holi Scripture to be doon, but that resoun techith it lijk weel and lijk fulli to be doon'.
[29] Ibid., pp. 17, 32.
[30] Ibid., pp. 39, 40: '[t]he more deel and party of Goddis hool lawe to man in erthe ... is groundid sufficiently out of Holi Scripture in the inward book of lawe of kinde and of moral philosophie, and not in the book of Holi Scripture clepid the Oold Testament and the Newe'.

The broad ideas that natural law is derived from the will of God and that it is ascertainable by means of reason were common. Gerson considered that the *lex divina* is revealed, but not every law revealed is part of divine law.[31] Some parts of divine law are revealed through scripture, others are deduced from those laws, and others are revealed to private individuals.[32] Natural law, on the other hand, though emanating from the divine will, depends for its knowledge upon human reason rather than divine revelation,[33] though Gerson agrees that the Old and New Testaments contain all the essentials of natural law.[34] Saint German, relying in part on Gerson, proposed a similar view.[35]

### THEOCRATIC LEGISLATION

The consequence of the theorists' use of the divine will and divine law, in their analyses of natural law, is a thoroughly theocratic conception of natural law. Natural law is fashioned by the divine will. A general theocratic outlook of law is also to be found in the practical sphere. There are many instances of the absorption of divine law into legislation, occasions upon which divine law is employed by legislators in such a way as to produce an apparent and explicit coincidence between the divine will and actual law. Frequently, legislation is designed to embody the requirements of divine law. Indeed, it must be remembered that when there is an absorption of this type, divine law, as a source of authority, is used alongside and in the same legislation as popular consent.

In the basic formula used by the theorists the commands of natural law are treated as the commands of God. An equivalent concept surfaces in parliamentary legislation in the late medieval period. In statutes and ordinances can be detected formulae which signify an *idea* of divine law. The idea is reflected in legislation by the incorpor-

---

[31] Pascoe, pp. 58, 59.   [32] Ibid., p. 59.   [33] Ibid., p. 60.
[34] Ibid., p. 61. D'Ailly's idea that both natural law and divine law derive from God's will, but that divine law is revealed in scripture and natural law known by reason, is at Oakley, p. 179.
[35] *Dialogue*, pp. 21–5; p. 21: 'a law is divine ... properly described, because it is revealed by God, and also because it directs a man by the nearest way to the eternal felicity'; ibid., p. 11: 'when the eternal law or the will of God is known to his reasonable creatures by the light of natural understanding or by the light of natural reason then it is called the law of reason. And when it is shown by heavenly revelation ... it is called the law of God'.

ation of such expressions as 'offence to God', 'against the law of God' and 'to the displeasure of God'. The usage of these epithets produces a theocratic style of legislation. The commands and prohibitions of human law, parliamentary legislation, are regarded *at the same time* as coinciding with divine commands and prohibitions.

The idea of an offence to God is used sometimes to condemn purely earthly conduct and sometimes to condemn conduct of a more obviously spiritual kind. Parliament in 1402 penalised individuals who constructed weirs across rivers for endangering the lives of those travelling by boat as well as endangering fish stocks. In the statute, the harming of the people and the destruction of the fish are described as offensive to reason and against the pleasure of God: 'the common passage of ships and boats is disturbed and many people harmed [*periz*], and also the young fry of fish destroyed, and against reason wasted and given to swine to eat, contrary to the pleasure of God [*encontre le pleisance de dieu*]'.[36] By way of contrast, in a quite different setting, the parliament of 1448 recognised that holding fairs and markets on Sundays and high feast days caused 'abominable injuries and offences done to almighty God', and ordained that fairs and markets should not be held on these days with the exception of four Sundays in Harvest. It is interesting to note that the statute describes the consequence for those holding fairs and markets as a 'defiling of their souls'.[37]

Two of the three statutes in which the term 'the law of God' appears in the fifteenth century concern the Lollards. Legislation of 1400 explains how the Lollards spread their heresy 'contrary to divine law [*contra legem divinam*] and [the law] of the church', making division among the people so that there is peril to souls and many other consequences 'which God prohibits' and 'to the hatred of right and reason, and utter destruction of order and good rule'. The measure permitted the arrest and imprisonment of all offenders by the church authorities whilst securing a fine to the king.[38] In 1414, whilst

[36] 4 Hen. IV, c. 11: the word *periz* is translated as 'harmed', though it may also mean 'perished'. From the same year, 4 Hen. IV, c. 22, reciting a statute of 1351 which dealt with improper presentments taking place 'against God and good faith'.
[37] 27 Hen. VI, c. 5: 'Item consideratis abhominabilis injuriis et offensis omnipotenti Deo'; see also 17 Ed. IV, c. 3, which penalises those encouraging games being 'evil-disposed persons that fear not to offend God in not observing their holy days'. For the phrase *que Dieu defende* ('which God forbid!'), an exclamation frequently appearing in non-legal sources (*MED*,'defenden', 11(c) ), see 27 Ed. III, St. II, c. 17; 9 Hen. V, St. II, c. 3; 3 Hen. VII, c. 9.
[38] 2 Hen. IV, c. 15.

parliament once more set out the procedure for the arrest of Lollards, the heresy was described as subverting the Christian faith and '*la leie Dieu* within this same realm of England', as well as the laws of the land.[39] The law of God also appears in a statute of 1496, the first in a series of enactments excluding large numbers of felonies from benefit of clergy.[40] It provides that James Grame be attainted of petty treason without benefit of clergy and that any lay person who murdered his master be denied the same: 'Where abominable and wilful prepensed murders be, *by the laws of God and of natural reason*, forbidden and are to be eschewed, yet nonetheless many and diverse unreasonable and detestable persons lacking grace wilfully commit murder, *to the high displeasure of God* and contrary to all the laws aforesaid.' What is more, parliament also described these killings as offensive to a 'natural duty' not to kill superiors; such people, it continues, 'against their *naturall and oblieged dutie* wilfully commit prepensed murders, in slaying their master or their immediate sovereign under whom he or they be or owe obedience'.[41]

The description of a state of affairs or conduct as being 'to the displeasure of God', which appeared in the last statute, is one which was frequently employed, particularly in the second half of the fifteenth century. A statute of 1455 (in a setting similar to the Grame legislation) explains how servants took and distributed the goods of their masters at the time of their death 'to the impediment of the execution of the will of their said lords and masters, and to the great displeasure of God [*dei displicenciam*], and also contrary to the faith and truth which they ought to have towards their said lords and masters'. The statute then creates a felony of the non-appearance of a servant in answer to a summons for the taking and distribution of his deceased employer's goods. (The legislation is curious as it is the non-appearance which constitutes the felony: default is felonious, not the taking or distribution.)[42] Legislation of 1488 empowered judges to

---

[39] 2 Hen. V, c. 7.
[40] Holdsworth, III, pp. 301, 315, and *CH*, p. 446.
[41] 12 Hen. VII, c. 7; *naturall reason* is also in 3 Hen. VII, c. 12. A related expression, *ley de naturell justice*, appears in 3 Hen. VII, c. 5 and 11 Hen. VII, c. 8: see below, chapter 4, n. 67.
[42] 33 Hen. VI, c. 1; it was common for statutes to create felonies sporadically, *IELH*, p. 426: for example, 5 Hen. IV, c. 5, 8 Hen. VI, c. 12, 18 Hen. VI, c. 19. For a statute concerned with the dilapidation of hospitals 'to the displeasure of God, and peril of the souls' of those misusing property given to maintain them, see 2 Hen. V, St. I, c. 1.

## Natural law: the superior moral law 69

examine and punish those involved in maintenance, embracery, riots, unlawful assemblies and other offences, by which the good rule of the realm was threatened, for its laws had not been effectively executed 'to the increase of murders, robberies, perjuries and unsuerties of all men living and losses of their lands and goods, *to the great displeasure of Almighty God*'.[43] In the same year, it was ordained that the taking away of women against their will constituted a felony. The women had then been married to their kidnappers and others 'to the great displeasure of God and contrary to the king's laws'.[44]

It is evident that the legislators present their legislation in such a way that it has the *appearance* of (incorporating) divine prohibitions. They do so by relating human conduct to the divine will. Conduct and its consequences are prohibited as 'contrary to the pleasure of God', as being 'offensive to God', as being 'against the law of God' and as being 'to the great displeasure of God'. The incorporation of these epithets into enactments creates a theocratic form of legislation, in which operates the idea of divine law. The prohibitions of human legislation are treated and represented as divine prohibitions. This theocratic sense of legislation is reflected in Fortescue's view that when law is enacted by king and community, when it becomes *lex statuti*, then it is 'made sacred [*sanctiatur*]'.[45] In Fortescue, human law generally is somehow *sacrosanct*. 'All human laws are sacred', he says.[46] Following the standard civilian idea, Fortescue sees jurisprudence as the knowledge of things divine and things human, and it is necessary for secular judges to be versed in divine as well as human law.[47] For this reason the ministers and teachers of human law are rightly called 'priests'.[48] In short, 'all laws that are promulgated by man are decreed by God'.[49] Thus, he argues, 'the law or laudable custom of any kingdom not contravening the law of God or the church is a law

---

[43] 3 Hen. VII, c. 1, the statute is discussed at Holdsworth, II, pp. 361–3.
[44] 3 Hen. VII, c. 2. Other illustrations of 'displeasure of God' are at 1 Ric. III, c. 2, 3 Hen. VII, c. 6, 11 Hen. VII, cc. 2, 3.
[45] *De Natura*, I, c. 30.
[46] *De Laudibus*, c. 3, p. 7.
[47] *De Natura*, I, c. 46. For Bracton, *De Legibus*, II, p. 25.
[48] *De Laudibus*, c. 3, p. 9. For Bracton, *De Legibus*, II, p. 24, and Roman Law generally, W. Kunkel, *An Introduction to Roman Legal and Constitutional History*, translated by J. M. Kelly (2nd edition, Oxford, 1973) pp. 95f.
[49] *De Laudibus*, c. 3, p. 9.

70  *Fundamental authority in late medieval English law*

published mediately by the Lord and approved which, by those who have from Him power to make law, is made and approved'.[50]

## THE JUDICIAL USE OF NATURAL LAW

The specific expression 'natural law' is never utilised in legislation during the fifteenth century. The nearest parliament comes to using a *concept* close to that of the natural law of legal theory (with the possible exception of an expression like 'the laws . . . of natural reason' appearing in the 1496 Grame statute) is in this diffuse idea of divine law reflected in the standard epithets described above. As a consequence, there emerges a basic dissonance between practice and theory, in which (as we have seen) natural law does play an important role. A similar dissonance in terms of emphasis exists between theory and the judicial usage of natural law. It is not common for the judges to appeal to the law of nature. The expression is used on only a handful of occasions in the Year Books, and then mainly in the latter part of the period (though the term had actually made its appearance a long time before).[51] And nowhere do they define the term. Nowhere do they say it is found in scripture or ascertained by reason and instinct. Consequently, it is impossible to say that there is a systematic and definite practitioners' idea of natural law. It is rather in the use of *conscience* and *reason* that we see their large moral idea of authority at work. Their idea of natural law is piecemeal, and our understanding of it can only proceed on the basis of isolated and individual statements. These are, roughly, of four types.

[50] *Works, De Titulo*, p. 86. There are no comparable remarks in Pecock. However, Thomas Smith claimed 'that which is done by this [parliamentary] consent is called firm, stable and *sanctum*, and is taken for law': *De Rep*, II, c. 1. Similarly for Hooker: see Davies, *The Political Ideas of Richard Hooker*, p. 52.

[51] The judicial use of natural law, mainly in the second half of the century, is at a time, of course, when the Chancellor's use of *conscience* makes its mark. The term *naturel ley*, however, can be found earlier in, for example, a case from 1313–14: W. C. Bolland, *The Eyre of Kent: 6 & 7 Ed II*, 24 Sel. Soc. (London, 1909) p. 126 per Ashby. For an interesting study see R. L. Jefferson, 'The uses of natural law in the royal courts in fifteenth-century England', unpublished Ph.D. thesis (University of Utah, 1972). Natural law in medieval thought is discussed, with a brief look at Fortescue (yet Pecock, though his *Repressor* is mentioned, is not thoroughly analysed). The study describes some judicial uses of natural law but lacks a full analysis of the Year Books and statutes. Its conclusion that the judges challenged parliamentary statute is questionable (chapter 4), but it has useful chapters on the chancellor, Yorkist appeals to natural law and its use in the sixteenth century. I am grateful to Professor J. H. Baker for drawing my attention to it.

First, natural law was used interstitially, to fill the gaps of the positive law. It was used in this way in a case of 1468. A device commonly used at this time by parties to an agreement was that of referring their disputes to the arbitration of a third party.[52] Sometimes the arbiter would award that one side pay the other a certain sum by a fixed date: it might also happen that the other party would claim he had not been given notice that the sum was due. Whether he would be discharged from payment through lack of notice was a question facing the Exchequer Chamber in this case.[53] Choke CJCP, Illingworth CB and Danby JCP decided that he will not be excused as it was his own folly to put arbitration in the hands of *that* person: it is wholly up to the parties to attend and have notice of the arbitration. On the other hand Yelverton JKB disagrees. It was not possible for him to perform without notice and, as there was no settled legal rule which did prohibit discharge from payment, even when no notice had been given, he should be excused. Yelverton states that 'we will do now in this case as the canonists and civilians do when a new case comes, *for which they have no law before*'. He explains that in such circumstances 'they resort to the *law of nature [al ley de nature]* which is the ground of all laws [*leys*], and according to that which is suggested by them *to be more beneficial to the common weal*, etc., they do, and so now we will do'.[54]

This passage is important for several reasons. Not only does Yelverton JKB propose to use natural law interstitially, when the case was not covered by existing law, but he also identifies the central purpose of natural law as something which is to be used to benefit the common weal. Unlike Pecock and Fortescue, here Yelverton concentrates exclusively upon the mundane function of natural law. Moreover, Yelverton proceeds to explain that if a *new* 'positive law' be made on this point, natural law requires that its effect upon the common weal must be estimated. Therefore, in this case, Yelverton maintained that it would not be beneficial to the common weal to insist on following arbitrements without notice, because the purpose of these is 'to appease disputes and wrongs among the people'. He is convinced of

[52] *HCLC*, pp. 173–7.
[53] P 8 Ed. IV, 1, 1; M 8 Ed. IV, 9, 9; 20, 35; Brooke, *GA*, 'Arbitrement', 37, Notice, 18.
[54] Only Pecock uses natural law interstitially, along with conscience, *Reule*, pp. 306, 307.

72    Fundamental authority in late medieval English law

the utility of this conclusion, 'for this case has never been seen before, and therefore our present judgment will be taken for a precedent hereafter'. For different reasons, Markham and Nedham JJCP agree, though the entire matter was adjourned.

This interstitial function of natural law was occasionally referred to in local custumals. A custumal of Rye, for example, stated that local judges should utilise natural law in cases of 'which there is no special remembrance or mention made in this book'. In these cases 'the mayor which is judge with his brethren the jurats, shall have recourse to the *laws of natural reason*, upon which and of which do proceed and are founded all the laws and customs according unto [that is, consonant with] the laws of England [the common law]'.[55]

Second, though very rarely, there are occasional statements in the practical sphere that *all* judicial decisions *ought* to be based on the law of nature. For instance, chapter 76 of the custumal of Fordwich declares that 'in *every case* the judge shall have recourse to the laws of nature [*jura naturalia*], upon which are founded and whence proceed all written laws [*leges scripte*]'.[56] And the Rye custumal recited that 'in all manner of causes and articles' the judge shall have recourse to natural law.[57] The common law judges never say this, though in 1489 the chancellor did imply the idea. In this case D was indebted to T who made two executors. One of these released D from performance of the agreement with T without the assent of the other executor.[58] *Subpoena* was sued in the chancery against the executor who released the debtor. The chancellor chose to require the executor to make amends. He gave two reasons. One was the normal idea: '*Nullus recedat a curia cancellariae sine remedio*, and it is against *reason* that an executor will have all the goods, and will make release alone.' The other reason he explained in this way: 'Sir, I know full well that *every law* is, or of right ought to be, in accord with the *law of God*; and the *law of God* is that an executor who is of evil disposition shall not expend all the goods.' Thus, if the executor did waste the goods and yet was able to make amends but failed to do so, 'he will be damned in

---

[55] 21 Sel. Soc. (London, 1906) p. 59.
[56] Ibid.: 'Et in omni casu habet recursum judex ad jura naturalia, super que fundantur et a quibus procedunt omnes leges scripte.'
[57] Ibid.
[58] H 4 Hen. VII, 4, 8; Brooke, *GA*, 'Conscience', 7; Fifoot, *Sources*, p. 304, and *HCLC*, p. 397; see also P 7 Hen. VII, 10, 2.

Natural law: the superior moral law 73

hell'.[59] To avoid this, the executor was to be compelled to make amends.

Third, though the common law judges did not state persistently that all decisions were to conform to natural law, occasionally they acknowledged that sometimes the requirements of human law and those of divine law *actually* coincided. This happened in *Gylys* v *Watterkyn* of 1485 in which P brought trespass against several defendants for assault, battery and imprisonment.[60] The defendants sought to justify their action by relying on a custom of London which permitted the inhabitants within its jurisdiction to seize adulterers: they showed successfully that P had committed adultery. P, on the other hand, responded that it could not be relied on in a temporal court because adultery was a spiritual matter. In the course of discussion, Townsend JCP preferred to allow the defendants' plea in reliance upon the custom, saying the custom afforded protection 'because it was good for the conservation of the peace and good rule'. Moreover, even though adultery was not a 'crime' at common law,[61] he rejected P's argument that the matter was spiritual and thus could not be pleaded, explaining how adultery was a temporal matter and prohibited by both divine and human law. He said: 'it is a great sin and peril by the *law of God and man*, and the occasion of this can destroy the city and borough'. The case was adjourned.

Lastly, there was one occasion when a judge expressed the view that human law could not revoke or abrogate natural law. In a Note of 1495 Fineux CJKB saw natural law as an independent moral force when he distinguished between a *malum prohibitum* and a *malum in se*.[62] A *malum prohibitum* would be when, for example, a statute prohibits an individual from making money: if he does make money he will be punished. This is a *malum prohibitum* because before the statute the

---

[59] H 4 Hen. VII, 4, 8 at 5: 'Sir, jeo scay bien que chescun ley est, ou de droit doit estre accordant al Ley de Dieu; et le Ley de Dieu est, que un executor qui est de male disposition ne expendera touts les biens.' For the chancellor's protection of the souls of wrong-doers, see *HCLC*, pp. 398, 399.

[60] H 1 Hen. VII, 6, 3: 'et il est un grand peche et peril per Ley de Dieu et home, et l'occasion de ce poit destruir tout le cite ou borough'. For justification upon suspicion, T 9 Ed. IV, 27, 39.

[61] *CH*, p. 492, n. 5. Also, M 13 Hen. VII, 10, 10. In the well-known *Carrier's Case* of 1473, P 13 Ed. IV, 9, 5, we meet the idea of statute coinciding with natural law.

[62] M 11 Hen. VII, 11, 35; Brooke, *GA*, 'Charters of Pardon', 76, 'Prerogative', 141. The case was used in the controversies of the seventeenth century: see D. L. Keir and F. H. Lawson, *Cases in Constitutional Law*, edited by F. H. Lawson and D. J. Bentley (6th edn, Oxford, 1979) pp. 93, 110.

act was lawful and afterwards unlawful. However, even though it is made unlawful later, the king can dispense with its application. Similarly, it is a *malum prohibitum* to ship wool to any place other than Calais as it is forbidden by statute. Again, the king can dispense with this. On the other hand, Fineux maintains that neither the king nor any other person (*ne nul auter* – presumably this includes the parliament) can dispense with a *malum in se*. A *malum in se* is independent and unalterable. For example, the king could not grant a licence beforehand to anybody to kill another or to commit a nuisance in the highway. These licences would be void, although if the above actions were done by individuals, the king may pardon them subsequently. In conclusion, Fineux states: 'And thus neither the king, nor the bishop, nor the priest can give licence to one to commit lechery, which is a *malum in se* in the *law of nature* [*en ley de nature*]; but when it is done, they can absolve well enough.'[63] In short, *mala* created by human enactment are transient and alterable, and their application can be dispensed with. Other *mala*, wrongs under the law of nature, cannot be erased, their validity is unchallengeable: it is only their application that can be affected by human action.

## NATURAL LAW AS A HIGHER LAW: THE STATUS OF ABHORRENT LAW

The voluntarist thesis advanced the view that law originates in the human will. The consequence of this was positivist in form. Rules consented to by the community or the judges acquired the status of law irrespective of their actual moral standing. Legislation offensive to conscience or producing a mischief was not void: it had to be repealed or amended before it lost its validity as law. Also (as we shall see), rules of the common law might produce a mischief or offend

---

[63] M 11 Hen. VII, 11, 35 at 12: 'Et issint le Roy, ne nul Evesque, ou Presbiter poit doner licence a un a faire lecherie, quia est malum in se en Ley de nature: mes quand 'il est fait, ils poient assoiler assez bien.' For further instances of natural law and divine law usage, see M 21 Hen. VI, 13, 28 (Srjt Yelverton, God forbids that it would be law); M 35 Hen. VI, 25, 33 at 29 (per Fortescue, God forbid); P 12 Ed. IV, 1, 3; 8, 22 at 9 (Srjt Catesby, who argues that the making of contracts at markets on Sundays is not contrary to the *ius naturale*: compare Srjt Pigot's argument, at 8, that it is against the law of God; see also Fairfax at 9); M 20 Hen. VII, 10, 20 at 11: an elder brother is bound by the law of nature to aid and comfort his younger brother, per counsel. See also Srjt Keble's use of the Old and New Testament in *Rollesley* v. *Toft* (1495): see Port, *Notebook*, 102 Sel. Soc. (London 1986) p. 32.

## Natural law: the superior moral law

reason or conscience, yet these too are treated as valid laws. This idea of authority, entirely mundane and rooted in the human will, was also to be found in legal theory. It opposes fundamentally the natural law thesis. Part and parcel of the natural law view is the idea that iniquitous rules, rules which offend natural law, the moral law, are no laws at all. They are null and void. This is the consequence of an outlook which postulates natural law as a superior species of law, deriving its authority from the divine will. The idea that abhorrent human law is void can be found in Fortescue, though not in Pecock, and it can be found in a limited sense in the practical field, as the practitioners use the idea in relation to local custom, not in relation to legislation and the common law.

### Legal theory

As the chancellor had argued in the case of 1489, Fortescue accepts that human law *ought* to conform to the requirements of natural and divine law. The *lex naturae* excels 'all other human laws' (it is human because it rules earthly things). Other human laws are obedient to it, as natural law is the mother of all laws.[64] If anything is contrary to natural law, then it is iniquitous (*iniquum*), since against natural law there can be no dispensation.[65] Fortescue also postulates divine law, with which he equated natural law, as a standard against which human law is measured. He says that divine law 'is more exalted and of greater authority than human law and by it is all human opinion measured [*mensuratur*], and if it be just, approved, and if unjust, condemned'.[66]

Fortescue goes even further. The moral law is capable of nullifying contrary and inferior human law. 'Where as it seems against the law made by God, [it] may not then be called *a law* but rather abusion, and in Latin called *corruptela et non lex*.'[67] He employs the fiction that

[64] *De Natura* I, cc. 5, 10, and see ibid., I, c. 29 and II, c. 29; *De Laudibus*, c. 15. Compare Marsilius, who seems to deny to natural law the full character of law unless embodied in human law, *DP*, II, pp. 164, 165, 168, 190: this accords with his view that there are no (earthly) sanctions for violations of divine law: ibid., p. 159.
[65] *De Natura* I, c. 5.
[66] Ibid., II, c. 26: 'Ipsa nanque celsior est majoris que auctoritatis quam lex humana, et per eam omnis humana censura mensuratur, et si juste fuerit approbatur, et si iniqua justissime condempnatur'; see too I, c. 46.
[67] *Works*, p. 498. For the modern view of abhorrent law, and the use of the natural law outlook by UK judges in relation to foreign law, see N. Doe, 'The problem of abhorrent law and the judicial idea of legislative supremacy', 10 *Liverpool Law Review* (1988) p. 113.

immoral law is deemed not to exist: it 'hastens into non-existence, as does everything which refuses to be led by natural law'.[68] This was a view which Fortescue seems to apply to all forms of law. It is a view which Saint German was to use early in the following century. Saint German expressly wrote that *any* law, local custom, common law or parliamentary law, was void if against natural law: '[a]nd therefore against this law, prescription, statute nor custom may not prevail and if any be brought in against it they be *no* prescriptions, statutes nor customs, but things void and against justice'.[69] Natural law, and its relation divine law, is treated as a superior law, as an ethical authority, against which the goodness of human law is to be measured. It also acts, and this exhibits its status as law, as a criterion of validity, vitiating those inferior human laws which are not in agreement with it. At this point we see a widening of Fortescue's definition of law. Law is not merely that to which people consent, but also that to which God, through the natural law, consents.

To illustrate the moral law as a yardstick against which human law is tested, Fortescue enquires whether procedure by jury under English law is repugnant to divine law.[70] The problem about the verdict of twelve men is raised, suggests Fortescue, because divine law requires proof of a disputed fact by only two witnesses who claim knowledge of the fact.[71] This, he argues, is to be found in the law of Moses, and 'to be contrary to this law is to break the divine law, and hence it follows that the law of England, if it differs from this law, differs from the divine law, to which resistance is not permissible'. He concludes that jury trial is not repugnant to divine law because the decision of the jury, the verdict of twelve men, will be given *in addition* to the evidence of available witnesses. Here Fortescue treats jurors as judging upon the truth of facts given in the evidence of witnesses possessing knowledge of those facts. Thus, 'the attestation of witnesses, if there were any, [will not] fail to have its due effect'.[72] Accordingly, English law requiring the judgment of twelve on the

---

[68] *De Natura* II, c. 34: 'et properat in non esse, sicut et omne quod legis naturae declinat conductum'; see also ibid., I, c. 5: customs contrary to natural law are *vana et irrita*; and I, c. 10.
[69] *Dialogue*, p. 15.
[70] *De Laudibus*, cc. 31, 32. For the biblical references, see John 8: 17; Matt. 18: 16; Deut. 17: 6; 19: 12.
[71] For Roman Law and canon law, see Holdsworth, IX, pp. 203–5.
[72] *De Laudibus*, c. 32, p. 77. For jurors as judges of fact, ibid., and generally, *HFCL*, pp. 68, 418, 424.

## Natural law: the superior moral law

truth of a disputed fact, in addition to the testimony of witnesses, does not conflict with divine law, which itself only provides that the testimony of two is sufficient proof of a disputed fact lying within their knowledge. Divine law allows two as witnesses to give evidence and prove a fact. English law also allows this, but in addition it requires a jury to decide whether the evidence given is true.

Whereas Fortescue and Saint German, in their analysis of the validity of bad law, deny a complete autonomy to human law, Pecock's view is less extreme. Pecock agrees that human law *ought* to reflect the moral law. The prince and the commonalty, he suggests, should not rule against God's law, 'but always with God's law',[73] for any law which is not in conformity with the law of nature is an 'unreasonable commandment [*maundement*]'.[74] Indeed, law does not take its moral goodness from its own substance, says Pecock, but from congruity to the dictates of reason.[75] Pecock develops the idea of natural law as a superior law in the conception of an all-embracing *legality* which might be conferred by natural law on all agreeing inferior positive law. For Pecock this legality is equivalent to an expression of moral validity. All actions, he claims, which touch upon morality, are either approved, disapproved or left undecided by reason. These he categorises as either 'lawful', 'unlawful' or 'indifferent'.[76] That which reason approves is *lawful* 'in the proper way to call a thing lawful', and that which reason forbids is *unlawful*. An indifferent matter is 'neither lawful nor unlawful for that it is so neither approved nor reproved by reason'. Yet indifferent things may be broadly called lawful.[77] Consequently, any law which fails to conform to natural law and thereby produces evil, either of its own substance or by man's abuse of it, is considered by Pecock to be *unlawful*, rather than a corruption or nullity as Fortescue said. These laws 'out of which come these said evils, are by right judgment of reason unlawful *and not worthy to be had and used*'.[78]

---

[73] *Donet*, p. 73; also *Repressor*, II, p. 453: as church law ought to conform to God's law so 'other politic men's laws might [*mowen*] be made and set to and with the same law of God'.
[74] *Repressor*, I, p. 100.   [75] Ibid., p. 105.   [76] Ibid., p. 135.
[77] Ibid., pp. 135, 136, 180; at p. 135: 'Ech doable thing ... which thing doom of resoun or ground of feith approveth, is leeful; and it is leeful in propre maner forto clepe a thing leeful, for that it is approved bi doom of resoun or bi ground of feith; and ech doable thing ... which thing doom of resoun or gound of feith reproveth, is unleeful.'
[78] Ibid., II, p. 432: those things 'out of whiche wallen the seid yvelis, ben bi right doom of resoun unleeful and not worthi to be had and usid'.

78  *Fundamental authority in late medieval English law*

In Fortescue we see a basic contradiction. At one point he says that laws are laws good or bad, and yet he says at the same time that abhorrent rules are not laws at all. Pecock, on the other hand, preserves a consistency in his concept of law. The human will alone is sufficient to create valid law. Agreement with natural law merely adds a further legality to human law. Bad human laws are not void; they are merely not to be used. There is a consistency in Pecock which is absent from Fortescue. However, it must be stressed that Fortescue's outlook tallies with those of his predecessors and contemporaries. Augustine argued that *lex injusta non est lex*; John of Salisbury that 'law is null and void that does not bear the image of divine law'; Gratian (Fortescue's acknowledged source) maintained that 'natural law absolutely prevails over customs and constitutions. Whatever has been recognised by usage, or laid down in writing, if it contradicts natural law must be considered null and void'. Though Aquinas (like Fortescue) acknowledged the existence of unjust laws (which ought not to be obeyed – this was the implicit positivism of Aquinas), he too said that if human law is 'incompatible with the natural law, it will not be law, but a perversion of law'.[79] During the fifteenth century, furthermore, D'Ailly and Gerson considered that in order to be valid *ab initio* positive law must conform to the will of God, since the divine will is the first law from which every law derives.[80]

### *The practical sphere: local customary law*

Though judges do not use natural law as extensively as the theorists, there is one basic point of contact on the few occasions when it is employed. Both claim that human law *ought* to conform to natural

---

[79] For Augustine, see C. J. Friedrich, *The Philosophy of Law in Historical Perspective* (2nd edition, Chicago, 1963) p. 39, and H. L. A. Hart, *The Concept of Law* (Oxford, 1961) p. 8. For John of Salisbury, *Policraticus*, IV, 6, edited by C. C. J. Webb (Oxford, 1909), and Gratian, E. Lewis, *Medieval Political Ideas* (London, 1954) volume I, p. 35. For Aquinas' assertion that unjust law 'is not law', see *Summa*, 1a, 2ae, 95, 2: this is at odds with Aquinas' view that unjust rules are still laws that ought to be disobeyed; again, to be capable of disobedience such rules must exist: see above, chapter 2, n. 121. Effectively, Aquinas has re-defined 'law', not as that which is produced simply by the human will, but rather, as 'an ordinance of reason made for the common good by him who has charge of the community, and promulgated' (*Summa*, 1a, 2ae, 90, 4), and, of course, 'the first rule of reason is the natural law' (ibid., 1a, 2ae, 95, 2).
[80] *MPT*, VI, p. 159; Oakley, p. 179.

## Natural law: the superior moral law 79

law. Yet, the theorists' use of the expression natural law as a higher law capable of nullifying *any form* of inferior human law is not to be found in the Year Books. The judges did not employ the term natural law to invalidate abhorrent human law, whether local custom, national custom or legislation. However, the judges did employ the same natural law *mentality*, though in a limited fashion. They did not use the expression *natural law* to nullify any form of bad law, common law or statute, but they did use analogous ideas of abstract right and wrong to nullify bad local custom. Any local custom, itself treated as *law*, which offended against *reason* or *common right* (*comen droit*) was void. These were more mundane ideas than natural law and divine law. *Reason*, as we shall see in a later chapter, was commonly used to signify *good sense* and *justice*, and *comen droit* often expressed an idea of abstract right or justice. Sometimes *droit* was equated with *reason*, and frequently they accompany each other as grounds of justification.[81] In form, then, the judges would allow (their ideas of) *reason*, for example, abstract right, to prevail over popular usage. The human will, on these occasions, is subordinate to the requirements of abstract right.

Using natural law, the basic idea is stated by Fortescue: 'if any custom has grown into use and it superadds anything to natural law which is repugnant to natural law, then by the canons it is void'.[82] Using *reason*, the idea is repeated by Littleton. For him, the local custom of gavelkind, by which male issue inherit equally, is allowable 'because it stands with some reason',[83] and, as to any prescription used, 'if it be against *reason*, this ought not, nor will be allowed before judges: *quia malus usus abolendus est*'.[84] In 1431, when D referred to a local custom that if the presentment of a local jury is found to be false, as lord of the manor, he was entitled to amerce each member of

---

[81] For *reason*, see below, chapter 5; for *droit* as abstract right, 1 Hen. IV, c. 12; 2 Hen. VI, c. 2; 1 Hen. VII, c. 2. For *reason* and *droit* together, M 9 Hen. VI, 44, 27; M 34 Hen. VI, 15, 28 per Srjt Littleton; M 3 Ed. IV, 24, 19 at 25B; H 14 Hen. VII, 17, 7 at 19: 'car comon droit est comon reason'; 4 Hen. V, c. 8: ordinaries taking for probate of a will excessive fees *encontre droit et ley*. Sometimes *comen droit* signifies 'common law': implied by Choke, T 8 Ed. IV, 5, 14. Sometimes these are distinguished: M 1 Hen. V, 11, 24 at 12 per Hill JCP; P 7 Hen. VI, 31, 27 per Cottesmore; M 9 Hen. VI, 43, 21 per Martin JCP; T 16 Hen. VII, 12, 5 at 13 per Keble: 'cest voucher n'est encontre common ley, ni comon droit'.
[82] *De Natura* I, c. 10. For the failure of the early Roman Law to develop a similar idea, see B. Nicholas, *An Introduction to Roman Law* (Oxford, 1982) p. 55. For medieval civilians adopting the same view as Fortescue, *MPT*, II, p. 32.
[83] *Tenures*, Bk II, c. 11, s. 210.     [84] Ibid., s. 212.

80     *Fundamental authority in late medieval English law*

the jury to the sum of forty shillings, 'all the court held that this could not be a custom, for this is against *common right* and is extortion'.[85]

Broadly, the idea that abhorrent customary law is void was used in relation both to customs attaching to a locality, and those attaching to a person or an institution, that is, to prescription. (Prescription itself is conceived as a branch or species of custom, personal custom or usage, giving rise to 'rights' vested in a particular body or person).[86] In relation to custom attaching to a locality the idea appears in a case of 1456. It tells of how T acquired the king's jewels and in return for a loan delivered them to S as a pledge. S claimed he did not know they were the king's and argued that by a local custom of London, those to whom goods were given in pledge are permitted to retain them until repaid. The court refuses to allow S to rely on the custom.[87] According to Moile JCP 'such a thing that is not *reasonable* cannot lie in custom: then here this matter is not *reasonable* that a stranger will charge my goods ... for it is *against reason* that one will put my goods in pledge and that I will be compelled to pay the money before I will have the goods'. Prisot CJCP adds, however, that 'a thing cannot lie in custom unless the same thing can be with *reason*; and if [it] can stand with *reason*, *notwithstanding that it be not according to the common law*, still it will well enough lie in custom'. In other words, for Prisot, when local custom agrees with reason, even if it contradicts the common law, it will be valid.

The superior authority of reason over the law of a locality rooted in popular usage and consent, was also used by Littleton JCP in a case of 1482.[88] P sued D in trespass for his close having been broken, land

[85] M 9 Hen. VI, 44, 27; Brooke, *GA*, 'Custom', 3, 'Fees', 17: 'Et tout le court tient que ce ne puit estre un custom: car ce est encontre commen droit, et est extortion.' Babington CJCP too uses *reason* and *common droit*. For presentment by the local (grand) jury and trial by the petty jury, see *HFCL*, p. 409, and *CH*, pp. 89, 90. For further uses, see H 42 Ed. III, 4, 16 at 5; M 7 Hen. VI, 12, 17; M 22 Ed. IV, 22, 2; and Srjt Littleton's analogous argument in M 34 Hen. VI, 15, 28.
[86] Co. Ltt., 113b; W. G. Salmond, *Jurisprudence*, edited by P. J. FitzGerald (12th edn, London, 1966) pp. 203–4. Note Littleton, *Tenures*, Bk II, c. 10, s. 170: 'no custom is to be allowed but such custom as hath been used by title of prescription, that is to say, from time out of mind'.
[87] M 35 Hen. VI, 25, 33: 'Car tiel chose que n'est reasonable, ne puit giser en custome: donq icy cest matter n'est reasonable que un estranger chargera mes biens ... car il est encontre reason que un mettera mes biens en pledge, et que jeo serai compelle a paier le monoie devant que jeo aurai les biens' (at 28).
[88] P 21 Ed. IV, 28, 23; P 22 Ed. IV, 8, 24; Brooke, *GA*, 'Trespass', 351, 'Custom', 51: 'car si un prescription soit encontre reason, il est void'. Brian CJCP disagreed: it was valid whether sown or not ('this is a custom used by all the realm of England', that is, common law).

ploughed and grass spoilt. D explains that the local custom allows those in ploughing their land to turn the plough on a piece of headland. P's land abutted onto this and it was upon this that D turned. In order to rely on the local custom, Littleton decides that D must show that the land was not sown. Otherwise, the custom 'is not of value' in allowing the crop to perish, 'for if a prescription is *against reason* it is void'. The case was adjourned. Indeed, in 1480, Brian CJCP went so far as to state that when the local customs of London were confirmed generally by parliamentary legislation,[89] any specific custom which was contrary to reason would not be considered as confirmed. It would exist merely as bad usage. He said that 'the customs which they [Londoners] use must be founded on *reason*, and although their customs are confirmed by statute, such things which they use for their customs, if they cannot lie in custom for default of *reason*, such usages are not confirmed for these are *not* customs but bad usage [*male usage*]'.[90]

The idea that personal custom, prescription, was void if abhorrent also appears frequently in the Year Books. In 1482 W brought false imprisonment against three defendants who justify that by prescription, upon suspicion of felony, the mayor of X is empowered to arrest and imprison for three days and then at the end of the three days to deliver the prisoner to the king's gaol.[91] Brian CJCP decides that the defendants cannot justify their acts by this prescription 'for it is wholly against *common right and all reason*'. Whereas W could offer mainprise in the king's gaol, the prescription did not allow this, which was against reason. Moreover, if the mayor could imprison for three days, so could the prescription permit imprisonment for three weeks or three years, 'which was wholly *against reason*'. The case was adjourned.

It was not always the case, however, that the practitioners saw conflict between local custom and the authority of reason, thereby enabling them to regulate the local custom. Occasionally they recognise agreement between them. For instance, in 1484, S and C brought

---

[89] See, for example, 14 Ed. III, St. I, c. 1; 14 Ed. III, St. II, c. 2.
[90] M 21 Ed. IV, 67, 50. There is no Brooke reference.
[91] H 22 Ed. IV, 43, 4 (and H 1 Hen. VII, 6, 3 at 7 for customs permitting detention for one or two days and in perpetuity). For a similar case, see M 2 Ed. IV, 23, 21 (the rest of this is at M 2 Ed. IV, 18, 13); Brooke, *GA*, 'Prescription', 65, 'Jurisdiction', 73. Here, had the charter not been produced the prescription, it seems, would have been void. See also H 12 Hen. IV, 12, 3 at 13: Hankford, 'and the king cannot make grant that will be in derogation of the people and it is against *common droit*'.

trespass against several defendants for taking the plaintiff's cygnets in Buckinghamshire. The defendants legitimise their action by relying on a custom of Buckinghamshire permitting individuals to take some of the offspring of swans coming off the Thames and nesting on their land (others of the offspring remaining the property of the owner of the swan). Serjeant Vavasour argues that the custom is against reason and as such void, but Fairfax JKB replies that 'as to the custom it seems good: for otherwise they can chase the cygnets out of their freehold if they wanted, and thereby it is *with reason* that he can have the three for the sufferance: and thus the custom is with reason'. Hussey CJKB concurred.[92]

Finally, it is to be stressed that the natural law view that abhorrent law is void is practised by the judges only in relation to local customary law. There are no explicit statements in the Year Books echoing Saint German's idea that if the common law or parliamentary legislation conflicted with natural law then it is void. Nowhere do the practitioners overtly invalidate national custom because it offended reason or common *droit*.[93] The nearest we have is an implicit suggestion of the idea by Littleton JCP in a case of 1467. Whilst addressing Choke's comments on the common law liability of an innkeeper for his lodger's goods, Littleton put the usual idea that 'custom that runs throughout all the land is common law'. And in a discussion of this, along with various local customs, he added, '[a]nd sir, a custom which can stand upon *reason* shall be allowed'.[94] Neither, as a matter of course, do the judges directly challenge the validity of parliamentary legislation on the grounds that it offends natural law or reason: there are no examples of this in the Year Books of the fifteenth century.[95] A rather curious arrangement seems to have been allowed by parliament in legislation from 1454. In order to combat a practice by which attorneys would stir up suits for their own private profit in East Anglia, the legislation provides for the official selection of only fourteen Norfolk attorneys by the two chief justices. Any appointment above that number would be void. The enactment concludes with the

[92] M 2 Ric. III, 15, 42. For other instances of conflict, see P 7 Hen. VI, 31, 27; P 12 Ed. IV, 1, 3; 8, 22 per Srjt Pigot, who also speaks of divine law (contrast Srjt Catesby); M 34 Hen. VI, 15, 28 per Srjt Littleton.
[93] They did, however, from time to time *relax* common law rules. See ch. 4, pp. 100–1 and ch. 6, pp. 141–2.
[94] M 8 Ed. IV, 18, 30; Brooke, *GA*, 'Custom', 46.
[95] For the relaxation of statutory rules, though, see chapter 4, pp. 104–6 and chapter 6, pp. 142–3.

following condition about its own application: 'provided always, that the said ordinance begin, and first take effect, at the feast of easter next coming and not before; if the same ordinance seem *reasonable* to the justices'.[96]

### CONCLUSION

The theorists' account of natural law is, on the whole, quite straightforward. They treat natural law as a law superior to human law. It is created by God, a form of divine law, composed of commands and prohibitions, ascertained by means of the human reason and through scripture. It has the nature of law insofar as any human law which conflicts with it is deemed, according to Fortescue and Saint German, not to exist. Abhorrent human laws are void. This is an entirely orthodox late medieval outlook. Indeed, the concept of a superior law also appears in legislation. Legislators commonly design enactments to incorporate divine prohibitions. Legislation often prohibits conduct or states of affairs described as offensive to God or as against the law of God. The authority of divine law sits alongside that of popular consent. However, whereas this divinely created authority is important in theory and legislation, natural law is not extensively employed by the judges. The practitioners do not define natural law, or discuss its location, but they sometimes use the expression as a rather vague and general idea of morality to fill the gaps of human law and to assert that human law ought to be morally acceptable. As we shall see in the following chapters, instead of natural law, the judicial idea of a moral authority is to be found rather in their usage of *conscience* and *reason*. Neither do the judges practise the general natural law idea that *all* abhorrent human laws are void. This mentality only arises in relation to local customary law. But this idea does make a dent in the emerging adoption of the positivist thesis. The will of the community, in its creation of customary law, is subordinate to the authority of reason. And it is from the presence of this general natural law outlook that the basic tension in late medieval thought arises. It is clearest in Fortescue, for, at the same time as saying 'law is that which is consented to by king and people', and 'bad rules are still laws', he also says 'law is that which is authorised by divinely created natural law', and 'bad rules, if they offend natural law, are not laws at all'.

[96] 33 Hen. VI, c. 7. For a similar idea in the private sphere, 15 Hen. VI, c. 6: guilds were not to 'make nor use no ordinance ... if it be not first discussed and approved for good and reasonable [*bone et resonable*] by the justices of the peace'; see also 27 Hen. VI, c. 6 for a statute to endure unless a 'reasonable cause' is shown for it not to.

# 4

# IUSTITIA, RIGOR IURIS AND AEQUITAS

Any description of medieval jurisprudence must take account of the concept of justice. It is a concept which amplifies the tension between the voluntarist and the theocratic-moralist conceptions of law. Like natural law, the concept of justice is pivotal, connecting law to the extraneous influence of abstract right and wrong. In legal theory justice is composed of a set of specific requirements, regulating not only the juridical relations but also the more general social and moral relations of individuals. However, it is not the human will which creates justice. Justice is not man-made: it is made by God. And it is a function of human law to disclose and give effect to this justice. Consequently, in its reflection of justice, human law obtains a justice of its own. Theory eagerly postulates a translation of justice into law. But when legal justice was strictly applied it might produce unwelcomed harshness. The use of equity articulates the general recognition that law was not static: equity expressed the need, from time to time, to relax the rigour of law. The concept of justice is important in legal theory, forming the basis of a major contribution by Pecock: the idea of a right. Yet, possessing many technical characteristics of the civilian and Thomist *iustitia*, as with natural law, justice is not used extensively in practice. (Though, as we shall see, there are some basic points of contact between the practitioners' *reason* and the theorists' *iustitia*.) On the other hand, some aspects of the theorists' *aequitas* do find something of a parallel in the practitioners' *equity*.

## THE SUBSTANCE OF JUSTICE

As with natural law, and in accordance with the common medieval opinion,[1] Fortescue proposes a theocratic conception of justice as created not by man but by God. 'Justice is the perfect judge of all human actions being so constituted by the high and omnipotent Lord.' It was conferred upon man at the moment of his creation: 'when God ordained the office of governing the world He ordained at the same time the creation of that justice by which the world should be governed'.[2] Without justice the world could not be governed: 'justice is the rule and model of governing'. Peace in society is preserved only through justice.[3] Gerson agrees: *opus iustitiae est pax*, for *iustitia et pax osculatae sunt*.[4] Fortescue considers that justice is achieved when society is ordered, rank upon rank, when man is set over man. Justice consists, in part, of society's system of order.[5] As Stillington LC said in 1468, 'justice requires every person to discharge the office that he is put in according to his estate or degree'.[6] Pecock too emphasised that a hierarchical ordering of society, 'an order of degrees and estates', was necessary for the institution of justice.[7] Both Pecock and Fortescue used the common view that it was for the king to ensure the prevalence of divinely created justice. As Serjeant Billing said in 1469, 'to every king by reason of his office, it belongs to do justice and grace, justice in executing the laws, etc., and grace to grant pardon to felons'.[8]

---

[1] For the civilians and canonists, *MPT*, II, p. 7. For Bracton, *De Legibus* II, p. 22 (*auctor iustitiae est deus, secundum quod iustitia est in creatore*). The view of Lucas de Penna (d. 1390?) is discussed by W. Ullmann, *The Medieval Idea of Law as Represented by Lucas de Penna: A Study in Fourteenth-Century Legal Scholarship* (London, 1946) p. 36.
[2] *De Natura* II, c. 1, and ibid., I, cc. 34, 35.
[3] Ibid., I, cc. 10, 35, 44. For Lucas de Penna on peace and justice, see Ullmann, *The Medieval Idea of Law*, p. 39, and Marsilius, *DP*, II, pp. 90, 95, 96.
[4] Pascoe, pp. 191, 192.
[5] *De Natura* II, cc. 34, 36, 59. For Gerson on order, Pascoe, p. 191.
[6] Chrimes, *English Constitutional Ideas in the Fifteenth Century*, p. 121.
[7] *Repressor*, II, p. 450; see also *Donet*, p. 75.
[8] P 9 Ed. IV, 1, 2 at 2. For Pecock, *Reule*, p. 336, and Fortescue, *De Laudibus*, c. 4, *De Natura* I, c. 25, and *Governance*, c. 4. Fortescue's 'twenty-two points of justice' which the king must observe are at *Works*, p. 477. For Aquinas, *Summa*, 2a, 2ae, 60, 1, and Bracton, *De Legibus* II, pp. 304, 305.

## Justice as virtue

The normal opinion saw justice existing in humankind as a virtue, a good quality of man: *iustitia quae virtus est*, asserts Fortescue.[9] According to Aquinas it is a cardinal virtue, the most excellent of all the moral virtues, and connected to all other virtues relating to human conduct, 'since justice concerns the relationship between men, all virtues which regulate the relations of one man to another have something in common with justice'.[10] Aquinas divides justice into *general* and *particular* justice. General justice coincides with legal justice, and concerns the fulfilment of the common good: in this, justice commands other virtues, drawing them into the service of the common good. Particular justice is either *commutative*, governing the relations between private individuals, or *distributive*, governing the relations between the community and individuals within it.[11]

The core of Aquinas' statements on general justice Fortescue accepts. But he does not employ Aquinas' notion of particular justice. The 'justice the human laws disclose is not of the kind that is called commutative or distributive or any other sort of virtue, but is itself the perfect virtue called by the name of legal justice'. This form of justice eliminates *all* vice and teaches every virtue, leading to the *summum bonum* of this life, happiness.[12] When man acts by his passions 'so also virtue, which is justice', ceases in man, for justice is the judge of *all* human actions and was so constituted by God.[13] In short, Fortescue considers that justice embraces the performance of all virtues, since it covers all human actions. Justice is a general virtue. The outlook is captured nearly in the *Three Considerations*, a fifteenth-century English translation of a French tract of 1347: 'justice is as the mother of all virtues, for all virtues have and comprehend in them the nature

---

[9] *De Natura* I, c. 40. For Bracton, *De Legibus*, II, pp. 25, 27, and Ockham, O. Suk, 'The connection of the virtues according to Ockham', *Franciscan Studies* (1950) pp. 9, 91.
[10] *Summa*, 2a, 2ae, 58, 11; 80, 1.
[11] Ibid., 2a, 2ae, 58, 6; 61, 1; 79, 1, and 1a, 2ae, 60, 3; 61, 5. There is an excellent discussion by G. del Vecchio, *Justice: An Historical and Philosophical Essay*. edited by A. H. Campbell (Edinburgh, 1952) pp. 33f., 52.
[12] *De Laudibus*, c. 4, p. 11: 'Iusticia vero quam leges revelant non est particularis illa que commutativa vel distributiva vocatur, seu alia quevis particularis virtus, sed est virtus perfecta que iusticie legalis nomine designatur ... perfectum quia omne vitium ipsa eliminat et omnem virtutem ipsa docet, que et omnis virtus ipsa merito nuncupatur.'
[13] *De Natura* I, c. 39, and II, c. 1.

of justice'.[14] Pecock, on the other hand, favours a separation of the virtues, though at times he too thinks of justice as a feature common to many moral virtues.[15]

## Justice and the consideration of others

At the heart of the concept of justice in medieval thought is the notion of *alteritas*, the idea that justice fixes relations between individuals.[16] As Aquinas said, justice exists 'to govern a man in his dealings towards others'.[17] Fortescue saw justice as ruling individuals in civil societies (*politiae*), and Pecock as operating 'betwixt person and person'.[18] The concept of a neighbour, culled from theology (and refined in Thomist thought), is central in Pecock's analysis. 'Wherever it is commanded of us to be just and rightful towards our neighbour, by the same it is forbidden for us to be unjust or unrightful towards the same neighbour.'[19] Justice, therefore, requires a species of love towards our neighbours, 'our virtuous fleshly love and our virtuous worldly love toward our neighbours'.[20] Indeed, a person cannot be just to himself, argues Pecock, otherwise it follows 'that this man should be therefore two men, for as much as justness asks necessarily to be between one person and him who is diverse and other than he is'.[21] The argument holds because injustice occurs when the person suffering does not consent to it: 'wrong and injustice is never done but when the sufferer dissents to the doer; and whenever the sufferer consents to the doer's

---

[14] Anonymous, *The Three Consideracions Right Necessarye to the Good Governance of a Prince*, edited by J-P. Genet, *Four English Political Tracts*, Camden Fourth Series, volume 18 (London, 1977) p. 174 at p. 196.
[15] *Donet*, pp. 60–7, 109.
[16] del Vecchio, *Justice: An Historical and Philosophical Essay*, pp. 12, 34, 54–5, 70–2, 77–81, 84, 91, 116.
[17] *Summa*, 2a, 2ae, 57, 1; and ibid., 58, 2. For Bracton, *De Legibus*, II, p. 23.
[18] *De Natura* II, c. 1, and *Repressor*, II, p. 450.
[19] *Donet*, p. 134. And *Repressor*, I, p. 39. The idea of a neighbour appears often in Aquinas: see for example *Summa*, 1a, 2ae, 72, 4: 'man is ordered to God by the theological virtues, to himself by fortitude and temperance, and to his neighbour by justice'; 'when a man sins in his social relations, for example, by theft or by homicide, he is said to sin against his neighbour'.
[20] *Folower*, p. 202, and for the basis of this as 'need', p. 209. For 'need' see also *Donet*, p. 68: 'bi lawe of kinde, of resoun, and of charite, right as ech man which hath superflue goodis more than is nede to occupie, ought frely geve of thilk superflue godis to his neighbore suffring nede, if thilk neighbore schal not be of power to agenquyte'.
[21] *Folower*, p. 218.

deed, the doer wrongs not the sufferer'.[22] A parallel can be found here with the practitioners' maxim, *volenti non fit injuria*.[23]

Pecock's argument has two important implications for the creation and application of law. First, because individuals consent to its creation law cannot be unjust. Law will be unjust only when it inflicts harm to which individuals do not consent. This jars against a theocratic view of justice, as all law consented to will *ipso facto* be just. Implicit is the idea that the human will in law creates its own form of justice. In point of fact, Fortescue himself said that in the *dominium politicum et regale*, it is 'the people that reserve such justice *as they desire*'.[24] The notion is only implicit, however.

Second, an idea related to the consideration of others as a requirement of justice is the principle that an individual, acting in a judicial capacity, must not be a judge in his own cause. When acting judicially he ought not to be partial to his own interests and, in consequence, act to the detriment of the interests of others. The principle implies the conception of judicial impartiality. Pecock considers that '[n]o man ought to be judge in his own cause which he has against his neighbour, neither [did] any man ought to be redressor of the wrong which his neighbour does to him'.[25] Littleton held a similar view when discussing distress damage feasant, the common law right to retain anything (such as cattle) doing damage on one's land.[26] He says that if the lord of a manor prescribes to distrain cattle doing damage on his land and retains them until a fine is paid to him for the damage *at the lord's will*, this is void 'because it is against reason, that if wrong be done any man, that he thereof should be his own judge; for by such means, if he had damages but to the value of a half-penny, he might assess and have therefor one hundred pounds, which would be against reason'.[27]

---

[22] Ibid.; see also ibid., p. 142.  [23] See above, chapter 2, n. 18.
[24] *Governance*, c. 2.
[25] *Repressor*, II, p. 381. For Aquinas, *Summa*, 2a, 2ae, 64, 5, and the custumals, 18 Sel. Soc. (London, 1904) p. 133 (Norwich, c. 28). At an early stage the canonists had developed a mature set of ideas concerning judicial impartiality: R. H. Helmholz, *Canon Law and the Law of England* (London, 1987) pp. 21–37.
[26] For distress damage feasant, see F. A. Enever, *History of the Law of Distress for Rent and Damage Feasant* (London, 1931) pp. 8, 77, 193, 224; *CH*, p. 383. The item could be retained until the other came to the distrainor 'with men of repute and in their presence was prepared to make good his damage *according to their view*': *De Legibus*, II, p. 445.
[27] *Tenures*, Bk II, c. 11, s. 212.

The basic idea was well established in the practical literature.[28] It commonly appears in cases relating to the validity of royal grants of franchise jurisdiction, grants to religious houses, or universities, for instance.[29] However, whereas Pecock and Littleton exclude judging in one's own cause by reference to *reason*, the practitioners often describe the practice as against *common right* (*comen droit*) or as an *inconvenience*, again essentially extra-legal justifications. In 1461, for example, Serjeant Billing argued that a prescription was void when 'he himself is party, by whch [it] is against *comen droit* that he will be judge in his own cause'.[30]

It was usually *defendants* to actions in the royal courts who challenged jurisdiction, arguing that a matter should be heard elsewhere, such as in the court of a franchise.[31] We do not normally find the plaintiff in a royal court pleading jurisdiction. This occurred in a curious case of 1411. The abbot of Glastonbury brought a royal writ of novel disseisin and his bailiff intervened demanding conusance of the plea, a demand resting on a charter of William the Conqueror.[32] The grant is allowed by Thirning CJCP and Hill JCP. Thirning explains that the abbot of Ramsey had jurisdiction in this way on a previous occasion 'and the bailiff of the abbot can do as good *droit* between his master and the tenant, as we can do between the king and another man of his people'. Hill argued that the grant is good on condition 'that *justice* be done to the parties'. However, Hankford JCP dissents: 'the king cannot make a grant that will derogate from his people, and it is against *commen droit*, that he by his servant will hold the plea, where he is the same plaintiff'. The case was adjourned.

[28] See D. E. C. Yale, '*Iudex in propria causa*: an historical excursus', 33 *CLJ* (1974) p. 80. See also, for example, M 2 Hen. IV, 4, 14; H 8 Hen. V, 5, 21 per Tirwit; M 7 Hen. VI, 12, 17 at 13 per Srjt Elderkar; M 17 Ed. IV, 5, 3; T 18 Ed. IV, 8, 8; see T 20 Hen. VI, 39, 9 at 40 per Newton CJCP for 'indifferent' juries. For 'indifferent' justice in legislation, 1 Hen. IV, c. 1 [*bone justice et owell droit soit fait a chescuny*]; for indifference generally, see 2 Hen. IV, c. 15; 3 Hen. VI, c. 5; 8 Hen. VI, c. 9; 7 Hen. VII, c. 3. The idea is, of course, an aspect of the modern principle of natural justice, as used in administrative law: see E. C. S. Wade and A. W. Bradley, *Constitutional and Administrative Law* (10th edition, London, 1985) pp. 642–51; for related ideas in early jurisprudence, see J. M. Kelly, '*Audi alteram partem*', 9 *Natural Law Forum* (1964) p. 103.
[29] D. E. C. Yale, '*Iudex in propria causa*: an historical excursus', at p. 85.
[30] M 2 Ed. IV, 18, 13 (and at 23, 21) at 19: 'per quel est encontre comen droit, que il sera judge en son case demesne'.
[31] Holdsworth, III, pp. 614, 629.
[32] H 12 Hen. IV, 12, 3; Brooke, *GA*, 'Conusance', 20.

The same principle was used in 1425 by Martin JCP. P sued trespass against four defendants who argued that P should not have the action because W had proceeded and recovered against P in novel disseisin for the same land where the trespass is alleged to have occurred. One of the defendants was on the jury which dealt with the previous novel disseisin action.[33] In reply, P denied that the land recovered then was comprised in the land upon which the present trespass is alleged. This is an issue which has to be tried by jury. The problem, though, is whether it will be tried by the same jurors who settled the novel disseisin matter. Though this case too was adjourned, Martin JCP explained that 'it will be harsh to try this issue solely by them who were in the first assise, for then one of the defendants in this writ will be one of them, and thus he must try his own issue, and thus in a way be his own judge, which would be unfitting and against law [*inconvenient et encontre ley*]'.

## Justice as giving each his due

Fortescue's *rectitudo*, uprightness, is the general behaviour required by justice, and, relying on Anselm, he says that 'if justice is rectitude of will it must be the case that a right will is justice'.[34] Fortescue also uses the more detailed formula from Roman Law, the celebrated definition of *iustitia*: 'justice is the constant and perpetual will to render to each his *ius*'.[35] This formulation is shared by so many medieval jurists.[36] Pecock does not explicitly adopt the Roman Law statement but explains in a broadly similar fashion that 'the office of justice, as it is a cardinal virtue, is to insist that a man by it yields to

---

[33] T 4 Hen. VI, 28, 12. See too H 8 Hen. VI, 18, 6 at 20 for Rolf's use of *inconvenience*, and *MED*: 'resoun', 1b(b): (1386) *Rotuli parliamentorum FM* (C&D) 36–101: 'The which with your rightful lordship y granted foremost principal remedy, as God's law and all reason will, that no doomsman stand together judge and party.' The same idea is repeated in 3 Hen. VIII, c. 23 (1511).

[34] *De Natura* I, cc. 35, 38: 'Si justitia sit rectitudo voluntatis, voluntatem rectam justitiam esse, necessario concedetur.' For Anselm, *Proslogium*, c. 9, and *Monologium*, c. 16 (for God's justice) and c. 8 (for creation).

[35] *De Natura* I, c. 35: 'Justitia est constans et perpetua voluntas ius suum unicuique tribuens'; and c. 39: 'Quid est justitia nisi voluntas in consentione perpetuae constantiae reddendi unicuique quod suum est.' For the Roman Law idea, see *Inst.*, Bk I, Tit, I, and its use in Bracton, *De Legibus*, II, p. 23.

[36] See, for example, Aquinas, *Summa*, 2a, 2ae, 58, 1; 58, 11; for Lucas de Penna, Ullmann, *The Medieval Idea of Law*, p. 38. For D'Ailly, Oakley, p. 188, n. 28, and for Gerson, Pascoe, p. 104.

every other person whatever thing is belonging of him to that other person to be paid or given'.[37]

Part and parcel of the view that justice requires giving each his due are ideas of reciprocity and restoration, concepts often associated with the medieval treatment of justice.[38] 'Where simple justice holds between people', writes Aquinas, 'we also find a simple relation of merit and reward', for people mark the 'balance of justice according to the recompense of thing for thing'.[39] Fortescue observes that 'justice is ever-present with us punishing, directing and rewarding according as our deserts require', always 'ruling [man] and paying him, one way or the other, the wages which he has earned'.[40] Again, for Pecock 'the said justice is none other than a willing of a man that his neighbour have his own goods and thereby [securing] an execution that his neighbour has his own goods',[41] and '[the] restoring of another man's goods unreasonably withdrawn or kept or occupied against his reasonable will; and also satisfaction or amends making over to our neighbour for [the] doing of anything ... excluded'.[42]

An interesting feature of Fortescue's analysis is the problem of the relationship of justice to the human will. Justice itself requires the will to render each his due constantly and perpetually, he says. Justice, like natural law, does not change. But justice is dependent for its operation in society upon the human will, and this does change. The human will can easily choose to allow injustice: 'so also virtue, which is justice, is said to cease in man so often as man's will ceases to be in accord with *rectitudo*'. Yet justice can never be extinguished. Man always knows what is just or unjust. In short, 'justice returns and departs at the pleasure of the human will'.[43] When the will, *voluntas*,

---

[37] *Donet*, p. 110: 'ffor whi sithen the office of rightwisnes, as it is a cardinal vertu, is forto that a man bi it yilde to every othire persoone what ever thing is longing of him to thilk othire persoone forto be paied or govun'; see also *Reule*, p. 254.
[38] See for example, Bracton, *De Legibus*, II, pp. 23, 298, 305.
[39] *Summa*, 1a, 2ae, 114, 1, 2a, 2ae, 62, 1. His views on the principle of proportionality in relation to harm, sin and punishment can be found, for instance, at 1a, 2ae, 73, 8. For Marsilius, *DP*, II, pp. 66, 67, 90.
[40] *De Natura* I, c. 39: 'sicque nobis semper ipsa praesens est, puniens, dirigens, vel remuneram secundum nostrorum exigentiam meritorum'; also, 'sic semper in homine et cum homine habitat justitia nuncquam effectu vacua, sed semper eum regens, et ei reddens stipendia utrorumque meritorum'.
[41] *Folower*, p. 185; see also *Reule*, p. 240, and *Donet*, p. 114.
[42] *Donet*, p. 64; and see *Reule*, pp. 150, 151.
[43] *De Natura* I, cc. 39, 40. For a similar idea in Gabriel Biel, see M. G. Baylor, *Conscience in Late Scholasticism and the Young Luther* (Leiden, 1977) p. 111.

ceases to allow justice then it ceases to be called just: it produces *iniustitia*.[44] These comments are of some significance. Humankind has the capacity to be just, to give effect to divine justice, but only when it so chooses. This concession may explain why Fortescue is able to make the positivist assertion that 'law is as often bad as it is good'. The virtue of justice is ever-present, but need not necessarily be embodied in law created by the human will. The human will, in its law, can discard justice.

### JUSTICE, NATURAL LAW AND THE IDEA OF A RIGHT

The elements of justice expounded by Pecock and Fortescue are basically orthodox. Like natural law, justice possesses a moral texture. It is treated as created by God and as a virtue. For Fortescue, the performance of all the virtues constitutes just action. According to Pecock, justice is only one of many moral virtues. It governs the relation of individual to individual, requiring that they render to each what is due. An interesting part of Pecock's theory is the idea that a person cannot be judge in his own cause. The idea is found in Littleton and the Year Books, but not in Fortescue. The fundamental defect in the authority of justice, however, is that its employment in society is wholly dependent on the exercise of the human will. Not all of their treatment of justice, though, is common stock. There are two aspects of their work which seem quite novel in medieval jurisprudence.

#### *Pecock's idea of a right*

The development of the idea of a right, based on the notion of a claim, is one of the major achievements of Pecock. It grows out of his analysis of justice. As we have seen, central to his concept of justice is the requirement that 'a man yields to every other person whatever thing is belonging of him to that other person to be paid or given'.[45] Justice also requires satisfaction and amends when injury is inflicted. Now, in addition to visualising the duties imposed on people as being required by justice (and, indeed, natural law), Pecock sees these duties as being

---

[44] *De Natura* I, c. 35.   [45] *Donet*, p. 110.

## Iustitia, rigor iuris and aequitas 93

in a sense *caused* by the existence of rights. In Pecock rights are institutive or causative of duties. Pecock considers that a central aspect of living justly towards God is for people to perform their promises to God 'because that by this bond grows to God *a right for to claim* that deed promised'.[46] He applies this to the relations of individuals in society. Living justly towards our neighbours involves performing (for example) covenants 'because by this bond there extends [*grows*] to our neighbour *a right of claim* [founded] upon our deed so promised to him in bond and covenant'.[47]

A person must perform an act, not simply because justice requires its performance, but because the other party has the ability to claim actively, the right to claim, the performance of that act. Pecock considers that this claim is actualised in the correlative duty to yield what is claimed. He explains that the duty arises by operation of the law of reason: 'since to our neighbours by clear judgment of reason we ought to be just and rightful in yielding to them what we owe to them to pay'. Moreover, as to those who are wronged, they are to receive 'of us', the wrongdoer, 'a just claim and also the goods which are theirs in just possession or in just claim', and that 'we [do] not withdraw the goods from them neither to treat the goods without sufficient authority against their will'.[48] Nevertheless, through consent and law an individual can abrogate or relax his right to claim something. People do not have a right to use anything belonging to another 'which is in his possession or in right claim, *against his licence or just will*, or without sufficient authority of law'.[49] And when a person as member of the commonalty assents to the making of a particular law, he 'renounces and foresakes all right *belonging to him* which is contrary to the execution of that law'.[50]

There is something of a parallel between Pecock and the earlier

---

[46] Ibid., p. 38.
[47] Ibid., p. 62: 'bi cause that bi thilk boonde there growith to oure neighbore a right of claym upon oure dede so bihestid to him in boond and covenaunt'.
[48] *Reule*, p. 254: 'sithen to oure neighboris bi open doom of resoun we ought be just and rightful in yelding to hem what we to hem owen to paie, and what to receive of us thei han just cleyme, and also that tho godis whiche ben heris in just possessioun or in just cleyme, that we not withdrawe tho godis fro hem neither trete tho goodis withoute sufficient auctorite agens the wil of hem'.
[49] *Donet*, p. 63: 'eny thing which is his in possessioun, or in right clayme, agens his licence or iust wil, or withoute sufficient autorite of lawe'.
[50] *Folower*, p. 142: 'and ech persoon of the same peple renouncith and forsakith al right longyng to him which is contrari to the execucioun of thilk lawe'.

civilians. Their concept of *iustitia* involved the idea that 'each be rendered his *ius*'. Implicit in *ius* is the notion of an entitlement. Azo, for example, said 'their *ius*' meant 'their due [*meritum*]', and it had been said that 'one has a *dictura* in something, if one can use it to claim [*petere*] the thing from all men'.[51] Similarly, Ockham identified *ius* with a power to claim things. The *ius utendi* was a 'licit power of using an external object, the unwarranted denial of which can be prosecuted in a court of law'. Also, *dominium* was 'a power of laying claim to a thing in court and of using it in a way not prohibited by natural law'.[52] The conciliarists too used *ius* as what appears to be a power to do something. D'Ailly argued that the church universal had 'the right of electing [*ius elegendi*] the one ruling over them', the pope.[53] The idea of *ius* as a *facultas* or *potestas* is to be found likewise in Gerson: 'a mortal sinner has the *facultas* or *potestas* of meriting eternal life'.[54]

Using the civilians' definition of *iustitia*, the concept of a right is, of course, implied by Fortescue, but it is not as elaborately developed as in Pecock. In his description of *ius* Fortescue maintains that 'every man who seeks to have back what is his own before a judge has the right [*ius*] but not the law [*lex*] of claiming it', for when one talks of possession or the having of a title (*habendo titulo*) then the term *ius* is to be used. After all, 'a rule of law is not a new publishing of a law but a brief statement of a previously existing right'.[55] The idea of a right also seems to appear in practice particularly in the usage of *droit*, as an

[51] F. W. Maitland, *Select Passages from the Works of Bracton and Azo*, 8 Sel. Soc. (London, 1895) p. 22; as Azo explained, 'for in law one is deprived of one's *ius* by a crime or a breach of contract'. See also E. Meynial, 'Notes sur la formation de la théorie du domaine divisé', *Mélanges Fitting*, II (Montpellier, 1908) p. 422.
[52] A. S. McGrade, 'Ockham and the birth of individual rights', *Authority and Power, Studies on Medieval Law and Government Presented to Walter Ullmann on His Seventieth Birthday*, edited by B. Tierney and P. Linehan (Cambridge, 1980) p. 150.
[53] Sigmund, p. 104, n. 65 (and see Oakley, p. 63, n. 50).
[54] R. Tuck, *Natural Rights Theories: Their Origin and Development* (Cambridge, 1979) pp. 25, 26.
[55] *De Natura*, c. 30. For the idea of a thing being connected to its claimant, see ibid., II, c. 33. Ibid., I, c. 31: 'Nam iuris regula non est nova legis edicio, sed iuris quod prius fuit brevis enarracio.'

*Iustitia, rigor iuris* and *aequitas*                                                 95

actionable entitlement in individuals: the notion of a duty is certainly present.[56]

### Fortescue on justice and natural law

Generally, medieval jurists implied rather than explicitly spelt out the relationship between natural law and justice. Gratian, for example, maintained that whatever conforms to natural law is just.[57] Bracton stated that 'natural law is a certain due which nature allows to each man', and that '*ius* is sometimes used for natural law which is always *bonum et aequum*'.[58] But it is left to the reader to infer that natural law is just because it is created by God who is just. The two are quite closely related in Pecock. The requirement that a person acts justly to his neighbour Pecock treats primarily as one of reason. Moreover, Pecock argues that the content of justice is to be worked out by means of the human reason, as with divine law. Justice is not to be found solely in scripture: 'what justice is and what are its species must be found in the judgment of reason, and not in holy scripture'. Pecock goes so far as to say that 'when any plea is between man and man, and every party thinks to have right, the judgment must be had in the doom of reason in the court by the judge, and not by holy scripture'.[59]

Whereas Pecock treats justice as an attribute of natural law, fixed by

---

[56] Work on the idea of a right in the Year Books needs to be done: see, however, the *droit* in someone to an expectant reversion in T 4 Hen. VI, 25, 4 at 26 per Martin JCP, and M 9 Hen. VI, 30, 1 at 31 for *droit* to an advowson per Srjt Paston; also 4 Hen. IV, c. 22 (presentment to a benefice in another's right (*en autri droit*)). And Simpson, *History of the Land Law*, pp. 103–5. See also 1 Hen. VII, c. 9: Richard II 'nient de droit Roy Dengliterre'. Townsend JCP used an interesting expression when he said in a case of 1493 that 'the defendant claims an interest in the thing [goods] mediately or immediately from the plaintiff [*le defendant clame enteresse en le chose*]': M 16 Hen. VII, 2, 7 at 3, and Port, *Notebook*, p. 100. The idea of an 'interest' can also be found at M 37 Hen. VI, 4, 6 per Prisot, and the notion of a claim at T 11 Hen. IV, 90, 46 per Hill JCP: 'en cest case il claime le chose d'ont l'action es pris'. See too M 8 Hen. IV, 16, 19 per Hill. For the 'brief de droit', 7 Hen. V. 5, 3 at 8; M 19 Hen. VI, 25, 48; M 33 Hen. VI, 45, 28 per Prisot. For Marsilius' idea of a right, *DP*, II, p. 191. Examples of duty can be found at 33 Hen. VI, c. 1 (duty owed by servants to masters); 7 Hen. VII, c. 15; M 8 Ed. IV, 9, 9 at 11A; T 11 Ed. IV, 8, 13; H 21 Hen. VII, 18, 30 at 19 per Tremaile: 'jeo riens n'avois sinon un droit in conscience'. See also *Three Considerations*, Genet, *Four Political Tracts*, p. 196. For the use of 'natural duty' and 'obliged duty' see 12 Hen. VII, c. 7: above, ch. 3, n. 41.
[57] *Decretum*, D. 1, c. vii; see Lewis, *Medieval Political Ideas*, I, p. 33.
[58] *De Legibus*, pp. 24, 27. For Aquinas, *Summa*, 1a, 2ae, 94, 3; 100, 2: 'all acts of virtue are of natural law' and 'divine law ... enjoins acts of all the virtues'. And for Saint German, *Dialogue*, p. 21: 'the lawe of God is always ryghtwyse and iuste'.
[59] *Repressor*, I, p. 17, and p. 13; see also *Folower*, p. 91.

the human reason, Fortescue connects the two concepts entirely. Now, as we have seen, there are many points of contact between his idea of natural law and that of justice. Both proceed from the divine will. Both are moral in character. Natural law requires that individuals do to others what they would have done to themselves. Justice covers similar ground, requiring people to render to others their due. In their essentials, the concepts overlap, together signifying a large and necessarily single divinely created system of morality. To the modern eye, one of the concepts appears to be superfluous. But Fortescue does not discard either of them. Constrained by the common store of inherited jurisprudence, in which the two concepts are included, he embraces both concepts in his philosophy of law. Something that is original in his analysis, however, is the explicit equation of the two ideas, an equation which, as has been said, is only implicit in other writers.

Like Pecock and earlier jurists, Fortescue asserts that 'what natural law adjudges is just', and actions contrary to natural law are unjust.[60] Again, like Pecock, Fortescue proposes that justice, as with natural law, can be known through the operation of the human reason. 'What else can natural law be but this: the truth of justice which is capable of being by right reason revealed?'[61] His conclusion is that 'justice and natural law are of one quality and of the same accidental essence'.[62] 'When the origin of justice is made clear, so too is that of natural law.' As a stream comes from its spring, he says, 'so does natural law come from justice, *so as not to be other than it*'.[63] Furthermore, and this may be unique in medieval thought, Fortescue expressly affirms that natural law renders to each his due.[64] Thus, 'now we consider that justice which is none other than natural law is the will to render each his *ius*'.[65] In short, for Fortescue, natural law *is* justice. It is for this

[60] *De Natura* I, cc. 10, 12.
[61] Ibid., c. 31: 'Quid tunc aliud potest esse lex naturae quam iustitiae veritas, quae recta ratione poterit revelari'; and ibid., c. 32, and II, c. 65.
[62] Ibid., I, c. 36: 'Justitia et ius naturae unius qualitatis sunt et accidentalis essentiae.'
[63] Ibid.: 'Sic jus naturae a justitia venit, ut non sit aliud ab ea'; 'Sic ius naturae cum justitia idem est in natura et eiusdem qualitatis bonitatis et efficaciae.' And c. 38: 'Ac cum justitiam et legem naturae unius esse substantiae licet accidentatis, unius qualitatis et naturae.'
[64] Ibid., c. 20: 'Natural law, unchanged, allots to each and every man that which is his own [*semper unicuique quod suum est ipsa tribuit*]'. However, D'Ailly implies the idea: Oakley, p. 188.
[65] *De Natura* I, c. 39: 'Jam quia recolimus justitiam que non aliud a lege naturae est, voluntatem esse ius suum unicuique tribuentem.'

reason that Fortescue substitutes for *lex naturae* the expression *iustitia naturalia*.[66] (Indeed, this is a term which actually surfaced in two statutes from the end of the period concerning usury: in both, usurious agreements were described as *contrarie a la ley de naturell justice*.)[67]

### JUSTICE AND HUMAN LAW

In legal theory law and justice are treated initially as separate. Whereas in populist theory law emanates from the human will, justice is created by God. As with natural law, though, the theorists use justice to re-assert and magnify the connection between law and morality. The connection is more conspicuous in Fortescue than Pecock. The basic idea is that human law ought to disclose divinely created justice.

### *Abstract justice and law*

It is a function of law, argues Fortescue, to disclose justice. This was a common opinion. The Italian jurist Lucas de Penna (d. 1390?) considered that *ius est iustitiae executivum*, and earlier Cynus de Pistoia (teacher of Bartolus) saw the relationship of justice to law as *producens et productum*.[68] Fortescue agrees that *ius* proceeds from *iustitia*. He maintains that 'human laws are none other than rules by which perfect justice is manifested'.[69] Simply put, 'law may be said to be the bond of right by which a man is constrained to do or suffer what is just'.[70] In somewhat optimistic fashion Fortescue adds that 'he who enjoys justice is made happy by the law', for it is by a knowledge of the law that justice is known: jurisprudence is the science of the just and the unjust, he says.[71] The educative role of law is not too far away.

[66] Ibid., Introduction, where they are treated as being of one essence. 'Natural justice' also appears in Aquinas, *Summa*, 2a, 2ae, 57, 2: people by common agreement establish laws if this is not contrary to natural justice; see *MPT*, V, pp. 39, 40.
[67] 3 Hen. VII, c. 5, and 11 Hen. VII, c. 8. For these, see Holdsworth, VIII, pp. 102, 103. For Pecock on the moral law as forbidding usury, see *Donet*, p. 68, and also *Repressor*, I, p. 16.
[68] Ullmann, *The Medieval Idea of Law*, pp. 35, 40. For Bracton, *De Legibus*, II, pp. 22, 23.
[69] *De Laudibus*, c. 4, p. 11: 'Leges humanae non aliud sunt quam regulae quibus perfecta iusticia edocetur.'
[70] *De Natura* I, c. 30: 'Unde lex dici potest juris vinculum quo quis constringitur facere aut pati quod est justum.'
[71] *De Laudibus*, cc. 4, 5, *De Natura* II, c. 46. For Bracton, *De Legibus*, II, p. 25.

A major aspect of Fortescue's relation of law to justice was his attempt to construct a coincidence of function. The starting point is the view that the object of human law is to disclose or reflect justice: law constrains individuals to do what is just. Now, as we have already seen, another principal purpose of law is to direct individuals to the performance of the virtues and to shun vice: law is a sanction 'commanding what is virtuous [*honesta*] and prohibiting the contrary'.[72] However, for Fortescue, the justice which law discloses 'is itself the perfect virtue called legal justice ... perfect because it eliminates all vice and teaches every virtue ... so that it is in itself justly called virtue'.[73] These are significant statements. From them we can reconstruct his idea: that law constrains what is just; justice teaches all virtue and eliminates all vice; likewise, human law promotes virtue and prohibits vice. There is here an exact marriage of function between law and justice. They share a common aim: the advancement of virtue. Once more, in his system of law, Fortescue equates concepts. He did it with divine law and natural law, with natural law and justice, and now with justice and human law. The idea is entirely antagonistic to the mundane view of law.

The single function of justice and law in Fortescue, the promotion of virtue, was not usually spelt out in the work of other jurists. It was, however, implicit in the civilian treatment of the 'three precepts of *ius*' in Roman Law: to live virtuously (*honeste vivere*), not to harm anyone (*alterum non laedere*), and to render to each his *ius* (*ius suum unicuique tribuere*).[74] There are both general and particular aspects to the three precepts. A width of purpose lies in the demand for 'living virtuously', the general pursuit of virtue. There is narrowness in the demand 'to render each his due', a requirement which necessarily includes the prohibition 'not to harm anyone'. The demand 'to render each his due' is, of course, the particular sort of virtuous living required by the virtue of justice. As the civilians considered that *ius* provides what justice commands,[75] then *ius*, in its promotion of general virtuous living, embraces the specific virtuous living described as justice. In short, the precepts of *ius* do the work of justice.

Fortescue's twin functions of law and justice, the promotion of all virtue, correspond to the civilian precepts of *ius*. Indeed, in the *Three*

[72] *De Laudibus*, c. 3, p. 9.
[73] Ibid., c. 4; see also *De Natura* I, c. 44, and above, n. 12.
[74] *Inst.*, Bk I, Tit. I, 3. For a statement of these in English jurisprudence, see Bracton, *De Legibus*, II, p. 25.
[75] *De Legibus*, II, p. 22. For Azo, 8 Sel. Sec. (London, 1895), p. 18.

*Considerations* what are actually the three precepts of *ius* are treated as requirements of justice. We read that 'justice gives to every man three commandments: the first is to live honestly and measurably; the second is to do wrong or injury to no-one; the third is to give and surrender to every man his right and duty'.[76] In much the same way, Lucas de Penna stated that 'the precepts of justice [*iustitia*] are the ten precepts of the decalogue, restitution, and living honestly, not harming anyone and giving each his *ius*'.[77]

The usage of the words *iustitia* and *justice* are almost entirely absent from the Year Books. In the fifteenth century it rarely appears, as when, in 1441 for example, Ascough JCP said that 'if the king granted that [a person] will not be punished for any felony nor trespass committed by him in times to come, this grant is void, because it is against *common droit* and justice, and cannot be with law'.[78] It is with some surprise that, in the early sixteenth century, in a case of 1527, we discover Fitzherbert JCP declaring that 'the common law of the realm is *justicia, quae tribuit unicuique quod suum est*'.[79]

*Rigor iuris*: the strict application of law

As human law was treated as the reflector of abstract justice, so Fortescue hints at the idea that lawful action was just action. In England, he said, people were brought to trial only before 'the ordinary judges where they were treated [*tractantur*] justly [*iuste*] *according to the law of the land* [*per legem terre*]', 'because that which is done *iure* is done also justly'.[80] The idea, which Fortescue does not develop, was not unique: Marsilius of Padua had seen justice as primarily fixed by law.[81]

However, nowhere do the judges refer to their decisions as being

---

[76] Genet, *Four Political Tracts*, p. 196. It is interesting to note the opinion of Aquinas, *Summa*, 1a, 2ae, 100, 2: 'the precepts of human law are concerned only with acts of justice; and if they prescribe the acts of the other virtues, that is only insofar as they take on the character of justice'. (Compare divine law which 'enjoins acts of all the virtues': ibid.)
[77] Ullmann, *The Medieval Idea of Law*, p. 38.
[78] P 19 Hen. VI, 62, 1 at 62.
[79] *Marmion's Case* (1527), see 94 Sel. Soc. (London, 1977) p. 118. For the use of justice in legislation, usually general in nature and of little import, see, for example, 2 Hen. IV, c. 1; 7 Hen. VII, c. 12; 11 Hen. VII, c. 12: 'indifferent justice to be had and ministered according to his comen lawes'. For the idea of a just weight, 9 Hen. V, St. I, c. 11.
[80] *De Laudibus*, c. 36, p. 89, and *De Natura* II, c. 49.
[81] *DP*, II, p. 108; see also pp. 37, 38, 57.

made in accordance with the *justice of the law*. Rather, frequently the common law judges simply relied upon strict law. They tended to the idea that law must be applied strictly. This is represented in their usage of the expression *rigor iuris*. In a case of 1406, for example, deeds creating a remainder were shown to the court when the donee in tail sought to pray in aid a remainderman. As aid was not granted, this showing was not put on record.[82] Consequently, it was held that if subsequently the remainderman wished to rely on the unrecorded showing of the deed, *de rigore iuris* he could not do so. The deed must be shown a second time. A similar problem occurred in 1440, when executors of T brought debt against D and showed the will to the court, a showing which was put on record. D imparled until another term at which time it was decided that the executors need not show the will a second time. In discussion Newton CJCP said: 'So it is for a deed of remainder when formedon in the remainder is brought, when the deed of remainder is shown proving the remainder, the action is maintainable always after, and the deed *de rigore iuris* will not be shown further.' In both cases, he said, 'the record proves that the testament and the deed of remainder have been shown'.[83] The same idea appeared in 1428 when Babington CJCP says in passing that the king can coerce by writ any man of forty pounds' heritage to be made a knight: 'and if they do not appear at the first day, but come afterwards ready to take the order and the honour, *de rigore iuris* they ought not to be received, but will make fine for the contumacy and deceit'.[84]

However, occasionally, the judges are prepared to reject *rigor iuris*. In this, as we shall see, they echo both the theoretical and practical uses of *equity*. In a somewhat complicated case from 1408, for instance, C sought abatement of a writ on the grounds that his joint tenant had not been named along with him in the writ. It was a settled rule that all joint tenants must be made defendants in real actions.[85]

[82] P 7 Hen. IV, 10, 1: Brooke, *GA*, 'Monstrance of Deeds', 30. For statute applied strictly, see Port, *Notebook*, pp. 115, 116: 'Ascunz estatutz construez strycte solonque lez parolles et ascunz serront construez si come ils fueront usez emmedyatly apres le feisauntz, quar lez justices quex fueront la avoient conusanz de lentent deuz quex fieront lestatut. Mez si une estatut reherse lentent, cest estatut ne poit estre construe autermen que lentent est reherce'; where statutes abridged the common law 'ils serront pris strycte' by the judges.
[83] M 19 Hen. VI, 7, 15; Brooke, *GA*, 'Estoppel', 80. See also M 38 Hen. VI, 2, 5, and, for a *quaere* about *de rigore iuris*, H 8 Hen. V, 4, 16.
[84] M 7 Hen. VI, 14, 24; Brooke, *GA*, 'Brief', 158. See also M 11 Hen. IV, 33, 61 per Hankford, JCP: *ex stricte iure* the usage of Kent is that a person of fifteen years or more may make a feoffment on sale, but no other alienation.
[85] *CH*, p. 411; Holdsworth, III, p. 126.

For reasons that we need not explore, Hankford JCP rejected C's plea in spite of the settled rule. He asserted: 'there is no doubt that you must have the plea *de rigore iuris*, but we do not wish to rule so strictly [*ruler cy strictment*]'.[86] The idea was also rejected in 1489 when Brian CJCP conceded that any contract entered into by a corporation without a sealed instrument *de rigore iuris nil valet*.[87] Despite the strict rule, he said that for day-to-day contracts no sealed instrument was required.[88] Townsend JCP agreed.

## JUSTICE AND EQUITY

Whereas the judges seem content to apply the idea of *rigor iuris*, the theorists are eager to acknowledge that justice and law can produce inappropriate conclusions (though their discussions are short on practical examples of these) when applied strictly. They overcome these effects by means of equity. This is an idea which the practitioners also employ. Both uses of equity, the theoretical and the practical, are concerned with the relaxation of law. Yet, and here we detect a further dissonance between theory and practice, whereas theory ascribes a largely moral function to equity, the practitioners' usage is more mundane.

### Legal theory: a moral outlook

Pecock's 'strict justice' consists of 'not willing or doing to that other man more or other than I am bound to will or do to that man, and not willing more to be had from him by any other creature than what is due'. Similarly, human law is not exhaustive, as 'circumstances ... stand in so great a variance that it is undeclarable by any one general rule thereupon to be made'. Therefore, 'it may not fall ... under any positive law or ordinance how often, how much [or] in what manner a sovereign should make his ruling and his attendance towards his subjects in executing the points of his sovereignty'. And, 'like cases neither may any one rule be made how and how much and when an

---

[86] M 10 Hen. IV, 6, 19; Fitzherbert, *GA*, 'Maintenance of Writ', 66.
[87] P 4 Hen. VII, 6, 2; Brooke, *GA*, 'Conditions', 128. Also 7 Hen. V, 5, 3 at 7 per Tirwit: '[i]l serra dure de doner judgment encounter droit'.
[88] For the basic rule that a sealed instrument was required, see *HCLC*, p. 551, M 22 Hen. VI, 4, 6, and M 4 Hen. VII, 17, 3. There were numerous discussions of this sort: P 12 Ed. IV, 9, 24; T 18 Ed. IV, 8, 11.

underling or subject ought in all cases obey his superior and sovereign by the strength of the law standing between them'. Thus, 'though some of those points are able to be specified and under positive law to be charged, yet *the law of nature and of natural reason and conscience* must needs be the chief deemer and ruler in every special case in this matter'.[89]

Here Pecock uses natural law and conscience interstitially, when the positive law is silent. In contrast Fortescue employs the more traditional idea of equity to overcome inappropriate results in applying law. He starts with the Aristotelian analysis of Aquinas. In essence, equity exists due to the limitation of positive law, the intention of the legislator and the advancement of the common good.[90] 'All cases will not be covered by statutes and customs', he says. Those uncovered cases are left to the king's discretion. The king remits punishments in special cases only if this does not damage his subjects or statutes and customs. Equity is left to the king's discretion 'otherwise the strictness of the words of the law should hurt the common good, thereby flouting the intention [*mentum*] of the law'. If this is not done, observance of the law would destroy the law along with its authors.

Accordingly, Fortescue defines equity as 'indulgence above what is just, for human nature always craves for pardon'. Moreover, equity is a virtue and does not detract from legal justice. It is 'a super-laudable relaxation of the strictness of law'. Equity does not, therefore, violate law. It perfects law. This is done, says Fortescue – and here he is close to Pecock – by reason of the law of nature. This is the case since 'often written law lies dead under a covering of words and the prince by equity arouses its vital spirit. The mind of the law-maker does not perceive all that the words of the law embrace. Thus, the good prince who is called a living law, supplies the defect of the written law.'[91] Fortescue relies on the common stock of medieval jurisprudence.[92]

---

[89] *Reule*, pp. 286, 306, 307.   [90] *Summa*, 2a, 2ae, 60, 5; 120, 1.
[91] For his general discussion, *De Natura* I, c. 24: 'Epiches, ut dicit Aegidius Romanus, est indulgere super justum, natura namque humana semper supplicat pro venia. Haec virtus, ut dicit Philosophus V Ethicorum, justum legale non diminuit: epikaia ... est ... quasi superlaudabilis laxatio rigiditatis legis.'
[92] For D'Ailly, see Oakley, pp. 160, 164, and for Gerson, Pascoe, pp. 65–7. And C. Lefebvre, 'Natural equity and canonical equity', 8 *Natural Law Forum* (1963) p. 122. Baldus' equity is discussed by J. Canning, *The Political Thought of Baldus de Ubaldis* (Cambridge, 1987) p. 156. See also Port, *Notebook*, p. 32 for Srjt Keble's view that 'the king is sworn at his coronation to keep his law with pity [*petie*]'.

*Iustitia, rigor iuris* and *aequitas* 103

But he fails to clarify his account of equity by discussing practical illustrations of the operation of the idea. Only at one point does he suggest a useful example. A man who climbs the city walls without licence, though he offends the law, should not be punished if he does so to repel enemies. This is required by equity.[93] Ever keen to produce a generalised symmetry, Fortescue concludes that 'justice begets law, justice and law produce equity, and law and natural equity are at one with justice'.[94]

### The practitioners' equity: a mundane outlook

Equity is very rarely used in the practical literature as a moral authority, a representation of general fairness, and then only in the latter part of the period. Legislation of 1477 attempted to restrict the jurisdiction of piepowder courts to matters arising within the limits of the fair or market and occurring during the time that these were held. It explains how the courts had been improperly used: pleas had been held not within the jurisdiction of the courts, and in relation to events occurring outside the time of the fairs. It also explains how individuals had brought feigned suits so that people coming to the fairs are 'grievously vexed and troubled ... contrary to *equity* and good conscience'.[95] As a measure obviating recourse to existing common law remedies for false litigation,[96] the statute provides that plaintiffs suing there had to swear that the cause of action occurred in the time and jurisdiction of the court. It is interesting to note that the statute, including the reference to *equity*, was made perpetual by legislation in 1484.[97] Similarly, in 1489, it was enacted that no-one shall sell woollen cloth in the realm for more than sixteen shillings per broad yard.[98] The provision justified the prohibition because, by selling cloth at excessive prices, these people obtained 'unreasonable lucre, to

---

[93] *De Natura* I, c. 24.
[94] Ibid., c. 36: 'Sic justitia ius parit, justitia et ius producunt equitatem, et sunt jus et naturalis equitas unum cum justitia.' For the use of equity by parliament in amending legislation, see *De Laudibus*, c. 53, p. 135. For the use of the law-makers' intention in practice, see P 4 Ed. IV, 3, 4 at 4A per Choke *et al.*; T 12 Hen. VII, 19, 1; M 13 Hen. VII, 4, 3; H 14 Hen. VII, 17, 7; M 16 Hen. VII, 2, 4. For earlier practices see T. F. T. Plucknett, *Statutes and Their Interpretation in the First Half of the Fourteenth Century* (Cambridge, 1922) pp. 49–56.
[95] 17 Ed. IV, c. 2. For the decline of piepowder courts, see Holdsworth, I, pp. 539, 540, 569, and V, p. 112.
[96] Holdsworth, III, p. 395f.  [97] 1 Ric. III, c. 6.  [98] 4 Hen. VII, c. 8.

the great hurt and impoverishing of the king's liege people, buyers of the same, *against equity and good conscience*'.[99]

The moral connotation implicit in these examples is exceptional. The normal usage of equity by the practitioners usually has little to do with morality. But it does have something in common with the theorists' equity insofar as it concerns the relaxation of law. In this they echo implicitly the idea of the inadequacy of law to cover all cases. The predominant judicial usage is found in the expression *equity of a statute*. This was a device used to enlarge the ambit of existing statutory rules. Practical equity relates to relaxation of law, but only as a method of legal expansion. The usage is static throughout the period.[100]

In 1424 P sued debt against the administrators of F, one of whom appeared. By a statute of 1335 plaintiffs could proceed against one executor alone in debt when the other failed to appear, and Cockayne JCP held that though 'the statute says nothing except of *executors*; yet the *administrator* will be taken by the *equity* of the same statute'. As he alone appeared, he alone would be compelled to answer the plaintiff.[101] The statute compelled executors alone to appear: its equity

---

[99] For a rare use of *equity* as signifying 'fairness' by a judge, in this period, see T 10 Hen. VII, 25, 2 per Brian CJCP: concerning the amendment of mistakes in pleas, 'if we do a thing that was not done, this is wholly against equity'. See also per Bereford CJ, YB 12 Ed. II (70 Sel. Sec., London, 1951) p. 147, for a statement made in 1319. And 3 Hen. VIII, c. 12 for 'good equity and righteousness'.

[100] For Littleton's use of the idea, see *Tenures*, Bk I, c. 2, ss. 21 and 31, and Port, *Notebook*, p. 116. For the judicial usage (and an examination of the following cases, which do not represent an exhaustive list, would be most illuminating), see T 7 Hen. IV, 16, 6; H 11 Hen. IV, 40, 2 (Horton: 'l'equite de le common ley'); H 11 Hen. IV, 45, 20 at 47; M 12 Hen. IV, 1, 3; P 12 Hen. IV, 20, 5; H 14 Hen. IV, 27, 37; T 4 Hen. VI, 25, 4 at 26; M 38 Hen. VI, 17, 43; M 3 Ed. IV, 19, 13; M 7 Ed. IV, 18, 12; T 9 Ed. IV, 30, 45: M 18 Ed. IV, 16, 18; P 22 Ed. IV, 2, 7; M 7 Hen. VII, 6, 9; M 8 Hen. VII, 7, 4; T 10 Hen. VII, 25, 2; M 13 Hen. VII, 11, 12; H 14 Hen. VII, 13, 2. Indeed, per Hals JKB at M 7 Hen. VI, 5, 9: 'the law moves by reason and equity'. Also, generally, W. H. Lloyd, 'The equity of a statute', 58 *University of Pennsylvania Law Review* (1910) p. 76. For the bold proposition that the judicial use of 'the equity of the statute' is evidence of the judges using a moral idea to challenge parliament's law, see R. L. Jefferson, 'The uses of natural law in the royal courts of fifteenth-century England', unpublished Ph.D. thesis (University of Utah, 1972) chapter 4, pp. 133f.

[101] M 3 Hen. VI, 14, 18; Brooke, *GA*, 'Administrators', 4; the statute is 9 Ed. III, St. I, c. 3. See also generally *CH*, p. 741. See also P 11 Hen. IV, 56, 2 and H 14 Hen. VII, 13, 2 for the view that administrators fall within the equity of 4 Ed. III, c. 7 (giving trespass to executors for wrongs committed to their testator).

allowed administrators to appear. Indeed, the terms of the 1335 statute expressly applied only to actions against executors *in debt*. In 1406 executors recovered against D who now brought *audita querela* against them in order to have the first judgment re-considered. The court extended the rule, applying to debt, to *audita querela*, and thus compelled the one executor who appeared to answer because, the text recites, '*equipollens lex est*, for similar cases are adjudged by the equity of the statute'.[102]

The theoretical basis used by the judges to justify the extension of a statutory rule by equity was *similarity*: the similarity between the problem before the court and the problem contemplated in that statute. Extensions are accepted because the matter in hand is an *equal mischief* to the one treated by the statute: 'although the statute does not give an action by express words, yet it is more than an equal mischief and will be taken by the equity'.[103] The fundamental point is that practical equity requires treating cases outside the statute, which are similar to those contemplated by the statute, in the same way as those within the statute. It is a notion equivalent to the modern idea that judges do not create new rules but discover them from principles already latent within existing law.[104] As Martin JCP said in 1426, '[w]hen a statute is made I say that all things can be taken *similar to the mischief* for the cause for which the statute was taken, and is helped by the *equity* of the *same* statute, notwithstanding that it was not in the express words in the statute'. For example, 'by the statute of Gloucester it is ordained that if a tenant in dower made alienation, he in the reversion will have a writ of entry *in casu proviso*'. Additionally, 'by the equity of the same statute, if a tenant for a term of life or a tenant by curtesy alienates, he in the reversion will have a writ *in consimili*

---

[102] T 7 Hen. IV, 16, 6; Brooke, *GA*, 'Executors', 48. For *audita querela*, Holdsworth, I, p. 224, II, pp. 344, 593. Stonore justified *audita querela* by using equity in the previous century: 17 Ed. III (RS) 37, and Holdsworth, I, p. 224, n. 7.

[103] M 7 Hen. VI, 5, 9 at 6 per Paston: 'Et comment que le statut ne donne action par express parols, uncore il est plus que ouel mischief, et sera pris par l'equite'. See also M 10 Hen. VI, 15, 51 per Martin JCP; M 31 Hen. VI, 11, 8 per Fortescue CJKB; H 14 Hen. VII, 13, 2 per Tremaile JKB: 'donq quand est in ouel mischief, semble que sera remedy par l'equite de ce statut'.

[104] R. M. Dworkin, 'Is law a system of rules?', *Essays in Legal Philosophy*, edited by R. S. Summers (Oxford, 1970) p. 25 at pp. 34f. Compare Hart: see R. W. M. Dias, *Jurisprudence* (5th edition, London, 1985) pp. 354, 355; R. Cross, *Precedent in English Law* (Oxford, 1977) pp. 214f.

*casu*; and this is taken by the equity notwithstanding that it was not express words'.[105]

There is obviously a parallel in this idea with Bracton's well-known assertion that 'if like matters arise let them be decided by like, since the occasion is a good one for proceeding *a similibus ad similia*'. For Bracton, equity itself 'desires like right in like cases and puts all things on an equality'.[106] As we shall see in the following chapter, the judges employed a similar idea of treating like alike in relation to the common law as an aspect of their usage of *reason*.

## CONCLUSION

In conceptual terms there is much in common between natural law and justice in the legal theory of this period. Both ideas are used to support the proposition that law has a moral basis. Like natural law, the theorists treat justice as a form of divinely created morality; and Fortescue saw them as identical. Justice requires citizens to render to each their due, and it requires them, in a general sense, to live virtuously. From the concept of justice Pecock constructs the idea of a right based on the notion of a claim. This was a mature contribution to legal philosophy. Moreover, justice is expressed as a morality which must be reflected in human law. Human law must disclose justice. For Fortescue the objectives of justice and law were the same: the advancement of virtue. However, there is a significant point of difference here between theory and practice. A great deal of energy is spent on the exposition of justice in legal theory. But the practitioners rarely use the term. As will be suggested, the common law judges' equivalent idea of justice is to be found rather in aspects of their usage of *reason*. Nevertheless, it is evident that a tendency to apply law strictly is to be found in the Year Books, in the usage of *rigor iuris*. In this context, whereas the theorists' *equity* is used to overcome inappropriate

[105] T 4 Hen. VI, 25, 4; Brooke, *GA*, 'Forgery of False Deeds', 14. The statute is 6 Ed. I, c. 7. By this, if a doweress alienated her dower, the reversioner could obtain immediate entry by the writ *in casu proviso*. But this did not apply to alienation by other life tenants. So 13 Ed. I, c. 24 and the writ *in consimili casu* provided for entry against alienees of tenants for life and by the curtesy. For similar mischief and similar cases see H 11 Hen. IV, 45, 20 at 47 per Hankford; M 18 Ed. IV, 16, 18.
[106] *De Legibus*, II, p. 25. For Littleton on the exchange of 'equal' estates in land, see *Tenures*, Bk I, c. 7, ss. 64, 65. For Aquinas and the idea that 'justice implies equality', see *Summa*, 2a, 2ae, 57, 1.

conclusions resulting from strict applications of law, the practitioners' use of equity is far less moral. The predominant judicial use of the term, a use running throughout the period, shares the theorists' idea of the relaxation of law, but merely as a device to expand the scope of pre-existing legislative rules to similar cases.

5

# JUDICIAL DECISIONS AND THE AUTHORITY OF REASON

The modern lawyer does not have to look far for authoritative statements of law. Today's practitioner turns for his authority to the law reports, to parliamentary legislation and to the many forms of secondary legislation. In the late medieval period the common law doctrine of precedent was in its infancy. Precedents, and for that matter statutes, were only beginning to be treated with any real degree of regularity in the courts as definitive sources of substantive rules: in the modern sense, as sources of authority. More frequently and persistently, and more naturally, the late medieval practitioners turned to more fundamental types of authority: large ideas of abstract right and wrong. Legislators used divine law to justify enactments and, occasionally, the judges used natural law, distinctly moral ideas of authority. Perhaps the most habitually employed idea of abstract right used in the common law courts is that of reason. It is used time and time again as a source of authority in argument and as the justifying basis for judicial decisions. Indeed, we have already met reason as a source of authority superior to local customary law: local custom offensive to reason was void. In this chapter we shall explore the practice of counsel and judges in exploiting reason as a source of authority in the disposing of individual law-suits and in the shaping of legal doctrine and principle.

LINGUISTIC BACKGROUND

*General usage in non-legal sources*

Appearing in a number of different forms,[1] *reason* is used in contemporary non-legal literature in a variety of ways, most commonly to

[1] *OED*, 'reason': for example, *reison, reyson, resun, resoun, reson, raison* and *reason*. The last three forms are the ones most commonly found in the Year Books. See also

## Judicial decisions and the authority of reason 109

signify the intellectual power and its exercise, logical consideration, wisdom, sound judgment and good sense.[2] Phrases such as *full of reason, reason willeth* or *reason wil excusen* denote 'sensible', 'reason requires' or 'good sense will excuse', or *as resoun askes* and *as resoun wille* signify 'as reason demands' and 'as common sense calls for'.[3] A typical usage would be 'we have found many men the which abound greatly in wisdom, reason and understanding'.[4]

The word was also used in terms of an action or matter agreeable to reason, that which is reasonable, a sense of what is reasonable or right. *Accordaunt to resoun* means 'sensible', 'reasonable' or 'proper', *ayen* (against) *resoun*, 'foolish', 'unreasonable' or 'wrong', and *oute of* or *withouten resoun*, 'senseless' or 'wrong'.[5] An example would be 'what man wolde bi resoun, kepyng a man in frenesie, gyve him a swerd or a knyf by which he wolde slee himsilf?'[6]

Equally important is the use of reason as signifying justice or just treatment, as with *don resoun*, 'to do justice', or *haven resoun*, 'have justice'.[7] It is used in this context to denote 'satisfaction', as with, again, *haven resoun*, 'to obtain satisfaction for a grievance'.[8] A typical usage being 'in that ile also er wonder rightwise iuggez, for they do *resoun* and trewth to like men, als wele to pouer as to riche'.[9]

These were the most predominant meanings. Its other meanings included a ground for an action or belief, or a statement offered as an

---

Baker, *Manual of Law French*, p. 176, *reson*, 1, right, reasonableness. 2, reason (that is, a point in argument), explanation. And *resonablete*, reasonable right, reasonable measure, due proportion.

[2] *OED*, 'reason', III, 10; *MED*, *resoun*: la(a) and (b).
[3] *MED*, 1a(c), 1b(b).
[4] Ibid., 1a(a): *c*. 1450.
[5] *MED*, 2(a) (b) (c): 'No medicine should be preued in a man's body but if it were according to reason', *c*. 1425, MS. Hunterian Museum, Glasgow, 95, 101a–b.
[6] *MED*, 2: a. 1425, *Wyclif's Sermons*, 1, 26, MS. Bodleian Library, Oxford (Arnold, 1. 1–412; 2. 1–376).
[7] *MED*, 3(a): 'Yef eny man fynt him y-greved... come and pleyne hym to the mair and alderman, and he shal have right and resoun', *Proclamation Brembre* (1384), in *A Book of London English: 1384–1425*, edited by R. W. Chambers and M. Daunt (Oxford, 1931) p. 31, line 33; *OED*, 'reason', III; 15.
[8] *MED*, 3(b): 'I complained to the potestate the pope himself, but I had nothing else but pleasant words: no other reason at Rome might I none have', 'The tale of the noble King Arthur' (1470), *The Works of Sir Thomas Malory*, edited by E. Vinaver, volume I (Oxford, 1967) p. 189, line 16.
[9] *Mandeville's Travels* (fourteenth century) (translated from the French of Jean d'Outremeuse), edited by P. Hamelius, Early English Text Society, 154, volume II (London, 1923) p. 141, line 24.

explanation, such as 'the wolf on a day came to the dog and demanded of him the *rayson* why he was so lean'.[10] It meant an account or reckoning, as when used in the phrase *yielden resoun*, 'to account for one's actions',[11] or as a statement of fact employed as an argument, as in 'she shewed so many good *resounes* unto the king her husband, that he forgave Absolen all his wrath'.[12]

## The theorists' and the practising lawyers' reason

As we have seen, the theorists' reason lies at the heart of their analysis of the moral law, the divinely created natural law. For Pecock, reason is the means by which humankind obtains a knowledge of natural law. It is the intellectual capacity to determine logically what is right and what is wrong. In point of fact, Pecock's use of reason results in an equation of the rules of natural law and the requirements of reason: what is commanded by natural law is also commanded by reason.[13] For Fortescue too reason has a highly moral function. Fortescue's *ratio* is the means by which natural law, and therefore justice, are known.[14] The standard meaning of reason in contemporary non-legal sources, as the intellectual faculty and good sense, is echoed in legal theory. But, as the means by which the rules of the moral law are known, in legal theory reason itself becomes the moral law.

Whereas the theorists explicitly related their *reason* to divine law and natural law, thereby fixing its moral character, the practitioners' *reason* is far more mundane. There is no express and regular joining of reason to natural law or divine law in the practical sphere. The practitioners do not define reason in moral terms. Nor do they postulate reason as an entity requiring the same conclusions as divine law or natural law, as in legal theory. Nevertheless, the practitioners' reason,

---

[10] *MED*, 5 (1484, Caxton, *Fables of Aesop*, v.xii); see also *MED*, 4(a) (b), and *OED*, 'reason', 5, 6, 7.
[11] *OED*, 2a; *MED*, 6(a).
[12] *MED*, 8(b), *The Book of the Knight of La Tour-Landry* (*c*. 1450), edited by T. Wright, Early English Text Society, Original Series 33 (London, 1868, revised 1906) p. 122, line 1. For a similar use in law, see A. Borthwick and H. MacQueen, 'Three fifteenth-century cases' [Scottish], *Juridical Review* (1986) p. 123 at p. 129. It also meant 'motto' or 'sentence', *MED*, 9(a).
[13] *Donet*, pp. 15, 16. Pecock himself used the expression the 'authority of reason', *autorite of resoun: Folower*, p. 143.
[14] *De Natura* I, cc. 31, 32.

## Judicial decisions and the authority of reason 111

like the theorists', is postulated as an idea of abstract right. It is only the expressly moral nature found in the theorists' connection of reason to natural law that is absent from the practitioners' reason. Certainly, reason is appealed to in the Year Books as an idea of abstract right in the invalidation of local custom, like natural law in theory. However, normally, the practitioners' reason is used in more everyday contexts, such as allowing or disallowing particular pleas, controlling delays or regulating the bringing of the actions. When used in these ordinary settings of litigation, reason also possesses fewer and narrower meanings for the lawyers than those which appear in non-legal sources. The materials seem to indicate, from the details of the law-suit in which the word is used, that, for the lawyers, reason connotes good sense, being used by counsel and judges to exclude absurd or inconsistent results, and justice, being used to exclude or correct imbalances between loss and recovery and imbalances between wrong-doing and punishment or the payment of compensation. It is when it is used in this way that we can detect points of contact between the practitioners' reason and the theorists' concept of justice, which was itself concerned with the exclusion of imbalances and the rendering to each of his due.

### Law and reason

Though substantive rules of the common law might have developed in a haphazard fashion, the view of reason as a fundamental basis for law seems to have been relatively constant in the late medieval period. Throughout the fifteenth century, in both the courts and in legislation, particular states of affairs or conduct are described extensively as *against reason*. It was against reason for fish stocks to be wasted, for actions to be feigned, for soldiers to be left unpaid, for drapers to be wrongfully put out of work.[15] Judges were under a duty to act reasonably, and process had to be continued as reason required.[16] In

---

[15] The enactments are: 4 Hen. IV, c. 11; 4 Hen. V, St. II, c. 2; 18 Hen. VI, c. 18; 3 Hen. VII, c. 11. Reasonableness was also used as the motivating force behind legislation: 1 Hen. VI, c. 6, 7 Hen. VII, c. 10, 11 Hen. VII, c. 20. For other instances of conduct forbidden by reason, 2 Hen. IV, c. 15, 11 Hen. VI, c. 7.
[16] For judges, 33 Hen. VI, c. 1, 7 Ed. IV, c. 1, 4 Hen. VII, c. 21, 11 Hen. VII, c. 7. For process, 1 Hen. IV, c. 12, 14 Hen. VI, c. 4. For conduct prescribed by reason 11 Hen, VII, c. 18. For reasonable prices, weights and costs, 4 Hen. IV, c. 25, 2 Hen. V, St. II, c. 4, 4 Hen. V, St. II, c. 3, 3 Hen. VII, c. 8.

substance, this usage of reason reflects a common practice of legal practitioners to base enactments, argumentation or decisions upon the requirements of reason. Frequently lawyers would urge that what reason enjoins the courts should provide.

An idea which is often repeated in the Year Books is that reason itself is the foundation of law. This was to be found, of course, in Roman Law. The civilians' *ratio legis* did not concentrate upon the letter of the law, whose application would lead to injustice, but a deeper interpretation of law-texts, to determine the logical connection between rules.[17] In the English Year Books we often meet statements and claims such as 'law is reason', or 'the law is founded of reason, and that which is reason is law'.[18] We also meet the claim 'common reason which is common law', and the view that 'nothing in the world speaks as reasonably as the law speaks'.[19] As Hals JKB stated in 1429, the law moves (*va*) by reason and equity.[20] And the judges fixed by their discretion what was reasonable.[21] Similarly, the Year Books abound with descriptions of states of affairs or conduct as *against law and reason*. When a monk gave a cloak to an infant whose father collected the child, the monk was not entitled to retrieve the cloak from the infant and leave him naked: that 'was against law and reason'; again, sheriffs were responsible for guarding their prisoners as law and reason required.[22] In short, the practitioners considered that what reason enjoined, the law *did* provide. They saw an actual coincidence between law and reason. In Saint German's view reason was the 'first

---

[17] Stein, *Regulae Iuris*, p. 129.
[18] 18 and 19 Ed. III (RS) 379 (*ley est resoun*, per Stonore J); and T 14 Hen. VI, 19, 60 at 21 per Vampage: 'le ley est fond' de reason, et ceo que est reason est ley'.
[19] H 35 Hen. VI, 52, 17 at 53 per Fortescue CJKB: '[d]onq comon reason, qui est comon ley'; P 13 Hen. VII, 22, 9 at 23 per Fineux CJKB: 'car riens deins le monde parle si reasonablement come le ley parle'.
[20] M 7 Hen. VI, 5, 9 at 7.
[21] T 9 Ed. IV, 22, 24 at 23, per Srjt Pigot: 'et cest reasonabilitie serra ajuge per nostre discretion'; M 20 Hen. VII, 3, 8 per Srjt Coningsby: 'et tiel cause serra adjuge reasonable per le discrecion des justices'.
[22] M 11 Hen. IV, 31, 57 per Thirning CJCP: 'que il fuit enconter ley et reason'; T 10 Hen. VII, 25, 3 at 26 per Srjt Keble: 'sicome la ley et reason veul' expound'. For other examples of coincidence between law and reason see M 22 Hen. VI, 28, 47 per Yelverton JKB; P 38 Hen. VI, 30, 12 at 31; M 3 Ed IV, 8, 1 at 9 per Nedham JCP; P 17 Ed. IV, 1, 2 at 2 per Srjt Catesby; T 18 Ed. IV, 10, 25 per Littleton JCP; H 3 Hen. VII, 19, 1 per Srjt Keble.

ground' of the law of England; and 'every law positive well made is somewhat of the law of reason'.[23]

THE AUTHORITY OF REASON AS GOOD SENSE

The cases dealt with in this section indicate two features of the practising lawyers' *reason*. First, and this is the principal end of the discussion, they tell us something of the influence of reason, appealed to as an authority to exclude absurd and inconsistent results, in the disposing by the courts of ordinary cases. Secondly, and this is essentially a by-product of the following discussion, the materials suggest the *meaning* of reason as 'good sense', a meaning common, of course, in contemporary non-legal literature. It is as a large idea, good sense, that the practitioners apply reason to the details of a law-suit.

*The appeal to reason*

Reason is used as good sense in an extraordinarily wide variety of cases. In 1412, for example, reason was used by Cockayne JCP to prohibit an individual from suing account for coins which did not belong to him.[24] In 1439 Serjeant Ascough stated the rule that if a person had seisin of an advowson, the right to present a parson, by virtue of an actual presentment, and he conveys that advowson, by common reason the grantee acquired that same right to present. This right he could enforce by *quare impedit*. In the same case Newton JCP considered that in *quare impedit*, as the entitlement to present depended on a past presentment by the grantor of the advowson (by which seisin of the advowson was recognised), then *ex necessitate* according to reason the grantee must allege and establish both seisin and presentment in the grantor.[25] Let us examine three cases in a little more detail.

---

[23] *Dialogue*, pp. 27, 31. The view is essentially Thomist: *Summa*, 1a, 2ae, 90, 4, where Aquinas defines law as 'an ordinance of reason made for the common good by him who has charge of the community, and promulgated'. Indeed, at one point Pecock stated: 'And as for the lawe of the kyng of englond, what is iugid bi iugis agens such constreyners, al is take to be lawe of resoun, which thei callen her common lawe': *Folower*, p. 143.
[24] M 1 Hen. V, 11, 21.
[25] M 18 Hen. VI, 24, 9. For seisin and presentment in advowson, see *CH* p. 360, P&M II, pp. 137, 138, and A. W. B. Simpson, *An Introduction to the History of the Land Law* (2nd edn, Oxford, 1986) pp. 32, 103, 104.

In 1420 a plaintiff sought to recover more than he had claimed in his writ.[26] According to the facts P sued *scire facias* to have execution of a judgment given in his favour on a writ of annuity. When execution was awarded P prayed not only damages but also arrears of rent which had fallen due pending the writ of *scire facias* and after judgment had been given on the annuity. The court decided not to award his prayer for arrears. He was to be awarded only that which was claimed in his writ and contained in the judgment, namely damages. Martin JCP explained that '[y]ou will not have your prayer, for your prayer is against *law*, for your demand is nothing except for a specific thing, and this is the form of your writ, and for you to have more than is comprised in your writ will be *against reason*'. As only damages were claimed and awarded, reason forbad recovery of arrears of rent, being neither claimed nor awarded. In Martin's statement, the requirements of reason and law are designed to coincide. It is important to note, however, that P could still sue a fresh action of debt to recover the arrears.[27]

Frequently, counsel would appeal to reason. It was sometimes used when the problem of inconsistency or contradiction arose. In 1423, for example, counsel argued from reason to obtain judgment of a writ. Debt was brought against two as *administrators* of J who died intestate. Serjeant Rolf seeks judgment of the writ, describing how the plaintiffs had another writ of debt of an earlier date against two as *executors* of J. Consequently, the second writ is bad. Rolf puts it this way: 'for it is self-contradictory [*contrariant en luy meme*] and also against reason that he can have two writs pending in one and the same court where each one is inconsistent [*contrariant*] with the other'. Martin JCP is not persuaded because this claim, he says, is simply an untried assertion of fact. But he does concede that had the plaintiffs recovered against the others then it might have been otherwise.[28]

Reason was also used to justify the requirements of existing law. Hussey CJKB used it in this way in 1482 in relation to the rule disallowing trial by battle in appeal of robbery, a 'private prosecution'

---

[26] M 9 Hen. V, 12, 13: 'Vous n'averes vostre prier, car vostre prier est encontre ley, car vostre demaund' n'est mes chose en certaine, et ceo est le forme de vostre brefe, et vous d'aver pluis que n'est compris deins vostre brefe serra encounter reason.' As to the technical law, see also Rickhill JCP at T 7 Hen. IV, 16, 4. Also H 12 Hen. IV, 16, 9 per Srjt Skrene on reason requiring a cause of action to be clearly comprised in a writ.

[27] *HCLC*, pp. 171, 300.    [28] M 3 Hen. VI, 14, 17; Brooke, *GA*, 'Debt', 3.

to recover stolen goods, when the appellor was physically incapable of combat.[29] Though trial by battle was well-nigh obsolete by the late fifteenth century, occasionally, such as in appeal of felony, it was proffered.[30] Hussey refers not only to the authority 'in our books' but also to that of reason. 'And I know well that it is said in our books, if the plaintiff be maimed by the appellee, then he will not wage battle, but certainly, as seems to me with reason that although he was not maimed by the appellee but by another if he is maimed, then it is reason that the appellee be ousted.' At this point Hussey claims for law its basic grounding in reason: 'for the law is not so unreasonable that it wills him to wage battle, whereas he is maimed and cannot fight, thus it seems to me in this case [that] it is reason that he should be ousted of battle'.[31]

## Treating like alike

The practitioners' *equity* was used to widen the effect of a legislative rule so that similar cases falling outside a statute were treated as if they were within its scope. Unlike the moral texture of the theorists' equity, practical equity was primarily to do with logic centred on the idea of similarity. The logic of practical equity is reflected in the usage of reason which, likewise, is sometimes used to justify treating like cases alike and different cases differently. However, whereas judges confine their use of equity (in treating like alike) to statutory rules, reason is applied to achieve the same end in relation to the common law. When in 1487, for example, four manors descended to four sisters jointly, with an advowson belonging to one of the manors, and they agreed to divide the manors equally, so *common reason* required

---

[29] For the rule, see P. R. Hyams, 'Trial by ordeal: the key to proof in the early common law', *On the Laws and Customs of England: Essays in Honour of S. E. Thorne*, edited by Arnold *et al.* (Chapel Hill, N.C., 1981) p. 90 at pp. 121, 124. And generally *HFCL*, pp. 403–10.
[30] 94 Sel. Soc. (London, 1977) p. 116, n. 6; *IELH*, p. 64.
[31] T 22 Ed. IV, 19, 46 at 20: 'et jeo scie bien que est dit en nostre livres ... car le ley n'est cy unreasonable que il voil' luy gager battail ... issint moy semble en cest case il est reason que il soit ouste de battel'. Also, M 21 Ed. IV, 38, 5 at 39 for Brown's view of law as being understood reasonably. An interesting example of its creative role can be found at P 38 Hen. VI, 30, 13 (misnumbered as 12) per Fortescue: 'Il n'ad este tenu ple en noz livres adevant, mes entant que il est or estre adjuge si nous puissons trover bon reason que il sera ple, il est reason que nous affirmons le jugement.'

116    *Fundamental authority in late medieval English law*

that they be entitled to enjoy the advowson equally and present in turn, in the absence of an agreement to the contrary.[32]

In the event that a tenant for life colluded with a demandant allowing judgment against him by default, thereby losing the land, the reversioner's remedy was a writ of right.[33] By statute, however, at any time before judgment the reversioner could pray to be received to defend his interest.[34] In 1454, W sued *praecipe quod reddat* against F who made default. D then prayed to be received to relate how he was seised and granted the land to F for a term of life with reversion to himself. W asserts that D did not make this grant. The problem for the court is whether W should have responded to the claim of the reversion instead of traversing the grant. Explaining that it had been accepted twelve times in the books that in receipt the grant, and not the reversion, was to be traversed, as W had done here, Prisot CJCP said that 'for the contrary there is no judgment', and that 'it would be unfitting [*inconvenient*] and against reason to try the cause *in one case and not in another*'. As with Hussey CJKB in the case of 1482, here Prisot relies on both the authority of precedent from 'the books' and reason. He then refers to legislation of 1385 entitling a reversioner to attaint or error on false verdicts or erroneous judgments had against tenants for life.[35] Here too a demandant traverses an alleged grant to the tenant rather than the alleged reversion. As the grant is traversed under the 1385 statute, so it is reason for it to be traversed in this instance: 'wherefore it seems to me that it is greatest reason to traverse the cause in this case at the bar, *as it is in all other cases that are given by the statute in a similar case*'. According to Prisot CJCP reason requires that like be treated alike.

The basis for essoins was the idea of an excuse. Bracton wrote that when 'one lawfully summoned does not appear he must be punished, unless he has legitimate grounds of excuse by which he may justify his absence'.[36] Excuses included being beyond the seas, pilgrimage, royal

---

[32] M 2 Hen. VII, 4, 17. For advowson 'in gross', severed from a manor, see P&M II, pp. 135, 137, and division of advowson between co-parceners, see Co. Litt., 164b. See also M 13 Hen. VII, 2, 2 for reason and permitting wager to people in 'equal positions': *arguendo*, Frowicke and Keble.
[33] *CH*, p. 411. Our case is M 33 Hen. VI, 38, 17 (Prisot is at 41): Brooke, *GA*, 'Counterplea de Receipt', 1.
[34] 13 Ed. I, St. of Westminster II, c. 3. See also 13 Ric. II, St. I, c. 17.
[35] 9 Ric. II, c. 3. Also M 12 Hen. IV, 1, 3 at 2 (Culpeper: 'it is reason to take the case here on the equity of the statute'), and P 5 Hen. VII, 16, 8, the *quaere*.
[36] *De Legibus*, IV, p. 71; see too pp. 72, 151, 152. And *De Laudibus*, c. 53, p. 135.

service, flood and sickness. They were also available when people pleaded non-summons and failed to appear to make their law on the issue of non-summons. This happened in 1459 when A brought *praecipe quod reddat* against B and B pleaded non-summons. A day was set for B to make his law, as permitted by settled practice, on the matter of the summons.[37] However, B failed to turn up, but the court was uncertain whether it had yet been decided that illness would excuse non-appearance to make law upon a matter of non-summons. The judges accept that both imprisonment and flood were good excuses in such cases. Thus, as there was no essential difference between sickness and, for instance, imprisonment, *reason* required that sickness be allowed. Danby JCP said simply that 'it is reason his default will be saved by infirmity as well as by imprisonment or flood of water', it is 'good reason that his default will be excused by common cause as by flood water'.[38] As Moile JCP stated: 'it is here greatest reason that he will save his default by infirmity *as by imprisonment*, etc., for infirmity is the imprisonment of God which is as sufficient cause to excuse the default as is the imprisonment of man'.[39] Sometimes, reason and practical equity were very much alike.

## Reason and delays

The problem of delays was rife in medieval litigation and often parliament addressed it.[40] Though sometimes slowness was treated as necessary for considered and sound judgment,[41] frequently the law itself, by permitting imparlance, view and receipt (for example), supplied the problem.[42] Nevertheless, the common law judges persistently sought to control *unnecessary* delays, noticeably in cases where there was a likelihood that a proposed delay would serve no useful purpose. Commonly, in such cases, judges forbad a proposed delay on the grounds that to allow it would offend *reason*. In 1452 D

---

[37] *De Legibus, IV,* pp. 64, 151–3; *CH,* p. 384; P&M II, p. 632.
[38] M 39 Hen. VI, 16, 20 at 17: 'il est reason que son defaut sera save per infirmite sibien come per enprisonment, ou creteine d' eau'; and M 38 Hen. VI, 11, 22: 'bon reason que son defaut sera excuse per comon cause come per creteine d'eau'.
[39] M 39 Hen. VI, 16, 20: 'Il est si grand' reason que il savera son defaut per infirmite come per imprisonment, etc., car infirmite est l'enprisonment de Dieu, le quel est si sufficient cause a saver le defaut come est l'enprisonment de home.'
[40] J. C. Holt, *Magna Carta* (Cambridge, 1965) p. 327 (c.40 of the 1215 Charter); 11 Hen. IV, c. 3; 4 Hen. V, St. II, c. 7; 11 Hen. VI, c. 6; 3 Hen. VII, c. 10.
[41] P 21 Ed. IV, 24, 11 per Fairfax JCP, and *De Laudibus,* c. 53, p. 133.
[42] 94 Sel. Soc. (London, 1977) p. 157.

was arraigned at the suit of the king for robbery, and the jury was ready to be sworn, when the robbed party appeared wanting the inquest delayed so that he could bring an appeal of robbery (a private action to recover the goods, as on indictment they would go to the king). Fortescue CJKB forbad the delay: if the robbed party subsequently chose not to proceed then 'the king must commence novel process against the jurors, which would be against reason'; and if the inquest were not taken at that moment, D would be detained in prison for a longer time 'which is against reason', as he might be acquitted there and then.[43]

The problem would arise, typically, when defendants attempted to exploit both voucher to warranty and aid prayer, pleas employed to delay actions for land. A demandant in a real action was obliged by law to bring his writ against the person who was seised. When a tenant for life was seised, he could pray aid of the reversioner to assist him in proving title. The reversioner would then be summoned by the court to undertake the defence.[44] On the other hand, in voucher to warranty a tenant called in another whom he would claim to have been his grantor, and who in the deed of grant would have warranted the title.[45] If in the same action a tenant were permitted to employ aid prayer, which had been unsuccessful, and then voucher to warranty, effectively he would have been allowed to delay the demandant twice. The judges often condemned this practice, saying that to allow voucher when aid prayer had been unsuccessful would be *encontre reason*. As Rickhill JCP said in 1405, in the course of discussion, if a tenant for life prays aid of another who makes default, the tenant cannot use voucher to bring the same person into court: '[t]he voucher will not be allowed after the aid, because it is not reason and to delay the demandant twice by the act of one same person, and for this he must stand for the one or the other at his peril'.[46]

This problem arose in 1444. X brought formedon against Y who vouches warrantors A, B, C and D. X objects explaining how in the

---

[43] M 31 Hen. VI, 11, 6; Fitzherbert, *GA*, 'Corone', 18. For appeal of robbery, Holdsworth, II, p. 361, III, pp. 320, 323. Similar instances of senseless delays and reason can be found at: T 3 Hen. IV, 18, 15 per Markham JCP; P 12 Hen. IV, 19, 4; T 4 Hen. VI, 26, 5 per Babington CJCP.
[44] Holdsworth, III, p. 121; *CH*, p. 411.
[45] *CH*, ibid.
[46] H 6 Hen. IV, 3, 22: 'Le voucher ne serra suffer puis l'aide, pur ceo que n'est reason et delayer le demaundant deux foits per l'act d'un mesme person, et pur ceo il doit estoyer a l'un ou l'auter a son peril'.

same case Y once already prayed in aid A, B, C and D as reversioners on a lease for a term of life. In that aid prayer the prayees were in default and Y was compelled to answer alone. And so X argues that Y should not be permitted his voucher. The court agrees. Markham JCP (rather optimistically) states that 'the law always eschews delays': in the time of Richard II it was adjudged always that if a person prays aid of a reversioner and also vouches that same individual as grantor, he will be ousted of his aid and put to his voucher: 'it seems that this was founded on greatest reason'. Law and reason are treated once more as coincident. Thus, if a tenant prays in aid the reversioner who then makes default, the reversioner will never be received afterwards 'because then the demandant will be delayed twice for one same cause'. Furthermore, Fulthorpe JCP admits the same conclusion when a tenant vouches Z and then seeks a stay in the matter because Z is within age, 'which is not reason that the demandant will be twice delayed on the same cause'. Consequently, in the case at hand, Y was denied his voucher.[47]

*The role of reason as good sense*

The instances discussed in this section are simple. They indicate two things about the practising lawyers' reason. First, they suggest a meaning, one which connotes good sense, a usage not peculiar to the lawyers: the word is commonly used to signify good sense in contemporary non-legal sources. Second, the cases suggest something of the influence of reason, good sense, as an authority appealed to in the treatment and disposing of ordinary law-suits. On each occasion, reason is being used to shape a result. Decisions and arguments are being designed to incorporate and conform to the requirements of reason. This practice, the *appeal* to reason, is in essence the exploitation of an abstract idea of good sense. It is this abstract idea of good sense which the practitioners represent or fix as a determinant requiring the exclusion of absurd or inconsistent results.

The judges tell us that it is abstract reason which prohibits an individual suing for coins which do not belong to him. The judges tell

---

[47] H 22 Hen. VI, 39, 12: 'que n'est reason que le demaundant sera ii fois delay sur mesme cause' (Fulthorpe); Brooke, *GA*, 'Voucher', 73. See also 3 Ed. I, St. of Westminster I, c. 40 (for delay and voucher). For other examples of reason and delays: T 2 Hen. VI, 15, 15 per Srjt Paston; P 20 Hen. VI, 23, 4 per Newton CJCP (double delays); M 34 Hen. VI, 9, 20 at 10 per Moile JCP; P 16 Ed. IV, 9, 10; and H 6 Hen. VII, 15, 9 at 16 per Hobbard AG (infinite delays).

us that it is against reason for a plaintiff to recover, at execution of judgment, more than had originally been claimed in the writ. Reason, as good sense, is a flexible concept. It is used in all sorts of contexts and to attain a variety of ends. When used to achieve like treatment of like cases, for example, in the case of 1459, concerning the saving of default, reason is employed to extend an existing rule. In the case of 1454, concerning the traversing of a grant, it is used to justify the continuation of an established practice. It is noticeable how often the authority of law and that of reason are treated as coinciding.

### THE AUTHORITY OF REASON AS JUSTICE

The relationship between the theorists' concept of justice and the practitioners' reason presents an intriguing problem. Whereas the theorists define their justice, the practitioners do not define their reason. They are certainly not equal concepts. When the theorist spoke of his *iustitia*, the practitioner would not immediately recognise this as his *reason*. Theory's justice is conspicuously moral: God-given, a virtue, and equated with natural law. There is nothing of this in the Year Books with reason. However, though they are not exactly the same, they are overlapping concepts. Overlapping in substance, in many respects they are equivalents.

According to legal theory justice consists in rendering to each his due, including what has been lost through injury.[48] Ideas of reciprocity and restoration are of central importance. Aquinas had commented that men mark 'the balance of justice according to the recompense of thing for thing'.[49] Pecock had said that the office of justice was to yield to people what was owed to them.[50] In essence, the work of justice was to redress imbalance. This was, of course, a major and intrinsic function of the courts. When a person suffered loss, recognised as such by law, the courts would insist upon recompense and provide a remedy.[51] Likewise, when a person committed a wrong, recognised as such by law, the courts would impose some form of penalty and insist upon the payment of compensation or punishment.

Reason is used extensively by common lawyers in these very contexts, when the problem of *imbalances* arises. Frequently it is employed to exclude imbalances, unjust results, to justify recompense

[48] Above Ch. 4, nn. 35, 42.   [49] *Summa*, 2a, 2ae, 62, 1.
[50] *Donet*, p. 110; *Reule*, p. 254. For Fortescue, *De Natura*, I, c. 17.
[51] *IELH*, for debt, p. 266, for *assumpsit*, p. 274.

when there has been loss, to justify the imposition of punishment when there has been wrong-doing. It is also used in the Year Books to justify the prohibition of double recompense and double punishment. In these and related contexts the practitioners appeal to reason, in a sense similar to the theorists' justice 'giving each his due', to ensure proportionality: to ensure that there are no imbalances between loss and recovery, wrong-doing and punishment. It is to be stressed that this usage as justice is not peculiar to the lawyers. Reason also had this meaning in contemporary non-legal literature.

## Recompense for loss

In the Year Books there appears to be at work a general principle that, for a plaintiff to be able to recover for loss, the wrong occasioning the loss must have been recognised as actionable by law and it must have been one which actually caused damage. In broad terms there would be no remedy for damage caused by a defendant if his conduct did not constitute a legal wrong. Thus, for example, economic loss may in fact cause damage, but if there was no wrong, if there was no *injuria*, it would not be compensated.[52]

There is also evidence of the general idea that loss caused by a defendant's action must of itself be compensated.[53] What is significant is that this principle, which was frequently observed in the common law courts, was one explicitly stated on several occasions to be prescribed by reason. By the beginning of the sixteenth century the idea was well used. A discussion took place at Gray's Inn in 1516 on the proposition that when a man covenants to build a house and does not do so, the person with whom the covenant was made shall have an action on the case. In the discussion Peter Dillon, a Reader at Gray's Inn, stated: 'for every *law* is grounded on *reason*, and *reason* wills that if a man has injury he should have an action. And now he has injury by this non-feasance, and so if he shall not have the action he shall be without remedy.'[54] The idea had been used by Littleton JCP in the celebrated *Case of Thorns* of 1466. Though no judgment is reported, the opinion of the court was that when D cut thorns and they fell against his will onto P's land, 'this falling was not lawful, and then his coming to take them away was not lawful'. For this P could

---

[52] 94 Sel Soc. (London, 1977) pp. 220–2.   [53] Ibid.
[54] Ibid., p. 272 (MS. Lincoln's Inn, Misc. 486(2)f.7v). Reason is interpreted as justice infrequently by legal historians: however, see A. K. R. Kiralfy, 'Law and right in legal history', 6 *JLH* (1985) p. 49 at p. 57.

bring trespass. Littleton agrees, adding, simply: 'if a man suffers damage, it is reason that he be recompensed'.[55]

As Dillon implied in 1516, this dynamic usage of reason was well suited to cases concerning the action on the case. This was a writ whose potential for supplying a remedy in novel circumstances provided fertile soil for large ideas of 'just' recompense inherent in this usage of reason. In 1472, for example, P sued an action on the case in deceit against a servant who had warranted cloth, in a sale for his master, to be of a certain length, whereas it was not of that length. The judges were unanimous that P should have an action on the case for the deceit. However, they were not agreed whether the master or the servant should be liable. Littleton JCP thought P should have the action directly against the servant. His justification is uncomplicated. Looking to the deceitful act of the servant, he argues that as P had been deceived, and may not have bought had he known the truth about the cloth, so 'it is reason that, if he be deceived, he should have an action of deceit'.[56] The majority, though, thought that when the warranty was given by a servant, this was to be treated as the act of the master whose sale it was and who could be sued.[57]

The basic concept, that reason requires recompense for loss, was expressed sometimes in a different form, in the idea that a failure to recompense a party for loss would be 'against reason': as was said by Richard Littleton in an Inner Temple reading from 1493, 'it would be against reason for the party to be without remedy'.[58] The idea can be found in a discussion from 1400. If A deposited money with B to keep and return on request, it was not settled whether A should sue debt or account in the event that B failed to return the money. Again, if A gave money to B to pay over to C (a payment by A to B 'to the use of C'), then if B retained the money, C could sue account against him as B was accountable because he received the money to C's use.[59] The

[55] M 6 Ed. IV, 7, 18 at 8: 'et si un home ad damage il est reason que il soit recompense'; see also Fifoot, *Sources*, p. 195 at 196 and Baker and Milsom, *Sources of English Legal History*, p. 327 at 331, where Littleton's *reason* is translated as 'right'.
[56] T 11 Ed. IV, 6, 10: 'il est reason s'il soit disceive que il aver action de disceit'. For reason and action on the case, Port, *Notebook*, in *Thomson v. Lee* (1498) p. 6 at p. 7 per Fineux CJKB.
[57] Fifoot, *Sources*, p. 336 (and pp. 349–51): the buyer must have relied on the seller's skill and knowledge, when the defect was not obvious, if the warranty was express and related to the existing state of the goods.
[58] Port, *Notebook*, p. 128: 'quar il fuit encontre reason que le partie serra saunz remedy'.
[59] For the basic problem see *HCLC*, pp. 183, 184; P 41 Ed. III, 10, 5; M 4 Hen. VI, 2, 4; M 18 Hen. VI, 20, 5; H 6 Ed. IV, 61, 6.

## Judicial decisions and the authority of reason 123

court in 1400 stated the rule that, on these facts, A's remedy, like C's, was account and not debt. However, in this case, *arguendo*, Markham JCP allows the same remedy to A if A delivered twenty pounds to B to bail to C who was to hold to the use of A. He says that, if B and C collude, A will be 'without [his] recovery, which will be against reason'.[60] For Markham JCP, therefore, in these circumstances A could bring a writ of account against B.

The same requirement of reason was also expressed in the form that if no loss had been suffered then reason forbad recover. The idea was often used by counsel in argument. In the *Case of Thorns* in 1466 Serjeant Young argued that, though there may have been damage to the plaintiff, the defendant had committed no wrong. When he cut the thorns, even though they fell onto another's land, the property in them was still in the defendant 'and thus it was lawful for him to take them'. 'Wherefore, notwithstanding that he has done damage, he has done no wrong [*tort*].' Consequently, said Serjeant Young: 'And in such a case, where a man has *damnum absque injuria*, in this case he shall have no action, for if he has [suffered] no wrong it is not reason that he recovers damages.'[61]

The idea was also used by Moile in 1450. In an action of maintenance it was alleged by P that D had delivered money to X and Y to distribute to jurors to maintain a suit between P and A. D argues that judgment should not be given for P, because the latter had not shown that the money had actually been distributed. Moile says: 'for he [P] is not endamaged, because the maintenance was not sent in fact. And to have an action *when he is not endamaged*, it would be against reason'.[62] However, Prisot CJCP disagrees. Not only is D's conduct forbidden by law,[63] but the delivery of the money alone is enough to constitute maintenance: had the two men actually distributed, that would have been a second maintenance.[64]

[60] M 2 Hen. IV, 12, 50; Brooke, *GA*, 'Account', 24; *HCLC*, p. 185, n. 2. For a related idea of the disturbance of something legally due as against reason, see 7 Hen. IV, c. 16.
[61] M 6 Ed. IV, 7, 18: 'et en tiel case lou home ad *dampnum absque injuria*, en ce case il navera action, car s'il n'ad tort il n'est reason que il recovera damages'.
[62] T 28 Hen. VI, 12, 28 (see also M 31 Hen. VI, 8, 1): 'Et a aver action quand il n'est pas endamage, il seroit encontre reason.'
[63] The statute is not named: but see 1 Ed. III, St. II, c. 14, and 4 Ed. III, c. 11 (this also contains references to *comen droit, droit* and *reason*); see also 20 Ed. III, c. 6, on maintenance, for its reference to *droit, ley et reson*.
[64] See too P 18 Hen. VI, 6, 6 (on 1 Hen. V, c. 3); at 6A per Srjt Fortescue: 'and for this wrong [*tort*] it is not reason that anyone will have an action except he who has [suffered] the wrong'.

## Satisfaction for loss and second actions: double recompense

There would, of course, be an obvious imbalance between loss and recompense if a person already satisfied for an injury was recompensed a second time for the same injury. Occasionally reason is used by the practitioners in this sort of context, to prohibit double satisfaction. Serjeant Godrede's use of the idea in 1431 was typical. When the court considered whether a plaintiff whose damages were assessed too low by a jury could have these increased and *also* have attaint against the jury (by which half the fine payable by attainted jurors went to the plaintiff), Godrede argued that 'it is not reason that the party has this advantage and attaint also'.[65] The idea is clearly visible in a case of 1413.

P sued trespass against two defendants,[66] one of whom sought to stay proceedings by *supersedeas*, as he was entitled to do by law because he was a clerk of the chancery which had jurisdiction over its officers in all personal actions.[67] Although the matter was adjourned, Hankford JCP decided that proceedings would not be stayed. It may transpire, he argued, that P would succeed in two separate actions, one by writ at common law against the one defendant, and a second by bill in the chancery against the other. 'Then it would follow that for one trespass he will recover double damages, for he must receive the entire damages here, and in the same way in the chancery, which will be against law and reason.' Thus, says Hankford, both must be put to answer and the matter must not be stayed by *supersedeas*. This is a simple illustration of the working of the idea: it is interesting to note, once again, that the denial of double satisfaction is described as against both law and reason.

In general terms, as Serjeant Godrede revealed in 1431, during the fifteenth century attaint was becoming unpopular. Punishments for the attainted jury were severe, complaints were frequently made, it was resorted to little and juries of attaint were often unwilling to find

---

[65] P 9 Hen. VI, 2, 5. Babington CJCP considered attaint available if damages were too low. Compare M 6 Ed. IV, 5, 16. For juries assessing damages, see 94 Sel. Soc. (London, 1977) pp. 114, 115 and for the problem whether judges could increase *and* diminish damages fixed by juries, see G. T. Washington, 'Damages in contract at common law', 47 *LQR* (1931) p. 345 at pp. 354–9. For half the fine payable to the litigant, see 34 Ed. III, c. 7; 38 Ed. III, St. I, c. 12; 11 Hen. VI, c. 4; and 11 Hen. VII, c. 24.

[66] H 14 Hen. IV, 21, 27.    [67] *IELH*, p. 38.

## Judicial decisions and the authority of reason

the first jury guilty.[68] Certainly, the court in a case of 1472 is reluctant to allow attaint.[69] The facts were these. D had successfully sued P in trespass for which P had paid damages. D later confessed to P that recovery had been false and therefore satisfied P for the loss by agreement out of court. P, the losing defendant in the original trespass action, now becomes the plaintiff in an action of attaint, and the question is whether P can bring attaint against D and the jurors. Now, of course, a successful attaint by P might not only have brought a reversal of the original judgment so that P would be 'restored to all that he had lost'[70] under the original trespass action, but it might also have meant that P received half the fine payable by the attainted jurors.[71] Donington, arguing for D against attaint, states that 'it will be against reason when the plaintiff is satisfied, and has extinguished his action against the party, that he will attaint the jury '.[72] The text concludes that 'it will be against reason that the plaintiff will be restored, where he is recompensed by agreement, for thus he will be twice recompensed'.[73]

### Reason, liability and punishments for wrong-doing

Two general principles often indicated in the Year Books are that a defendant committing a wrong must be punished, or pay compensation (indeed a person having to compensate was commonly described as *puni*),[74] and that a person would be punished or made to pay compensation by the courts only for conduct recognised as punishable in law, or for which he was compellable in law to compensate. Persistently, reason was treated as the authority for these basic principles.

---

[68] *De Laudibus*, c. 26, p. 63; J. B. Thayer, *A Preliminary Treatise on Evidence at the Common Law* (Boston, 1898) pp. 137–40; Holdsworth, IV, p. 516.
[69] M 13 Ed. IV, 1, 3 and 5, 14; Brooke, *GA*, 'Attaint', 91, 118.
[70] *De Laudibus*, c. 26, p. 63.
[71] Above, n. 65.
[72] M 13 Ed. IV, 1, 3 at 2: 'il serra encounter reason quant le plaintiff est satisfie, et ad extient son action vers le partie, que il atteindr' le jure'.
[73] M 13 Ed. IV, 5, 14: 'il serra encounter reason que le plaintiff serra restore, ou il est recompence per accord, car issint il avera ii. recompensations'. The text also has the statement that 'le ley n'est cy unreasonable de punisher le petit jure': ibid.
[74] 94 Sel. Soc. (London, 1977) p. 222, n. 8. For cases where reason is expressly related to punishment and burdens: M 11 Hen. IV, 18, 43 at 19 per Horton JCP; H 8 Hen. VI, 26, 16 Srjt Elderkar; M 34 Hen. VI, 3, 8 per Prisot CJCP; M 3 Ed. IV, 15, 10 at 15 per Brian CJCP: 'car si le plaintiff luy voyle punisher per le ley, il est reason que il luy punish droitelment, et nemy a tort'; H 5 Hen. VII, 10, 2; M 14 Hen. VII, 5, 11 Srjt Yaxley.

The idea was usually expressed in these forms. First, it is considered 'against reason' *not* to punish or require the payment of compensation if there had been wrong-doing. Second, when a person does something damaging *lawfully*, it is *not* reason to hold him liable. Certainly, in the first the idea of reciprocity is not too far away: in that sense it is not dissimilar to the theorists' 'rendering to each his due', the crux of justice. In the second, on the other hand, there seem to be connotations of both justice and the familiar good sense.

The idea that it is 'against reason' not to punish when there had been wrong-doing appears in an interesting case of 1413. Excommunicates were generally disabled from suing in court.[75] D sued P in Rome on an advowson. P is then excommunicated but brings *praemunire* claiming D had sued in Rome on a prohibited matter. Advowsons fell within the jurisdiction of the royal courts.[76] Hankford JCP was faced with two competing legal rules. D was forbidden to sue on an advowson in Rome. But P was an excommunicate, and as such had lost his capacity to sue. He decided that excommunication would not disable P from suing *in these circumstances*. To disallow *praemunire*, he argued, would mean that D's wrong, suing in Rome when forbidden by law, would go unpunished. His justification is simple. Every excommunicate would be denied the use of *praemunire*, 'so that the suit will be unpunished, which will be a mischief, and against law and reason'.[77] (Again, the requirements of law and reason are designed to overlap.)

The same idea is visible in the well-known case of *Orwell* v *Mortoft* (1504).[78] In general terms judges were beginning to allow *assumpsit* for non-feasance around 1500.[79] Yet, still judges clung to the old ways. In *Orwell* v *Mortoft* the majority adopted the old idea that debt, and not case, was the proper action when A paid money to B for a purpose which was not carried out.[80] Only Frowicke CJCP favoured the view that A be entitled to elect debt *or* case. Reason is prominent in Frowicke's decision. In the case P paid D for barley which, P alleged,

---

[75] Holdsworth, I, p. 631; Bracton, *De Legibus*, f. 426b; see too M 8 Hen. VI, 3, 8; P 13 Ed. IV, 8, 3.
[76] 16 Ric. II, c. 5.
[77] H 14 Hen. IV, 14, 4; 'issint serra le suit dispuny, que serra mischiefe, et encounter ley et reason'; Brooke, *GA*, 'Praemunire', 15; Fitzherbert, *GA*, 'Excommunication', 21. We cannot, of course, ignore the jurisdictional aspect of the case: see also Holdsworth, II, p. 305, n.3. and *CH*, p.409.
[78] M 20 Hen. VII, 8, 18; Fifoot, *Sources*, p. 351.
[79] *HFCL*, p. 332; *IELH*, p. 279.   [80] *IELH*, p. 303.

## Judicial decisions and the authority of reason 127

D undertook to keep safe and deliver to P on an arranged day. P sued case for non-delivery claiming that D had wrongfully converted the barley to his own use. For the majority debt was the proper action: the old view.[81] Frowicke, though, emphasising the wrongfulness of D's conduct, thought P should be allowed debt or case. He conceded that P could recover and be satisfied for his loss in debt, but, he argued, reason required that D be 'punished' for the deceit he had practised. He says: 'for [if] he [D] has done a thing to frustrate my bargain and to my deceit, whereby I am put to loss, and so it is reason that he should be punished for this misdemeanour by the action on the case which has been brought'.[82]

The second proposition is that the courts treat as contrary to reason the imposition of liability upon a defendant when the conduct complained of is of a type permitted by law. When conduct is lawful it is against reason to punish or compel compensation.[83] As Hill said in *Beaulieu* v *Finglam* (1401) '[it] will be against all reason to put blame or default in a man, where he has none in him' according to the custom of the realm.[84] At the close of the period, in 1504, Yaxley argued, 'when one does a lawful act, it is not reason to punish him'.[85]

The writ of *capias* was a process by which a sheriff was ordered to imprison the defendant to bring him into court to answer the plaintiff.

---

[81] *HCLC*, pp. 57–8: debt was available where fungibles, goods not specifically identified, were claimed by weight or measure.

[82] M 20 Hen. VII, 8, 18 at 9: 'car il ad fait une chose a determiner mon bargain, et in deceit de moy, per quel jeo suis mis a un per[d] per que est reason per cest misdemeanour que il soit puni per accion sur le cas qui ad este mis'. (It is interesting to speculate whether Frowicke considered that the defendant would not be 'punished' with debt.) The idea was approved at M 21 Hen. VII, 41, 66: see, however, *HCLC*, p. 250, for later traces of the old idea.

[83] For reason and the idea that people must not be punished without fault, see the *Case of the Marshalsea* (1455), Fifoot, *Sources*, pp. 159, 168, 169 per Danby JCP; see also H 22 Hen. VI, 38, 8 per Portington JCP, and P 16 Ed, IV, 2, 7 at 3; and Townsend's use of fault in T 17 Ed. IV, 3, 2 (as counsel), and H 2 Hen. VII, 11, 9 (as JCP).

[84] P 2 Hen. IV, 18, 6: 'Ceo serra encounter tout reason de mitter culpe ou default en un home, lou il n'ad nul en luy' (Fifoot's translation of 'luy' as 'law' is mistaken: *Sources*, p. 166). See also Baker and Milsom, *Sources of English Legal History*, p. 557 at 558.

[85] M 20 Hen. VII, 4, 12 (along with Pollard): 'uncore cest loial act, et quand on fait loial act, il n'est reason de luy punir' (see also 2, 5; 4, 14). The case concerned the question whether executors will be repaid from the estate when they discharge the testator's debts with their own goods: the case is also notable for the comment of Vavasour JCP: 'this payment of their money is a lawful act, and more than they must have done, and then it would be against all reason that they will not be repaid' (4, 14 at 5).

128  Fundamental authority in late medieval English law

After arrest the sheriff was obliged to certify what he had done touching the execution of the writ. This was the 'return of the writ'.[86] In 1468 D imprisoned P when commanded to do so by X, a sheriff.[87] However, the writ of *capias*, commanding imprisonment, was not returned by the sheriff. P now sued D for false imprisonment.[88] Danby JCP held against P. D ought not to be sued successfully in this way, 'for when he made the arrest at the time lawfully it will not be reason that by the act of his master he will be charged'.[89] On the same facts, this approach was adopted by Rede CJCP in 1504, 'for he [D] has executed his warrant according to the law and then it is not reason that the act and default of his master, to which he is not in any way privy, will be prejudicial to him'.[90] Rede CJCP repeated the idea in 1506: 'every servant is held to do the precept of his master in all that is lawful, and when he does this lawfully, it is not reason to punish him, although there is default in his master, but sooner to punish the master in whom the default is'.[91]

Lawfulness of the conduct and being privy to the wrong are all-important here. And on these occasions we see connotations of the two meanings of reason. In the talk of punishment is implicit the idea of what is due. In the talk of lawfulness and privity there seem to be ideas of good sense. Once again, the notion of imbalance is implied, for otherwise when conduct is lawful someone would be punished, and when the defendant is not privy he would be punished: these reason forbids.[92]

---

[86] G. Jacob, *New Law Dictionary* (fifth edn, printed by H. Lintot, 1744), 'Writ'.
[87] M 8 Ed. IV, 17, 24.
[88] See M 20 Hen. VI, 5, 15, T 20 Hen. VI, 33, 3 for the view, per Markham JCP that when a court erroneously awarded a writ to arrest X and the sheriff executed the writ, the sheriff is not liable 'because he took him by authority of the law'. In T 18 Ed. IV, 9, 18, Littleton JCP held likewise that a servant acting under the ostensible authority of a writ cannot be sued if the sheriff subsequently fails to return it: but the sheriff might be sued later.
[89] M 8 Ed. IV, 17, 24 at 17: 'car quant il fist l'arrest a un temps loialment il ne serra reason que par l'act de son master que il serra charge'.
[90] M 20 Hen. VII, 13, 23: 'car il ad execute son garrant accordant a l'ley, et donq n'est reason que l'act et defaut son maistre, a quel il n'est in ascun maner prive, serra prejudicial a luy'. For an analogous problem and the use of reason, see 36 Hen. VI, 7, 4 at 8 per Prisot CJCP.
[91] P 21 Hen. VII, 22, 14 at 23: 'chescun servant est tenu de faire le precept de son maistre in tout ce que est loial, et quand il ce fait loyalment, il n'est reason de luy punir, coment que il y ad un defaut in son maistre, mes plustost de punir le maistre in que le defaut est'; Brooke, *GA*, 'False Imprisonment', 12.
[92] See also M 14 Hen. VII, 1, 4 per Rede JKB.

## Liability and double payments of compensation for a single wrong

Another obvious occasion of imbalance, between the exaction of compensation and wrong-doing, would be if a defendant were compelled to compensate twice for a single injury or loss. Occasionally the courts forbid this form of imbalance by appealing to reason. In 1400 the plaintiffs were tenants-at-will and sued trespass against two defendants for cutting trees.[93] The question was whether the tenants could sue when there was a possibility that the freeholders of the same land could also bring trespass against the same defendants.[94] Counsel argues that the tenants cannot have their action 'for from this would follow that a man would be two times punished for one same trespass, which is against reason'. Markham JCP, though, was not persuaded. When someone assaults a servant, the servant could sue trespass and the master could sue for the injury to his servant 'whereby he loses his service [*per quod servitium amisit*]'.[95] So here: 'it is not unfitting [*inconvenient*] that a man will be punished twice for one and the same trespass'.[96]

The idea was more successful in 1409, when it was held that if a husband H and wife W sued jointly for disseisin, they could recover the land and damages in common.[97] However, if goods were taken also, as W could not own goods during H's life, H alone could recover for these. Hankford JCP agrees with counsel who argues in the course of discussion that if A takes B's goods and this is found by the assize, he will be adjudged a disseisor 'with force and arms' and imprisoned. Counsel continues: 'and if the party afterwards recovers by writ of trespass, he will again be imprisoned, which will be against reason' when the taking was inquired by the assize beforehand.

---

[93] M 2 Hen. IV, 12, 49: 'car de ceo ensueroit que home serra deux foits puny pur un mesme trespass, que est enconter reason'.

[94] For trespass and cutting trees see S. F. C. Milsom, 'Trespass from Henry III to Edward III', 74 *LQR* (1958) pp. 195, 407, 561, at pp. 201–2. If the incident here is the same as that in the previous case (M 2 Hen. IV, 11, 48) (but we are not told whether it was) the same defendants might also have been sued in assize of nuisance by the freeholders for disturbance of a right of way. At M 2 Hen. IV, 11, 48, the freeholders had unsuccessfully sued case against these defendants. As freeholders they had to bring assize of nuisance, not case: Fifoot, *Sources*, p. 93.

[95] See G. H. Jones, '*Per quod servitium amisit*', 74 *LQR* (1958) p. 39; *IELH*, pp. 382, 383.

[96] Srjt Fortescue at M 19 Hen. VI, 44, 94 at 45, says that in this sort of case 'the trespasser will be twice punished for one same trespass'.

[97] M 11 Hen. IV, 16, 38; Brooke, *GA*, 'Judgment', 20, 'Joinders in Action', 98.

Reason was also used to prohibit double procedural vexation. In 1460 P sued detinue of charters against D, counting for a box and charter.[98] D said that P had already sued detinue for the same box and charter and that whilst process continued on that occasion P had made this second claim. D argued, therefore, for abatement of P's second writ. The court agreed. As Danby JCP said, when D appeared and answered the first writ 'now it is reason that this [second] writ will abate'. Reason is used here in the conventional manner, as good sense, in a way similar to that discussed earlier in a case of 1423, to exclude the absurd result of two writs being employed for one and the same thing.[99] Prisot adds a further justification. By both writs D will be summoned and distrained, and twice lose issues, and 'it is not reason that one will be twice vexed for one same cause *simul et semel*'. He continues, 'for by both writs he will be summoned and afterwards distrained, and thus twice will lose issues, and this is not reason'. Generally, he says, 'it is as great damage to the defendant to lose damages twice, as to plead to two different writs, thus can he be as well vexed by process as by plea: wherefore it is reason that this writ will abate'.[100]

CONCLUSION

Certainly the late medieval lawyer turned to established practice. He was beginning to turn to the law 'in the books' in much the same way as the modern lawyer turns for his 'authority' to precedent, and the authoritative texts of statutes. Yet, in addition, the medieval lawyer habitually turned to the more fundamental authority of reason as a determinant in the disposing of ordinary cases.[101] His reason, however, possessed fewer meanings than that appearing in contemporary non-legal sources. The lawyers' reason does not possess the overtly

---

[98] M 39 Hen. VI, 27, 40; Brooke, *GA*, 'Brief', 255; Fitzherbert, *GA*, 'Brief', 142 (for the rest of the case, M 39 Hen. VI, 12, 16).
[99] Above, n. 28, M 3 Hen. VI, 14, 17.
[100] M 39 Hen. VI, 27, 40 at 28.
[101] For a perceptive view, where 'reason' and 'authority' (in today's sense) are distinguished, see J. H. Baker, *The Legal Profession and the Common Law: Historical Essays* (London, 1986) p. 467: 'They [the medieval lawyers] rely on "reason" rather than authority, on the inherent rightness of the reasoning rather than the impressiveness of the footnotes. They show lawyers thinking about the law as a coherent whole, rather than as a series of accidental and unconnected byproducts of litigation.' It is submitted in this chapter that 'reason' *is* their 'authority'.

## Judicial decisions and the authority of reason 131

moral texture of the theorists' reason. For the lawyer reason, the foundation of the common law, simply meant good sense and justice. The appeal to reason is used to exclude absurd and inconsistent results, and it is used to exclude unjust results. As good sense, it appears extensively in a great variety of cases and contexts: to prohibit senseless delays, to ensure that like cases are treated alike (and here there is a link with practical equity), for example. Sometimes its use is successful, sometimes it is not.

When used to exclude unjust results, reason is employed to prevent imbalances between loss and recovery and imbalances between wrong-doing and the payment of compensation or punishment. In these contexts, its meaning is close to the theorists' conception of justice, rendering to each his due. We are not supplied, of course, with a dictionary compiled by the practitioners telling us that their reason was the same thing as the theorists' justice. Yet it seems that, founded upon ideas of proportionality, reason does resemble justice in this, a conceptual aspect. It seems to be the case, therefore, that, like divine law, natural law or consent, reason is used by lawyers as a source of authority which is in terms abstract (though more mundane than, for example, natural law), existing as ideas of good sense and justice. It is used in this way certainly to dispose of every-day problems facing the courts. Sometimes, indeed, it is also used to justify the creation of new legal doctrine, to justify the preservation of established rules, and sometimes (as we saw in chapter 3) to invalidate local customary law. What was important to the common lawyer was that his law conformed to reason.

6

## CONSCIENCE IN THE COMMON LAW

Most commonly, in the study of legal history today, conscience is considered to have been the preserve of the late medieval chancellor. The function of the chancellor, and the principal basis of his jurisdiction, was to provide remedies for loss and wrong-doing as conscience required.[1] Conscience was not the concern of the common lawyer. Nor was it the basis of authority for the common law. It is the purpose of this chapter to suggest that conscience, representing a large moral idea, was of comparable importance outside the chancery. Certainly conscience formed the basic authority for the chancellor's jurisdiction. But, along with reason (as justice), divine law and natural law, conscience also was extensively employed as a moral authority fundamental to the common law. Tracing the usage of conscience outside chancery, in the decisions of common law judges and in parliamentary legislation, re-inforces the late medieval view of law in general as having a moral basis. Whereas reason may have been something of a technical idea of right understood largely by the common lawyers, conscience was a distinct moral force known directly, principally through the pulpit and the confessional,[2] by the ordinary citizen. Indeed, for the citizen, the psychological incentive to obey legislation was enhanced through promulgation in the counties when the authority of a statute was seen publicly to be built on conscience. Everyone knew that to offend one's conscience would imperil the soul.

[1] Holdsworth, I, p. 451; *HFCL*, pp. 86, 89–91; *IELH*, pp. 88, 89; W. P. Baildon, *Select Cases in Chancery: 1364–1471*, 10 Sel. Soc. (London, 1896) pp. xxix, xxx.
[2] G. R. Owst, *Literature and Pulpit in Medieval England* (Oxford 1961), pp. 185, 238, 459, 522, 571, 574, 593 (for conscience in preaching), and pp. 237–8, 373–4 (for confessions); for the early seventeenth century, see E. G. Moore and T. Briden, *Introduction to English Canon Law* (2nd edition, Oxford, 1985) p. 100 (for confessions). See also generally J. Martos, *Doors to the Sacred: A Historical Introduction to Sacraments in the Christian Church* (London, 1981) pp. 328–45.

## LINGUISTIC AND THEORETICAL BACKGROUND: SAINT GERMAN

Appearing in a variety of forms, *conscience* is a word which frequently appears in non-legal literature of the period. Derived from *conscientia* (*con*: with; *scire*: to know), the word implies a privity of knowledge with another. It signifies an inward knowledge or consciousness of right and wrong, a moral sense of the rightness or wrongness of one's actions: it was a knowledge which was shared, principally, by God.[3] As Fortescue explained in 1452 'conscience comes from *con* and *scioscis*. And so together they make "to know with God"; to wit: to know the will of God as near as one reasonably can'.[4]

In medieval thought conscience provided a standard topic of discussion focussing immediately upon the moral life of individuals.[5] Theorists divided conscience into two parts, *synderesis* and *conscientia*.[6] For Philip the Chancellor (d. 1236) *synderesis* affects a person's free choice by telling it to do good and refrain from evil.[7] For Aquinas *synderesis* is the natural disposition by which humans apprehend the basic principles of behaviour found in natural law.[8] When individuals applied *synderesis*, their knowledge of these first principles, to concrete situations, this he called *conscientia*. Conscience was an act of judgment about particular conduct which derives from a naturally given knowledge of the first principles of right and wrong, a knowledge identified with *synderesis*.[9] Aquinas went on to distinguish the consequent conscience, which determined the correctness of what has already been done, and the antecedent conscience, which determined the moral rightness of proposed actions.[10] When individuals offended

---

[3] *MED*, 'conscience', 2: 'The worm of conscience may agrise of wicked life, though it so privy be that no man woot thereof but God and me', *Canterbury Tales*, 'The physician's tale' (*c*. 1390), *The Works of Geoffrey Chaucer*, edited by F. N. Robinson (2nd edition, Oxford, 1957) p. 145 at p. 147, line 280.

[4] Statham, *Abridgement* (printed at Rouen *c*. 1490 and attributed to Nicholas Statham, d. 1472), edited by M. C. Klingelsmith (1915), 5lb, 'Conscience'; the citation given, though this does not appear in the YB, is M 31 Hen. VI.

[5] T. C. Potts, *Conscience in Medieval Philosophy* (Cambridge, 1980) p. 1; M. G. Baylor, *Conscience in Late Scholasticism and the Young Luther* (Leiden, 1977) pp. 27f.

[6] Potts, *Conscience in Medieval Philosophy*, p. 2; T. C. Potts, 'Conscience', *The Cambridge History of Later Medieval Philosophy*, edited by N. Kretzmann, A. Kenny and J. Pinborg (Cambridge, 1982) p. 687.

[7] Potts, *Conscience in Medieval Philosophy*, pp. 101-2.

[8] *Summa*, 1a, 79, 12; 1a, 2ae, 94, 1.

[9] *Summa*, 1a, 79, 13.    [10] Baylor, *Conscience in Late Scholasticism*, p. 42.

their consciences, then that was also an offence to the law of God.[11] For Aquinas, the conscience was binding on individuals, as people are bound by the commands of a ruler, by the threat of divine sanctions for disobedience.[12]

Neither Pecock nor Fortescue discusses conscience in any comparable depth. Pecock, however, did equate the 'law of conscience' with the 'law of reason', which he saw, of course, as coincident with divine law; and he did use conscience to deal with cases left uncovered by the positive law.[13] The implicit connection between the law of conscience and the law of God and reason in Pecock is similar to the view of Gabriel Biel (d. 1495) who argued that conscience was the 'messenger' of divine law: 'conscience is in truth like the command of the law', 'pronouncing some action to be done, or to have been done, or to be omitted, or to have been omitted'.[14]

Saint German, on the other hand, employed conscience extensively in his analysis of actual law in the *Dialogue*, between a doctor of divinity and a student of the common law, which concentrated on the relationship between conscience and the common law.[15] In his treatment of conscience, Saint German follows the traditional medieval outlook, using both *synderesis* and *conscientia*.[16] For Saint German conscience is not a subjective understanding of right and wrong but something determined by revelation and reason: the 'art of translating this general rule into specific rules of conduct to be followed in particular situations, is ... a form of applied knowledge'.[17]

---

[11] Potts, *Conscience in Medieval Philosophy*, p. 56.
[12] *Summa*, 1a, 2ae, 19, 5; Potts, *Conscience in Medieval Philosophy*, p. 134, and *Cambridge History of Later Medieval Philosophy*, pp. 700, 703.
[13] *Reule*, pp. 227, 229, 307 (also p. 166 for God allowing a person to act by conscience); see also *Folower*, pp. 141, 143.
[14] Baylor, *Conscience in Late Scholasticism*, pp. 92, 99, 104, 110 (a German theologian); for D'Ailly, see Oakley, p. 188.
[15] *IELH*, p. 164; *HFCL*, p. 89; J. A. Guy, *The Public Career of Sir Thomas More* (Brighton, 1980) pp. 43, 44; and J. A. Guy, *Christopher Saint German on Chancery and Statute*, 6 Sel. Soc. Supplementary Series (London, 1985) pp. 19f. For an excellent and succinct description of the various theories advanced about the *Dialogue*, see J. H. Baker, *Doctor and Student: Christopher Saint Germain*, The Legal Classics Library (Birmingham, Ala. 1988) pp. 3–5. Professor Baker prefers the idea that the *Dialogue* was 'but a first step in the legal debate about the ultimate authority and self-sufficiency of the law of England. Saint Germain set out to refute the notions that equity and conscience were outside or above the law ... English law had exactly the same foundations in divine law as the Canon Law': ibid., p. 20.
[16] *Dialogue*, pp. 81, 83, 87–95.   [17] Ibid., pp. xxvi, 81.

## Conscience in the common law 135

It is conscience which ought to mould the conclusions of the common law. With the common law this produces the customary fusion with morality: he often says that 'conscience in this case ought to be formed upon the law of the land' (as, he says, conscience must always be grounded upon some law).[18] For example, at common law and in conscience, if land is demised for a term of life with remainder to the heirs of S, then if the tenant for life dies within the lifetime of S, the land will revert to the donor (because this sort of remainder 'is void in law').[19] Saint German explains that 'practically the whole body of the law consists of cases of this sort'. And so, 'English lawyers hold that where there is any law duly had and ordained for the disposition of things real, personal or mixed, which the law is not contrary to the law of God or the law of reason, that then that law is binding upon all who are subject to it, in the tribunal of conscience.'[20] Although he conceded from time to time the possibility of dissonance between them,[21] for Saint German, broadly, there was agreement between the conclusions of common law and those of conscience.

Certainly, the theoretical influences on Saint German, in his discussions of conscience, were supplied principally by Aquinas, Gerson and D'Ailly.[22] And his adoption of conscience in the context of the common law, and its application to specific common law rules, may

---

[18] Ibid., p. 133 and pp. 163, 207; *IELH*, pp. 93, 94; and Guy, *The Public Career of Sir Thomas More*, p. 44.

[19] *Dialogue*, p. 129. And Simpson, *History of the Land Law*, pp. 95f.

[20] *Dialogue*, p. 129; see also pp. xxvii, 120–1 for the idea that a purported conveyance passes nothing because of some formal defect: the donee has no more right in conscience than in human law; for similar illustrations see pp. 139, 207. Aquinas had said that unjust law did not bind in conscience: *Summa*, 1a, 2ae, 96, 4.

[21] For example, see *Dialogue*, pp. 290–2. In *A Little Treatise Concerning Writs of Subpoena*, he also discusses whether a parliamentary statute (4 Hen. IV, c. 22 or c. 23), which was said to provide that judgments given in the king's courts could not be questioned in chancery, was against conscience: the student defends the statute as it imposed merely a procedural limitation on equitable relief in the interests of the legal value of certainty: see Guy, *Christopher Saint Germain on Chancery and Statute*, p. 117; see also Baker, *Doctor and Student: Christopher Saint Germain*, p. 17 (as Professor Baker points out, 'Saint Germain does not quote the statute correctly, because it does not expressly refer to the Chancery but to the *conseil du Roy*': ibid., p. 17, n. 58).

[22] R. J. Schoeck, 'Strategies of rhetoric in St. German's *Doctor and Student*', *The Political Context of Law*, Proceedings of the Seventh British Legal History Conference (London, 1987) p. 77 at p. 79. It has been argued that Saint German's reliance on Gerson was something of a departure from standard canonical learning: Z. Rueger, 'Gerson's concept of equity and Christopher St. German', 3 *History of Political Thought* (1982) pp. 1–30.

clearly have been influenced by canonist ideas and techniques, particularly the canonists' works of casuistry, written as manuals for confessors.[23] Yet it is not remarkable that a writer on the English common law should draw so heavily from theology and canon law. Fortescue, and of course Pecock, had done the same. This was the way of medieval jurists. It must also be remembered in the case of Saint German that he was writing for a lay audience, and much of his work concerned the extent of the spiritual jurisdiction of church courts as well as the chancellor's jurisdiction.[24] As a simple device of justification the moral focus was obvious and standard. However, at the same time, Saint German's use of conscience (along with divine law and reason, it must be remembered) reflects merely the concern, shared by Pecock and Fortescue, to stress the moral basis of law in general.

Perhaps more importantly, his use of conscience was an articulation of a more fundamental and a more practical influence. The connection of conscience and the common law, so evident in Saint German, frequently appears in the practical sphere of the common law. Time and time again practitioners, the legislators and the judges, employed conscience as the basis for their decisions. In Saint German we see something of a parallel with the techniques of Fortescue. As we saw in chapter 1, he wrapped up the contemporary English system of lawmaking, rooted predominantly in popular consent, in terms of populist theory: he articulated the practice of consent in populist language. So with Saint German. He wraps up the conclusions of the common law in terms of conscience, and in the theory of Aquinas, Gerson and D'Ailly, at a time when his practitioner predecessors and contemporaries, as a matter of habit, cast their decisions in terms of conscience. Conscience was part and parcel of the moral legitimation of legal decisions. It is to practical conscience in actual law, and it seems Saint German had some experience in the practical sphere

---

[23] *Dialogue*, pp. xxviii, xxx, xxxvii, xxxix; *HCLC*, pp. 377–81 for an excellent discussion of the fifteenth-century confession manuals, the *Summa Rosella* of Baptista Trovomara (or Trovamala), and the *Summa Angelica* of Angelus Carletus.

[24] For his place in the royal propaganda campaign, see *Dialogue*, pp. xiif., and D. S. Berkowitz, *Humanist Scholarship and Public Order* (Washington, 1984) pp. 19f. For the controversy with More, see J. W. Allen, *A History of Political Thought in the Sixteenth Century* (3rd edition, London, 1951) p. 165. For the contrary view that it is remarkable for a writer on the common law to draw on theology and canon law, see R. J. Schoeck, 'Strategies of rhetoric in St. German's *Doctor and Student*', p. 77 at p. 79.

(though it is doubtful whether he was 'prominent as a practitioner'),[25] that we shall now turn.

## CONSCIENCE AND SUBSTANTIVE LAW

In order to explain the usage of conscience in practice it is convenient to distinguish the different categories of decision-making in the process of law. There are, broadly, two levels. Conscience was often used upon the substantive level, being incorporated into the content or substance of law. Conscience was also used upon the formal level, with regard to the administration of law, as an authority to regulate the conduct of participants in the legal process as it relates to the decisions of judges, jurors and litigants. First, we shall examine those occasions in legislation and in the Year Books when practitioners build the content of their decisions on conscience.

### Legislative decisions

Reason was often used to connect the substance of law to abstract right. The common law was founded on reason. However, there was little use of reason *alone* to justify legislation. A device more commonly used by parliament, particularly in the latter half of our period (a time of course when chancery was asserting its jurisdiction in conscience), is the combination of reason *and* conscience, and the combination of *droit* and conscience.

An ordinance of 1455 described how officers in the exchequer received excessive gifts and fees from sheriffs and others (for entering pleas and judgments), in addition to their normal fees, 'against all reason and conscience'. The ordinance fixed the size of the extra fees and penalised those in receipt of more.[26] In 1489 hatmakers and capmakers sold caps at outrageous prices. Hats costing sixteen pence

---

[25] A useful discussion of the apparently minimal extent of Saint German's practical experience can be found in Baker, *Doctor and Student: Christopher Saint Germain*, pp. 6–9. Though it is suggested that 'there is no hard evidence of his engagement in legal practice', it must be remembered that he was trained as a 'practising' lawyer: ibid., pp. 3, 6.
[26] 33 Hen. VI, c. 3 (*contra omnem rationem et conscienciam*). The majority of statutes found were enacted after 1452: further research is necessary to identify a consistent usage before our period; see, for example, 20 Ed. III, c. 1 (1346) for legislation moved by conscience and created *sauver nostre conscience*.

138  *Fundamental authority in late medieval English law*

to make were sold for three shillings or forty pence, and caps made for the same sum at four or five shillings. Because the makers of these 'knew well that every man must occupy them, they will sell them at no easier price, to the great charge and damage of the king's subjects and against good reason and conscience'. The ordinance fixed the price, for hats twenty pence and for caps two shillings and eight pence, and penalised sales above.[27] Similarly, in 1495 it was enacted that those 'bound' to serve the king in time of rebellion shall not be attainted for treason subsequently. It was 'not reasonable but against all laws, reason and good conscience' for those under a duty to serve the king to be guilty later of treason.[28] It is interesting to note that the ordinance stated that any law made contrary to it was void: an explicit fetter on later parliaments.

The following enactments contain the combination of *droit*, reason and conscience. In 1452 parliament legislated against people compelling women, sometimes having been taken forcibly, to be bound in obligations (or to marry) involuntarily. The legislation asserts that those guilty of such conduct have been 'moved with insatiable covetousness, against all *droit*, humanity, integrity and good conscience'. Any agreements entered into in this way were declared void.[29] Here parliament attacks conduct which is described as against conscience, and so on. In legislation from 1439 it is the consequence of conduct, not the conduct itself, which is described as offensive to conscience. It is explained how individuals held offices by letters patent bearing a date *before* the king actually made the grant. The effect was to deprive previous occupiers of those offices prematurely. This was 'against all *droit*, good conscience and reason'. Consequently, warrants were to be sent to the chancellor (according to which an office would be granted) bearing the date of delivery to the chancellor and the letters patent must then bear that date (not an earlier one).[30] Here the conduct attacked is ante-dating grants untruthfully. It is the consequence of this conduct, the premature depriving of previous office-holders, which is contrary to *droit*, conscience and reason.

Finally, in 1483, legislation was passed to regulate those who empanelled jurors, in order to improve the quality of jurors. Grand juries had been procuring wrongful indictments and failing to indict

[27] 4 Hen. VII, c. 9; see also Holdsworth, IV, p. 377.
[28] 11 Hen. VII, c. 1.   [29] 31 Hen. VI, c. 9.   [30] 18 Hen. VI, c. 1.

Conscience in the common law 139

those who should have been indicted. This was *contrarie al comen droit et boon conscience*. So, officers could empanel only those of good name who held land of twenty shillings per annum. Any officer who returned insufficient jurors was penalised and any indictment by insufficient jurors was void.[31] It was not the jurors' conduct that was against conscience, but the consequence of their conduct, people being wrongfully indicted or not indicted when they should have been. This is dealt with obliquely via the direct treatment of the officers' actions.

On these occasions, and along with reason and *droit*, conscience functions as an expression of morality and operates as an integral part of the legislative decision. It is used to influence explicitly the substance of the legislation. Each statute or ordinance provides that on X facts Y result must occur. If A does B, then A will be penalised. The legislative arrangement represents a substantive rule. The common feature of the enactments is this. First, we meet the moral rule: with reason and *droit*, conscience prohibits conduct itself (charging excessive prices, compelling women to enter contracts involuntarily) or the consequence of particular conduct (the deprivation of office-holders, for example). Second, we meet the legal rule of the legislation itself which repeats or duplicates this ostensibly moral prohibition. The legal rule and the moral rule are made to coincide explicitly. The psychological impact for the citizen, at promulgation, is clear. The legislation has acquired its own justification publicly.

## Judicial decisions

The precise role of conscience in the common law courts is revealed not only when we analyse the method by which judges reasoned and justified their decisions, but also when we recognise the relationship between conscience and a conception of lawfulness. Like reason, the appeal to conscience was a mode of fundamental justification. Broadly, the cases can be classified into four types.

In the first class the courts determine the lawfulness of conduct in virtue of the fact that both law and conscience require the result. In general, executors were obliged to satisfy the debts of their testator,

---

[31] 1 Ric. III, c 4; see also Holdsworth, I, p. 80; for other occasions upon which conscience is used, see 39 Hen. VI, c, 1; 4 Hen. VII, c. 8; 7 Hen. VII, c. 15; 7 Hen. VII, c. 20; 11 Hen. VII, c. 34; 12 Hen. VII, c. 6.

140    *Fundamental authority in late medieval English law*

otherwise the testator's soul would be in peril.[32] To this end, executors could sell the testator's property to provide a fund from which to pay his debts.[33] In 1481 Choke JCP considered that an executor was entitled to buy the testator's property himself if no-one else wished to pay as much for it, 'for this stands with good conscience, and with our law'. There was no conflict of interest: the executor's act was neither unlawful nor unconscionable.[34]

To perpetuate a union prohibited by canon law was considered to be an offence to the conscience of a husband and wife, by reason, for instance, of a subsisting valid marriage.[35] In 1505 a wife wanted a divorce and certain defendants helped her escape to Westminster Abbey to procure it. Her husband sued trespass against the defendants and the question for the court was whether their conduct was lawful. The court held that it was. Fineux CJKB explained that the aim of their conduct was to effect a divorce so that the wife might (for whatever reason) relieve herself from an unconscionable union with the plaintiff, 'to be divorced in discharge of her conscience'. Such conduct was lawful.[36]

In the second class of case the judges use conscience *alone* to produce a particular outcome. For example, originally the common law did not recognise the validity of a will bequeathing freehold land.[37] So freeholders would convey land before death to a third party in trust instructing him to convey according to directions in a will prepared in advance.[38] It had not been settled whether such wills could be revoked, though wills bequeathing chattels could.[39] In 1452 Illingworth decided in the Exchequer Chamber that when A conveyed land to feoffees to convey to B his daughter, and B refused to be

---

[32] *HCLC*, p. 559; *Dialogue*, pp. 197, 200: executors bound by divine law to do what was profitable for the testator's soul.
[33] Holdsworth, III, p. 586.
[34] H 21 Ed, IV, 21, 2 at 22: 'car ce estoit ovesque bon conscience, et ovesque notre ley'. For a similar problem, see T 9 Ed. IV, 12, 4 and M 20 Hen. VII, 4, 14. The equation of conscience and law is also to be found in P 34 Hen. VI, 38, 9 at 39 per Danvers JCP; P 22 Ed. IV, 6, 18 per Hussey CJKB.
[35] R. H. Helmholz, *Marriage Litigation in Medieval England* (Cambridge, 1974) p. 63; see ibid., p. 63, n. 131 for a woman in 1455 marrying another mistakenly believing her husband to be dead 'but according to conscience' leaving him to return to the other.
[36] M 20 Hen. VII, 2, 4; Brooke, *GA*, 'Trespass', 440 (the case is cited in H 21 Hen. VII, 13, 17: but then conscience was not used).
[37] *HFCL*, pp. 118, 207; Holdsworth, IV, pp. 422, 438.
[38] Simpson, *History of the Land Law*, pp. 62, 135, 136, 138, 139.
[39] Holdsworth, III, p. 540.

governed by him, 'it is not conscience nor reason that she [B] should have the land', and A must therefore be able to change his will. Fortescue CJKB agreed: in conscience B should not have the land and A should be able to revoke, for, he said, 'we are not arguing the law in this case but the conscience'. There was no rule of the common law upon which the court could rely and both judges permitted changing the will because this was required by conscience.[40]

A similar use is found in 1465. P sought execution of judgment against A, B, C and D in debt, brought by separate writs on one obligation.[41] A and B defaulted: only C and D appeared. P then sued *capias ad satisfaciendum* against A *only*, as judgment debtor, to secure his arrest and imprisonment. A challenged this seeking a stay by *supersedeas* until either P relinquished execution against the others or else until C and D who appeared lost their challenge to execution of judgment. It was held that proceedings would be stayed in conscience. If execution was awarded against A, there may be further satisfaction for the same debt (imprisonment against the judgment debtor was treated as 'satisfaction')[42] in the event that execution was also had against the others. Moreover, there was general antipathy towards judging against absent defendants: the court was not going to award against a defaulting defendant when there was a possibility of executing judgment against one who appeared.[43] The text concludes that '*supersedeas* was awarded, *et haec causa consciencie*, for condemnation was by default'.

The third class of case was when the judges saw a tension between conscience and the requirements of the common law.[44] A case in point

---

[40] Statham, *Abridgement*, 51b: 'Conscience': the citation given, though this does not appear in the YB, is M 31 Hen. VI; see also Fitzherbert, *GA*, 'Sub Poena', 23, and *HCLC*, pp. 337–9. For the Roman Law idea of gifts being revoked for ingratitude, see *Inst.*, Bk II, Tit. VII, 2. Alternatively, the case may mean that the testator may revoke because the beneficiary has now no claim in conscience. See P 8 Ed. IV, 1, 1 at 2 per Markham for the idea that it is against reason and conscience to compel someone to do a thing of which he has no notice.

[41] M 4 Ed. IV, 38, 22, T 5 Ed. IV, 4, 9; Brooke, *GA*, 'Executions', 96; see *Dialogue*, p. 139 for an analogous problem.

[42] M 4 Ed. IV, 38, 22 at 39 per Danby JCP; see also *HCLC*, pp. 588, 590 and Holdsworth, VIII, p. 231.

[43] P&M, II, p. 590; *CH*, pp. 385, 386.

[44] The problem is similar to that of customary law offensive to reason (see above ch. 3). On the rare occasions when the judges treat conscience as superior to law (as below, n. 50), of course, the developing positivist thesis suffers a set back: the heteronomist thesis prevails.

was that of *Doige* in 1442. The facts are well known.[45] P agreed to buy land from D and paid the purchase price. D conveyed to C and so deceived P. P then sued a bill of deceit and D demurred arguing that P should have sued covenant. Judgment was eventually given for P. Covenant could not be sued as the agreement could not be performed since the land had already been conveyed. D had disabled herself from performance. Deceit was appropriate. For Fortescue CJKB and Newton CJCP P was entitled 'in conscience' to the land itself. But, of course, by *law* the land could not pass as it no longer belonged to D.[46] As Newton CJCP said: 'in conscience and in right the plaintiff ought to have the land, although the property cannot pass to him by law without livery of seisin'.[47] The conclusions of conscience and law opposed each other. In conscience P should have a conveyance of the land, but in law this could not be. Rather than choose between opposite requirements the judges admitted a compromise, the separate remedy of deceit, an action well established in the city of London.[48]

In a case from 1506, on the other hand, we see the judges clearly preferring to apply conscience over the requirements of law. By a statute of 1445 sheriffs could take nothing from a prisoner to pay for his comfort except sums fixed by the statute.[49] P argued that D, an under-sheriff, took more than the fixed sum. But D replies that by the usage of his county he was entitled to take this larger sum as a 'bar fee'. The court is faced with what appeared to be a conflict between local custom and parliamentary legislation. In the case the court concluded that the custom conformed to reason and conscience and as such allowed receipt of the larger sum. For the under-sheriff to be recompensed for his labour in providing for prisoners 'it is with reason and

---

[45] T 20 Hen. VI, 34, 4; Fifoot, *Sources*, p. 334; *HFCL*, pp. 328–32; *HCLC*, pp. 255–9.
[46] *HFCL*, p. 330. Fortescue CJKB says, therefore, at 35: 'car mesque le plaintiff ad droit d'aver cel terre en conscience, uncore la terre ne passe sans liverie'. For other occasions of land owed in conscience, see, for instance, T 12 Hen. VII, 19, 1 at 20 per Mordant; H 21 Hen. VII, 18, 30 at 19 per Tremaile.
[47] T 20 Hen. VI, 34, 4 at 34: 'en conscience et en droit le plaintiff doit aver la terre mesque le propriete ne peut passer en luy par ley sans liverie del seisin'. The suggestion that *Doige* was based on a 'principle of conscience' (94 Sel. Soc. (London, 1977) pp. 267, 293, 294) may be putting it a little too high: it was essentially a compromise between law and conscience.
[48] *HFCL*, p. 329.
[49] 23 Hen. VI, c. 9: twenty pence for a sheriff, four pence for an arresting bailiff, and so on. For other statutes regulating the office of sheriff, see Holdsworth, II, p. 448.

good conscience also that this sum be given to the under-sheriff'.[50] The case is unusual in that the judges relax the strict prohibitions of the statute in favour of custom rooted in reason and conscience.

In the fourth category of case, the judges apply the conclusions of law in preference to those of conscience. For example, in 1489 it was explained how A's executor B sued debt against C for forty marks on a bond made between A and C.[51] C confessed the debt. However, C alleges that he, and not B, was A's executor, and that D had borrowed one hundred pounds from A and D gave to A forty marks in usury for the loan. C also alleges that, as A's executor, he repaid the sum to D on A's behalf to relieve A's conscience from the usurious arrangement: 'in discharge of the conscience' of A. In other words, C argues that he is discharged from the debt by paying the same to D to extinguish the usurious pact between D and A, thereby saving A's conscience. On the other hand B argues that *by law* the debt still prevails unless there was written evidence that C had repaid it to A. It was settled law that a debtor under a bond had to show written evidence that he had been released from the obligation: the law regarded the bond as incontrovertible evidence of the debt.[52] C could not do so and the court found against him. It mattered not that he had acted for the good of A's conscience. The original bond still registered a debt.

There seems to be considerable evidence that the appeal to conscience, in parliamentary legislation and in judge-made common law, was extensively used in the fifteenth century. The appeal to conscience was often central to the justification in legislative and judicial decisions. It was used to shape the substance of rules. Conduct was permitted or prohibited in a legal form, in legislation or the judges' law, because it conformed to or was offensive to conscience. Hatmakers must not charge excessive sums for their hats because conscience forbad it. Individuals would be excused in trespass if they took another's wife, at her behest, to secure a divorce in discharge of her conscience. As with reason, by and large the practitioners were keen to produce the appearance of coincidence between their law and

[50] H 21 Hen. VII, 16, 28 at 17: 'et sic il este ove reason, et bon conscience auxy, que cel summe seroit donne al sousviconte'. The judges said they considered that this is what parliament would have intended.
[51] T 4 Hen. VII, 13, 12; Brooke, *GA*, 'Debt', 139. Usury was, of course, condemned generally: *HCLC*, pp. 510f.; Aquinas, *Summa*, 2a, 2ae, 78, 1–4.
[52] *HCLC*, pp. 99–101; *IELH*, pp. 87, 88, 270, 271. See also P 11 Hen. VI, 27, 7; P 22 Hen. VI, 52, 24; T 5 Ed. IV, 4, 10. The case is also interesting for the reference to *stricti iuris*.

conscience. This was happening outside the chancery, where similar ideas were at work.[53]

CONSCIENCE AND THE ADMINISTRATION OF LAW

Conscience was also used by the common lawyers on the formal level, in the context of the administration of law. It was used extensively as a means of governing the conduct of those who participated in the process of law. Conscience was often employed to regulate the way in which participants in the legal process, judges, jurors and litigants, made their respective decisions. All these must act according to conscience. Once again, the moral principle comes to the fore.

*The judicial conscience*

In *Manley's Case* (1544) Serjeant Saunders asserted that the office of a judge was to execute justice according to his conscience.[54] Some earlier theorists took the same view. Both Giraldus Cambrensis and Wyclif considered that a judge ought to decide according to his conscience as opposed to what had been alleged.[55] The chancellors too adjudged *secundum conscientiam et non allegata*, and in canonist jurisprudence conscience was crucial.[56] Though at common law a judge must decide not upon his private knowledge but upon matters

---

[53] Similar types of decisions can be found in chancery. For both law and conscience requiring a decision, see M 18 Ed. IV, 11, 4; for conscience alone, see T 11 Ed. IV, 8, 13, and H 4 Hen. VII, 4, 8; for conscience applied over the formalism of law, see T 9 Ed. IV, 14, 9; M 9 Ed. IV, 41, 26; T 14 Ed. IV, 6, 8; for rejection of argument from conscience, P 4 Ed. IV, 8, 9, and P 21 Ed. IV, 24, 10. See also L. O. Pike, 'Common law and conscience in the ancient court of chancery', volume II, *Select Essays in Anglo-American Legal History* (Boston, 1908) p. 722. Also, Port, *Notebook*, pp. 13, 14.

[54] 94 Sel. Soc. (London, 1977) p. 41, n. 5 (36 Hen. VIII, Gell, f.36).

[55] M. Radin, 'The conscience of the court', 48 *LQR* (1932) p. 506 at pp. 511, 517: a discussion mainly on the later civilians' and canonists' treatment of the problem of admitting evidence known (largely by the judge) to be false.

[56] T 9 Ed. IV, 14, 9. See for the canonists' use of conscience R. H. Helmholz, *Canon Law and the Law of England* (London, 1987) pp. 54, 109–110, 287, 337. For example, according to canon law a proctor had to dismiss a case when cause was shown during the hearing that it was one which he could no longer defend in good conscience: ibid., p. 54, n. 56 (Hostiensis, *Summa Aurea*, I tit. *de postulando* no. 5).

proved before him,[57] some issues lent themselves well to interference by the judge's conscience: such as the question of assessing damages. In 1405, for example, P sued conspiracy against D and others for conspiring to indict him for trespass.[58] The defendants defaulted and damages were assessed by the jury at forty pounds. P now demands judgment. Gascoigne JCP felt that the damages were too high and says that if P did not release the defendants from part of the damages, then the judges would decrease the damages as their conscience dictated, 'for as well as being able to increase damages, we have the power to abridge according to our conscience'.[59] P then released twenty pounds and had judgment for the remainder, 'and otherwise the court would have abridged by their conscience'.

In general terms trespass *vi et armis* was treated as a wrong to the plaintiff and an offence to the king. A writ of *capias* was available to make the defendant answer. If he was found guilty *capias* issued a second time to imprison him until he satisfied the plaintiff and until he paid a fine to the king.[60] In 1464 P successfully sued D in trespass *vi et armis* and *capias pro fine* was issued after judgment. But before D had actually satisfied either P or the king, the king commanded that process be discontinued and that D be released.[61] It is explained that the king did this so that D would not be vexed twice, as he had been convicted previously for re-disseisin. When P challenged the king's release, the judges appeared uncertain. They admitted that they must do as reason and conscience counsel them, and that it was not honourable for someone to give judgment one way in one term and another way in the next: 'and therefore we wish to give judgment now as we gave before, in like manner, and so it seems to us what reason and

[57] Holdsworth, IX, p. 136 and H 7 Ed. III, 4, 7. But for judicial notice see Thayer, *Evidence at the Common Law*, pp. 277f.; also see P 7 Hen. IV, 41, 5 per Gascoigne CJCP.
[58] M 7 Hen. IV, 31, 15; Brooke, *GA*, 'Abridgement', 23, 'Damages', 44.
[59] Ibid.: 'car auxibien come nous poiomus encreaser damages, nous avomus poyar d'abridger selonque nostre conscience'. For judges abridging excessive assessments of damages by juries, see G. O. Sayles, *Select Cases in the Court of King's Bench under Edward I*, 57 Sel. Soc. (London, 1938), p. cxi; C. T. Flower, *Introduction to the Curia Regis Rolls: 1199–1230*, 62 Sel. Soc. (London, 1943) pp. 473–9; H. Potter, *An Historical Introduction to English Law and its Institutions*, edited by A. K. R. Kiralfy (4th edition London, 1958) p. 330.
[60] It is uncertain for how long the *contra pacem* allegation carried a real penalty: see *HFCL*, pp. 293, 294.
[61] The case was very long drawn out: P 4 Ed. IV, 16, 28; 19, 36; T, 21, 4; M, 32, 14; H, 40, 1; For the many references in Brooke, *GA*, see 'Supersedeas', 26; 'Execution', 95; 'Escape', 33; 'Discontinuance of Process', 36; 'Parliament', 54; 'Amendment', 70.

146  *Fundamental authority in late medieval English law*

conscience is, and according to this we will act'.[62] Nevertheless they chose to postpone a definite decision until the return of Markham CJKB: 'and when he comes', they said, 'we will show the matter to him, and hear the reason and conscience of him'. On his arrival Markham CJKB gave effect to the king's commandment.[63]

## Conscience and jurors

The medieval jurists considered that the factual decision which jurors had to make, 'to declare upon their oaths whether the fact be such as one of the parties says' (Fortescue), was to be governed by conscience. According to Bracton, if the oath of a juror is foolish he should not be sued in attaint 'though in truth the matter is otherwise than he has sworn, because he swears according to conscience, since he does not go against his understanding'.[64] Any false verdict, however, intentionally so returned, would offend conscience. The juror, as an ordinary citizen, knew what that meant. As Saint German met conscience in the manuals written for confessors, so the citizen met conscience in his confession.[65] To offend conscience would imperil the soul.

The conscience of jurors was sometimes mentioned in legislation. A statute of 1414 fixed a property qualification for jurors because, it recites, there had been a predominance of false verdicts returned by those of a low income, 'whereby they offend their conscience the more'.[66] By legislation of 1433 dwellers of Southwark were prohibited from being jurors. This was because they were people 'without conscience and of an evil governance'. The statute explains how they had qualified as jurors through the acquisition of wealth by harbouring

[62] P 4 Ed. IV, 19, 36: 'Et pur ceo voillomus doner judgement a ore, sicome donomus a devant ore en autiel matter, et issint moy semle que reson et conscience est, et selonque ceo nous voillomus faire ove grace de Dieu durant le temps que nous sumus les justices del roy en cest place.'

[63] Ibid.: 'et oyer le reason et conscience de luy'. For further references to the judicial conscience, see M 8 Hen. VI, 4, 11 (the rest of the case is at 11, 28) per Martin JCP at 5; H 5 Hen. V, 6, 13 per Thirning CJCP. For conscience and lesser officers of government, see 9 Hen. V, St. I, c. 5; 18 Hen. VI, c. 14; 4 Ed. IV, c. 5; 12 Ed. IV, c. 9; 4 Hen. VII, c. 16. Fortescue too said 'it were also greatly against his [the king's] *consciens*, that ought to defend them and their goods, if he took from them their goods without lawful cause': *Governance*, c. 12.

[64] *De Legibus*, III, p. 337; and see p. 346. For Fortescue, see *De Laudibus*, cc. 25, 26; for the juror and conscience in Saint German, see *Dialogue*, p. 292.

[65] Above, nn. 2 and 23.

[66] 2 Hen. V, St. II, c. 3 ('ils le puis legierment offendent lour conscience'); see Holdsworth, IX, p. 186 for disqualification.

## Conscience in the common law 147

murderers, robbers and thieves, 'without pity, loyalty and good conscience'. In this event, as these persons without conscience 'may not by reason be intending to bear witness of truth there where truth shall be inquired', they were not to be permitted to sit on juries.[67] Only those possessed of good conscience could be jurors.

In general, if jurors 'found in their conscience' that what a plaintiff or a defendant said was true, they could 'give their verdict in conscience' and 'save their conscience'.[68] As Catesby JCP stated in 1482, if T had been summoned as a matter of fact, then 'they [the jurors] must find in their conscience that he was summoned'.[69] In a case of 1455, for instance, P (a prior) sued a writ of annuity against D (a prior) for rents.[70] P said he and his predecessors had been seised of the rents for time out of mind and showed a deed of 1242 reciting that a predecessor of D had granted an annual rent. He adds that the deed did not create the annuity: that existed before the deed which merely confirmed it. D urges the court to treat the deed as creating the annuity. Then the annuity would have arisen after time out of memory (fixed at 1189) and P's claim would be defeated.[71] Prisot CJCP says that if the jurors think there is no evidence denying P's claim then they must find that the annuity existed from time out of mind and find for P: in so doing 'they give a good verdict for their conscience'. He adds that P will 'do evil for [his] conscience' if he knows that the deed created the annuity, as D suggested, and makes the jurors perjure themselves. Danby JCP agrees. Without knowledge to the contrary (that the annuity existed for time out of mind) the jurors can give a good verdict 'according to their conscience'.[72]

In short, here the judges do not command the jurors to give a verdict according to their conscience. They merely point out, and in a sense advise, that when there is no evidence to the contrary the jurors

[67] 11 Hen. VI, c. 1. Also 8 Hen. VI, c. 29; and 1 Ed. IV, c. 2 for jurors having no conscience.
[68] M 6 Ed. IV, 5, 14 per Brian for the defendant; T 22 Ed. IV, 19, 45 per Starkey for the plaintiff. See also M 1 Hen. IV, 1, 1 ('le quel il esteme en sa conscience'), M 1 Hen. IV, 5, 10 per Thirning, and M 15 Hen. VII, 13, 1 per Frowicke. The same applied to witnesses: T 14 Hen. VII, 29, 4 per Vavasour: 'car l'evidence n'est pas done, mes per eux informe in leur conscience del droit'.
[69] T 1 Ed. V, 2, 3.
[70] P 34 Hen. VI, 36, 7; Brooke, *GA*, 'Prescription', 6; Fitzherbert, *GA*, 'Challenge' 43.
[71] For 'time out of mind', see Simpson, *History of the Land Law*, p. 109.
[72] P 34 Hen. VI, 36, 7 at 36, per Prisot: 'ils donent un bon verdit pur lour conscience'; 'en cest cas vous faits mal pur votre conscience de faire eux estre perjures'. For Danby, ibid., at 37: 'Verament en votre cas ils font bon verdit solonque lour conscience.'

can find for P with no offence to their consciences. To return a false verdict would imperil the soul. Rather than command obedience to conscience, the judges merely describe the consequence of an untrue verdict in terms of an offence to conscience. As we read in the *Paston Letters*, the courts could only 'desire them [jurors] to do as conscience wills, and to eschew perjury'.[73]

### Conscience and litigants in general

In the case of judges and jurors conscience governs decisions *after* the legal process has begun. Conscience also functions *before* the legal process begins. It regulates litigants in their decisions to bring legal action. In legislation of 1449, when individuals took goods by colour of distress, having no right or cause to take them, their conduct of feigning actions to aggrieve others was 'against law, reason and conscience'. All such takings were penalised as felonies.[74] Here the physical taking constituted the felony, but it was the false use of distress, the invention of disputes, which was offensive to law, reason and conscience. Legislation of 1455 dealt with wrongful suits brought in local courts against the abbot of Fountains, who had 'against conscience been grievously disturbed and vexed without cause by feigned actions'.[75] By covin between litigants and court officials the abbot would be required to wage and make his law personally in different actions on the same day in different courts. The abbot lost, therefore, 'where neither by law nor by conscience any cause of action was had'. As wager of law was a personal defence (defendants must wage in person as they alone knew the truth of their denial),[76] the statute permitted the abbot to wage law by attorney and allowed a monk and six others as compurgators. Court officials who failed to allow wager by attorney were penalised.[77]

Whilst both these statutes penalised particular conduct (taking by way of distress without cause, and disallowing wager by attorney), they contain implicitly the idea that bringing false legal action offends

---

[73] *Paston Letters* (London, 1904) vol. III, no. 438; edition by J. Gairdner (Westminster, 1900) no. 373.
[74] 28 Hen. VI, c. 4. For the general problem of unfounded litigation, see Holdsworth, II, pp. 457f., and 9 Hen. V, St. I, c. 1; 6 Hen. VI, c. 1; 1 Ric. II, c. 13.
[75] 33 Hen. VI, c. 6.
[76] *IELH*, p. 271; 62 Sel. Soc. (London, 1943) p. 123.
[77] The statute increased the penalty fixed by 15 Hen. VI, c. 7. The usual number of compurgators at common law was eleven: *IELH*, p. 64; *HCLC*, p. 138; for an exception to this, see Thayer, *Evidence at the Common Law*, p. 27.

conscience. This, via their actual prohibitions, they condemn. The conscience of litigants also appears sometimes in the Year Books. In 1433 D brought *praecipe quod reddat* against T who failed to appear. Seisin was granted to D and three days later T came to court showing how he had recovered the same land in an assise two years before. Moreover, T explained how he lived in Wales and had no knowledge of the writ and that the sheriff who purportedly served it was cousin to D. The sheriff had returned that T had been summoned: T said he had not. T's counsel argued that, without T's knowledge of the writ, 'it will be against conscience that the tenant will be disherited to lose his land by covin of the demandant and of the sheriff who is his cousin'.[78] No decision is reported: Babington CJCP chooses to speak with Hals JCP.[79]

Counsel's argument in this case can be contrasted with the use of conscience in a case of 1454. P sued debt on a bond against D for ten pounds. D says P has no action showing an indenture that if D on an agreed day paid twenty shillings to P the bond lost its effect.[80] If D did not pay the primary debt of twenty shillings, the penal sum of ten pounds fell due. D alleges that on the appointed day he offered the twenty shillings and P refused it: and ever since D has been ready to pay and offers the sum in court. Prisot CJCP asserts that as P refused the twenty shillings when offered he is barred forever. Serjeant Littleton, appearing for D, concedes that this is correct. But, recognising the larger sum under the penal bond was at stake, explains that D is still willing to pay the original debt of twenty shillings according to conscience, because he knows it is owed: 'but still from conscience we are ready to pay the twenty shillings because we know well that he is owed'.[81] The case ends with P arguing that D did not offer the original sum as agreed and D denying this. This is an interesting case. In it the litigant aspires to do more than the law requires: to do what conscience requires.[82]

In 1456 Moile JCP seems to influence the conscience of the party directly.[83] Trespass was brought against an infant. Counsel argues that the infant has no discretion to know malice and Moile JCP,

[78] P 11 Hen. VI, 42, 38: 'il serra encounter conscience que le tenant serra disherite a perdre sa terre per covin le demandant, et del viconte qui est son cosin'.
[79] M 19 Hen. VI, 3, 5: it seems the first judgment was annulled.
[80] H 33 Hen. VI, 2, 8; Fitzherbert, *GA*, 'Debt', 55; 'Estoppel', 52.
[81] Ibid.: 'mes uncore de conscience nous sumus prest a paier les xx s. pur ceo que nous conusons bien que il est deu'.
[82] For an analogous problem in Saint German, see *Dialogue*, p. 115.
[83] M 35 Hen. VI, 11, 18; Brooke, *GA*, 'Corone', 6.

150    Fundamental authority in late medieval English law

addressing the plaintiff replies: 'Can you find it in your conscience to declare against this infant of such tender age? I believe he does not know any malice, for he is not a person of much power, and this you can see for yourself.' Moile then lifted up the child in front of the court.[84]

### Conscience and litigants: wager of law

In debt or detinue, for example, a defendant could elect wager of law or trial by jury. Wager of law involved first the defendant pleading to the action, usually *non debet* or *non detinet*, and second offering to wage his law by which he would swear that he did not owe or detain. His oath-helpers would then testify to his credibility. If these swore successfully, the defendant won the action.[85] However, the defendant's choice of wager of law was subject to an essential condition. He must be satisfied that he would swear truthfully. A false swearing would constitute an offence to his conscience and imperil his soul.[86] A defendant ought to make his law only if he considered his denial to be true: if he swore falsely he offended his conscience. As Hankford JCP succinctly pointed out in 1410, 'he [the defendant] can have his law, if the truth be such in conscience'.[87]

Although wager of law lay at the option of the defendant, as an alternative to jury trial, it was by no means automatically chosen.[88] Sometimes there were discussions about the propriety of wager of law in which it might be debated whether the defendant should make his law because of the possibility of him swearing falsely. Again, it was the false oath that offended conscience. These discussions would revolve around whether wager of law would be 'bad and perilous in conscience', or whether the defendant could 'safely in conscience' make

---

[84] For further illustrations of conscience and the bringing of actions, including false suits, see H 7 Ed. IV, 29, 15; P 9 Ed. IV, 2, 5; P 10 Ed. IV, 9, 24; P 21 Ed. IV, 22, 3 per Brian CJCP; 17 Ed. IV, c. 2; 1 Ric. III, c. 6, and *Yorkshire Star Chamber Proceedings*, edited by W. Brown, The Yorkshire Archeological Society, Record Series, volume XLI, (Leeds, 1908) p. 10, *Re George Oglethorp* (1499).
[85] *IELH*, p. 64; J. B. Thayer, *Evidence at the Common Law*, pp. 24f; *HFCL*, pp. 39, 86; 62 Sel. Soc. (London, 1943) pp. 123f.
[86] Pecock, *Reule*, p. 166: 'Holy writ says, "whoever does against conscience, he buildeth helward".'
[87] H 11 Hen. IV, 50, 27: 'il puit aver son ley, si le verity soit tiel en conscience'; Brooke, *GA*, 'Detinue of Charters', 20.
[88] *HCLC*, p. 139 (for instance, H 33 Hen. VI, 7, 23).

his oath.[89] It is important to remember, moreover, that these near-casuistic debates took place at a time when there was no offence of perjury: perjury was merely a spiritual offence with no temporal sanction.[90] Its spiritual sanction was, of course, that anyone swearing falsely would imperil his soul.[91]

Most commonly the courts simply declare upon the advisability of wager of law by referring to the likelihood of an offence to the conscience by false swearing. If the court considered that there may be an offence to conscience, it would *advise* that the defendant should not make his law, though the choice ultimately was his. If there were no likelihood of an offence to conscience, it would *advise* that he could safely make his law. For example, if P bailed a horse to D and counted on the bailment of an ox, D would then plead that he did not detain in the manner and form of P's count. Thus D could safely wage on the ground that the action had nothing to do with the *thing* which is the subject of the true bailment. Because of the formal misstatement D can swear truthfully that he did not detain as alleged.[92] There is no offence to his conscience.

An interesting development of this is found in a case of 1442 when the court considered a misstatement, in the plaintiff's count, of the *place* in which the bailment occurred. P sued detinue for two bonds alleging the bailment was made in Middlesex. D replies that the bailment was made to him not by P alone but by P and T upon certain conditions which he specified. T comes to court showing the delivery was made by P and T but on a condition different from the one alleged by P and in London rather than Middlesex. The question is whether D could safely wage his law. Counsel argues that D ought not to wage in the light of T's explanation. It is true that P's bonds have been detained, 'thus it seems that it will be bad and perilous in conscience to

---

[89] See P 21 Hen. VI, 35, 2 at 35 per Markham; P 38 Hen. VI, 29, 12 at 30 per Ashton JCP; P 8 Ed. IV, 1, 1 at 2 per Nedham JCP; M 2 Ric. III, 14, 39 per Catesby JCP. See generally, *HFCL*, p. 86. L. A. Knafla, 'Conscience in the English common law tradition', 26 *University of Toronto Law Journal* (1976) p. 1 notes a handful of YB cases on this matter, but fails to explain precisely the extent and role of conscience in wager of law.
[90] *HCLC*, p. 138.
[91] See 18 Sel. Soc. (London, 1904) p. 52, Cinque Ports Custumal, c. 37: 'The judge shall exort him or them that they swear, to take heed to themselves what danger it is to foreswear himself willingly, to forsake Almighty God and their baptisms and all this good work and their part in heaven and give themselves to the devil to hell.' See also *Dialogue*, p. 232.
[92] S. F. C. Milsom, 'The sale of goods in the fifteenth century', 77 *LQR* (1961) p. 257 at pp. 267, 268.

put this in issue'.[93] In other words, as T has explained that D did *in fact* detain, though not in the form and place actually counted, D could not in conscience deny the truth of detaining, which he would ordinarily do by the general plea *non detinet*. Newton CJCP was not persuaded. If the bailment was made in London, then D did not detain in the manner and form that P alleged. Thus, D can 'well and lawfully' wage his law. Once more, D is simply denying that the action has anything to do with the actual bailment. Newton directs that D can safely wage, if he so elects, for in so doing he does not untruthfully reply to P's actual allegation and misstatement.[94] There was no offence to his conscience.

Effectively wager of law was available, as Brian CJCP observed in 1485, only to one who knew the facts involved in the issue.[95] If a defendant was not certain of the facts about which he swore, he may make an oath which is in actual fact untrue: that would offend his conscience and imperil his soul.[96] In 1482, when a defendant consulted the court on whether he could wage his law, Brian said this. If P alleges that D detains a white horse, then, if he actually detains a red horse, D can in conscience wage his law, 'for it is true in fact that he does not detain any horse of such colour'.[97] In the case of 1442, though, it was the misstatement of the place of bailment which was sufficient for a successful denial by way of *modo et forma*.[98] However, in the 1482 case Brian CJCP decides that in detinue for a chain a defendant could *well with conscience* wage his law if the count misstated the *weight* of the chain, but not if it misstated the *value* of the chain. Weight, like place and colour, was knowable with certainty, as raw fact: value was not. Accordingly, Brian offers the following statement: if P counts for a horse which he alleges D detains as worth twenty pounds, although in reality it is worth only twenty pence, 'still he is not able by conscience to wage his law, for he cannot know the value of the horse'.[99] Once more, the judge is concerned to prevent false swearing and an offence to conscience. This hypothetical in-

[93] P 21 Hen VI, 35, 2 at 35 per Markham: 'issint semble que il serra malveis et perilous en conscience de mettre ce en issu'; Brooke, *GA*, 'Ley Gager', 48.
[94] See Milsom, 'The sale of goods', pp. 267, n. 63, 268, n. 71; *HFCL*, pp. 257, 354.
[95] P 1 Hen. VII, 25, 18; Milsom, 'The sale of goods', p. 262, n. 28.
[96] *HCLC*, p. 138.
[97] P 22 Ed. IV, 2, 8; Brooke, *GA*, 'Ley Gager', 78.
[98] Above, n, 94.
[99] P 22 Ed. IV, 2, 8: 'uncore il ne poit per conscience gager son ley, car il ne poit value le chival'. For the conscience of witnesses in canon law, see Berman, *Law and Revolution*, pp. 251, 253.

stance anticipates a number of cases in the latter half of the sixteenth century in which defendants were examined or sought guidance as to whether it was 'safe in conscience' for them to wage their law.[100]

It is crucial to note that these judicial advices against wager of law, because there may be an offence to conscience, were actually without legal sanction; they were unenforceable at law. Ultimately, even if there was advice to the contrary, the choice to wage lay with the defendant. He was legally free to ignore the advice even when this may possibly imperil his soul. In any event, the principle is implicit. Defendants when using wager of law must swear according to their conscience. Decisions about the propriety of wager of law, therefore, are frequently dependent upon whether there is an offence to conscience. In short, advice about wager of law is determined by the effect upon the conscience of the defendant, in conformity with which they are encouraged to act.

## CONCLUSION

The appeal to conscience was not confined to the chancery. The common-law judge knew as much about conscience as the chancellor. Everybody did: the parliamentary legislator and the ordinary citizen. And, like the chancellor, the common law judge would often explicitly weave his decisions around the requirements of conscience. So did the makers of statute. Conscience was used to mould the substance of rules: rules prohibited this or that because conscience prohibited it. The common-law judge would also encourage the litigants before him and the jurors in his court to decide in the same way. Indeed, the common-law judge himself must act according to his conscience. It seems to be the case that in the substantive setting an idea of public conscience is used, and the idea of a private conscience is used on the formal level.

The appeal to conscience, then, was an extensively used mode of justification in the courts of common law. In general, the justification, as part of legal reasoning in the Year Books, was dominated at common law both by the appeal to reason and the appeal to conscience. The appeal to reason, perhaps slightly more prevalent than that to conscience, signified a mundane idea of good sense and justice, whereas the appeal to conscience was more distinctly moral. When

[100] J. H. Baker, 'New light on *Slade's Case*', 29 *CLJ* (1971) p. 213 at p. 230, n. 93.

Saint German discusses the conclusions of the common law in terms of conscience, he may be so doing under the influence of Aquinas, Gerson, D'Ailly, the canonists and the emergent chancery jurisdiction. But in essence he was merely articulating a tradition firmly rooted outside chancery in the common law. For the practitioner the common law was shaped, along with reason, by conscience. Casuistic debates about conscience in the chancery found a direct parallel in the common lawyers' arguments about the requirements of conscience in the building of substantive rules and the regulation of such things as wager of law. In the realm of secular law, conscience was not the preserve of the chancellor.

7

MISCHIEF AND INCONVENIENCE

With the autonomist thesis, which separates law and morality, the essence of a judicial decision is simply its conformity with law. This formalism, typified in the use of *rigor iuris* and the rejection of argument from reason or conscience, might produce a particular abstract wrong or injustice. But what counted was law not morality. As decisions repugnant to law are excluded in positivism, so an idea of coherence emerges. Successive decisions will make sense together when they are not repugnant to each other. By using *inconvenience* the medieval common lawyer sought to exclude inconsistent results. In contrast, *mischief* related to abstract right and wrong, but a narrower and less moral idea than that of reason or conscience. At common law mischief specifically meant being without redress or procedural vexation: these too the practitioner sought to prevent. Whereas inconvenience concerned established practice and avoiding inconsistency, mischief concerned right and wrong. In cases where different arguments from mischief and inconvenience occur together, and in competition, we find a confrontation between two opposing claims. The mischief argument excludes injustice to an individual; the inconvenience argument excludes inconsistency, to maintain consistency in the application of law. The judicial preference, at this time, was the positivist value of excluding inconsistency, not upsetting established practice, at the expense of allowing injustice: 'a mischief will be suffered sooner than an inconvenience'. The two views of law, the voluntarist thesis and the moralist thesis, usually existed on separate levels. In the mischief and inconvenience cases they clashed.

MISCHIEF AS A WRONG: A NARROW CONCEPT

In contemporary non-legal sources *mischief* was used to signify all sorts of ideas: misfortune, trouble, the effect of sin, disease, poverty, and disaster.[1] It was also used to denote some form of harm, injury or evil considered to be the work of an individual or as due to a particular cause.[2] In the legal sources, frequently mischief functioned as the *sine qua non* of legislation. Statutes and ordinances would be designed expressly to eradicate mischief. The legislators' use of mischief was in some respects close to the more general idea of wrong appearing in non-legal literature. Certainly in legislation mischief signifies an idea of wrong, but often taking a variety of forms.

Sometimes it is used without any explicitly moral connotation, simply expressing a mundane form of wrong constituted by doing harm. Legislation of 1423 recites how 'many mischiefs now of late have been done in destruction of people, ships and merchandises and of fry of fish, by weirs, kydells and trunks [on the Thames] being harmful [*esteantz noesantz*]'. The ordinance authorises justices of the peace to enquire into the obstructions and initiate proceedings against those offenders (*trespassers*) who were responsible.[3] Sometimes it is used with moral connotations. Harm would be called a mischief which was also forbidden by God. Parliament had addressed itself to the same problem of obstructions on rivers in 1402. On this occasion the harming of people, goods and fish was described as a mischief against reason and 'contrary to the pleasure of God'.[4] Occasionally mischief signified wrongs already designated as such by

---

[1] *MED*: 'mischief': for example, Wyclif, 'Jesus Christ ... gave his heart blood ... to bring us out of mischief of sin and pains', *The Lay Folks' Catechism* (c. 1400), edited by T. F. Simmons and H. E. Nolloth, Early English Text Society, Original Series, 118 (London, 1901) p. 73, line 1105.
[2] 'This false thief has done this lady yet a more myschef', 'The legend of good women' (Philomela) (c. 1385), *The Works of Geoffrey Chaucer*, edited by F. N. Robinson (2nd edition, Oxford, 1957) p. 480 at p. 514, lines 2330/1; 'Great myscheyf have I do, and much yll as to robbe and slea', *Roberte the Devyll* (1480), a metrical romance, found in W. C. Hazlitt, *Remains of Early Popular Poetry in England* (1864) p. 31; 'Thou shall do no myschief, that is to say, in avoutrie [adultery] nor in fornication', *The Epistle of Othea to Hector* (c. 1440), edited by G. F. Warner, Roxburghe Club Publications, 141 (London, 1904) p. 52, line 31. For mischief in Pecock, in a spiritual context, *Folower*, p. 139.
[3] 2 Hen. VI, c. 12. The statute is one of several providing for free passage on rivers at this time: 45 Ed. III, c. 2; 17 Ric. II, c. 9; 1 Hen. IV, c. 12.
[4] 4 Hen. IV, c. 11.

## Mischief and inconvenience

law: legal wrongs, such as disseisin or murder,[5] wrongs for which law was created to suppress. In relation to robbery, counterfeiting and other offences, for example, 'for the repressing and avoiding of the said mischiefs, sufficient laws and ordinances be made, by the authority of many and divers parliaments held within this realm'.[6] Sometimes mischief denoted both a legal and a moral wrong. In 1496 legislation described the 'mischief' of wilful premeditated murder as 'by the laws of God and of natural reason forbidden'.[7]

Whereas mischief in non-legal sources and in legislation sometimes signified a large idea of moral wrong, akin to the practitioners' idea of divine law or that of conscience, for the common lawyer mischief was more specific, less moral and more mundane. In the main, when used in the common law courts, mischief related to being without redress and procedural vexation.

### Mischief as being without redress

One of the requirements of reason was the idea that loss and injury must be recompensed, and occasionally being left without a remedy was treated as 'against reason'.[8] More usually mischief was used to denote the wrongful condition of a party being without redress when this was legally or justly due. The idea was presented in two ways: being without an action and being without a remedy. As Fortescue CJKB observed in 1453, '[t]hus mischief would ensue on another mischief that I will not have the effect of my suit; and thus more mischiefs would follow from this'.[9] The idea appears in Littleton's *Tenures*. If a disseisor died and his heir entered the land, the disseisee's right of entry disappeared. He then had to sue a writ of entry

---

[5] 1 Hen. IV, c. 8; 4 Hen. VII, c. 12. The word was used in similar ways in the courts: P 1 Hen. V, 4, 4; P 9 Hen. VI, 2, 6 at 3 per Srjt Rolf; M 35 Hen. VI, 18, 27 per Moile JCP for covin and fraud as mischiefs; M 37 Hen. VI, 4, 6 (failure to repair a bridge is damage and a mischief); M 1 Ed. IV, 1, 5 at 2 per Srjt Littleton (disseisins).
[6] 4 Hen. VII, c. 12. For legislation conceived to be created to erase mischief *per se*: M 10 Hen. VI, 15, 51 per Martin JCP; P 22 Hen. VI, 52, 20 per Newton; M 31 Hen. VI, 11, 8 per Fortescue CJKB; M 37 Hen. VI, 1, 2 per Prisot JCP. See also 2 Hen. IV, c. 9; 7 Hen. IV, cc. 8, 17; 18 Hen. VI, c. 6. For statute erasing a mischief at common law see Port, *Notebook*, p. 116.
[7] 12 Hen. VII, c. 7. The statute deprived Grame of benefit of clergy (in petty treason): above ch. 3, n. 41. For similar statutes see Holdsworth, III, pp. 301, 315.
[8] Above, ch. 5, n. 58.
[9] M 32 Hen. VI, 10, 17 at 10B; see also M 35 Hen. VI, 25, 33 at 29 per Fortescue CJKB: if A steals B's goods and A sells them in open market to C, then B can upset the sale otherwise he 'serra sans remedy; le quel serra grand mischief'.

158  Fundamental authority in late medieval English law

*sur disseisin* against the heir.[10] The disseisee need not resort to this, however, if he could not actually enter, by making continual claim to the land, by going to it and professing the claim once a year as long as the disseisor lived: by so doing he saved his right of entry beyond the disseisor's death.[11] Littleton states that continual claim was to be enjoyed by a sick person, for instance, otherwise, by not being able to go to the land by virtue of his infirmity, he suffers the mischief of being unable to make the claim.[12]

The same idea was employed in 1409 when Serjeant Norton argued against abatement of a writ. The writ recited an assignment by W alone whereas the fine put before the court recorded an assignment by both W and R. For the plaintiff Norton argued that 'if we will be without action, we are at great mischief'. The court abated the writ.[13] In 1466 P sued trespass against D for taking his goods. P said they were due to him as tithes.[14] D replied that he acted as servant to a parson, to whom the goods were due as tithes, and therefore the court had no jurisdiction to try this essentially spiritual matter. It ought to be resolved in the church courts.[15] For P, Serjeant Young argued that if the court did not have jurisdiction, 'then the plaintiff would be at great mischief', because trespass could not be sued in the church courts. The judges agreed with Young. P could not sue trespass in a spiritual court as, for that, D could have prohibition.[16]

When an alternative method of redress was available, the practitioners considered that there was no mischief. As June JCP said in 1429, 'one is not at mischief where he has a clear remedy by the common law or by the statute'.[17] For instance, to establish that a debt

[10] *Tenures*, Bk III, c. 6, s. 385.
[11] Ibid., Bk III, c. 7, ss. 414, 417, 418; Holdsworth, II, p. 585, VII, p. 21.
[12] *Tenures*, Bk III, c. 7, s. 434.
[13] M 11 Hen. IV, 1, 1: 'si nous serromus sans action, nous sumus a grand mischief'; Brooke, *GA*, 'Waste', 64; 'Brief', 420. Thirning CJCP and Hankford JCP disagreed: actions must be brought according to the record.
[14] M 6 Ed. IV, 3, 7.
[15] The allegation was common to oust the royal court: *CH*, p. 492, and H 20 Hen. VI, 17, 8; M 35 Hen. VI, 39, 47.
[16] 'si cest court n'averoit jurisdiction, donques le plaintiff serroit a grand mischief, par ceo que il ne poit aver action envers luy en court spirituel'. For prohibition, 94 Sel. Soc. (London, 1977) p. 66; *IELH*, p. 112. See too 13 Ed. I (*Circumspecte Agatis*); 9 Ed. II, c. 1.
[17] M 8 Hen. VI, 12, 30: 'le party pur ceo n'est a mischief: car on n'est a mischief, ou il ad overt remedy par le common ley, ou par le statut'. For examples of the idea of no mischief when a remedy is available, see M 9 Hen. VI, 44, 24 per Martin JCP; M 3 Ed. IV, 15, 10 per Nedham JCP; P 5 Ed. IV, 3, 26 per Heidon; T 18 Ed. IV, 10, 25 per Littleton JCP (dissenting).

## Mischief and inconvenience 159

*sur obligation* was extinguished, the defendant must adduce written evidence.[18] In 1404 P sued debt on a bond and D confessed the debt but said that J had paid the sum on his behalf. There was no destruction of the bond or written acquittance. Yet, D also said that P took back the same bond *vi et armis* and he relies on this to escape liability.[19] The court finds against D. As the debt was confessed it would be a mischief to P 'if one would be received to avoid such obligation by such averment by nude parol'. The common law requirement prevailed. However, the court explained that there was 'no mischief to the defendant, in this case if his plea is true', as he could sue trespass *vi et armis* on the forceful re-taking of the bond.[20]

In a case from 1456 counsel argued successfully that being without a remedy was a mischief.[21] Losing land in a *praecipe quod reddat* brought by T, P sued deceit against T and the sheriff to whom the *praecipe* had been directed. P claims the sheriff never served the writ and to establish this proposes an examination of the summoners (who allegedly served it).[22] Of the four summoners, three are dead and one appeared. T's counsel argued that this summoner should not be examined as his story may differ from the other three had they lived. Serjeant Wangford, for P, replied that if the summoner were not examined 'the plaintiff will be at great mischief, and the other party to no mischief, for if he were not examined the plaintiff will be without remedy for his land; the which will be great mischief, inasmuch as the recovery may have been wrongful, perhaps without good title'.[23] The court agreed and when the summoner was examined he said that the writ was not served by him.[24]

### Procedural vexation

Whereas in legislation mischief concerned the direct infliction of harm by one party upon another, in terms of substantive wrongs such as

[18] *HCLC*, pp. 99–101; P 11 Hen. VI, 27, 7; P 22 Hen. VI, 52, 24; T 5 Ed. IV, 4, 10.
[19] The facts are close to those of *Donne* v. *Cornewall* (1485) P 1 Hen. VII, 14, 2.
[20] H 5 Hen. IV, 2, 6.
[21] H 35 Hen. VI, 46, 11.
[22] Examination of summoners is discussed in *Fleta*, edited by G. O. Sayles, 99 Sel. Soc. (London, 1983) volume IV, Bk V, c. 3, p. 6, and Bk VI, c. 6, p. 118; and see *CH*, p. 384.
[23] H 35 Hen. VI, 46, 11 at 47: 'le plaintiff serra a grand mischief, et l'auter partie a nul mischief : car si ils ne serront examines, le plaintiff serra sans remedy pur sa terre; le quel sera grand mischief, entant que le recoverie fuit per tort, peraventure sans bon title'.
[24] Fitzherbert, *GA*, 'Deceit', 18; Brooke, *GA*, 'Deceit', 7.

160  *Fundamental authority in late medieval English law*

robbery or murder, mischief was also used in the context of procedural wrongs: vexation which resulted from invoking the legal process. The usage appears throughout the period. In 1430 Paston JCP abated a second writ for the same land because having 'to come and answer twice for one acre of land by two original writs' was 'a great mischief'.[25] Similarly, in 1460, when P sued successively two writs of detinue for the same box and charters, Prisot CJCP considered that, even if the first writ is no longer pending, 'if two separate writs are purchased for one same thing, then he [D] will lose issues on the one writ and on the other, and thus always until he appears, or be arrested twice by *capias*, then he is at mischief by vexation of the process, as he will be by the plaintiff, and all is one same mischief'.[26]

Indeed, in 1462 the processes of distress and arrest themselves, when used to secure the appearance of a defendant *properly* named in a writ, were described by Choke and Nedham JJCP in terms of mischief.[27] Here the defendant *Wir*bolt sought to abate a writ of debt by pleading misnomer because in it he had been misnamed as *Wri*bolt. Process had been carried out against *Wri*bolt: the writ had been returned *non est inventus*. The defendant had come voluntarily to court and the question was whether he could plead misnomer. Adhering to earlier precedents,[28] it was held that he could not. Only those who came in by compulsion could so plead. Thus, it was explained that if an individual who is misnamed in the writ appears voluntarily, he is 'not to mischief nor to any loss, for he is not to lose here goods on attachment, nor issues on distress, nor will he be put in prison'.

In broad terms, being subject generally to the temporal law, all the ordinary civil actions could be brought against a cleric. However, when sued it was difficult to employ the usual process to compel the cleric's appearance at court in the same way as a member of the laity. He may have no lay fee by which he could be distrained, nor could he be arrested by the king's officer, the sheriff. Instead, therefore, the secular courts would compel appearance by a writ of *venire facias*

---

[25] M 9 Hen. VI, 50, 34. For a similar use, M 19 Hen. VI, 3, 6 per Ascough JCP (continued from H 8 Hen. VI, 30, 26).

[26] M 39 Hen. VI, 12, 16: 'il est a mischief par le vexation del proces'; Brooke, *GA*, 'Brief', 255 (for the rest of the case, M 39 Hen. VI, 27, 40).

[27] M 3 Ed. IV, 15, 10; Brooke, *GA*, 'Misnomer', 54. On distress and arrest, see *CH*, p. 385.

[28] Per Choke JCP at 16, explaining that it had been adjudged 'two or three times' that D could not plead this. For general discussions: M 19 Hen. VI, 43, 89; H 19 Hen. VI, 58, 23; and H 21 Ed. IV, 78, 14 when the plea was allowed.

*Mischief and inconvenience* 161

*clericum* directing the bishop of the diocese to cause the clerk to come.[29] In 1471, a writ of annuity was sued against D who, the sheriff returned, was a cleric without lay fee.[30] As he could not be compelled to appear by distress,[31] *venire facias clericum* was needed. But, to avoid this process, the cleric appeared voluntarily. Both Brian JCP and Choke CJCP decide that he will be received. The latter explains that the extraordinary process involving the bishop had effectively begun upon the sheriff's return of 'no lay fee', 'and it will be a mischief to the defendant if he will not be received to appear, for here *venire facias clericum* will issue, by which the profits of his church will be sequestered, etc., this will be a mischief to him'. So, 'where a man is vexed in his goods, he will be received to appear as where he is vexed in his body'.[32] Littleton JCP takes a harder line, concentrating on the non-functioning of the ordinary process of attachment and arrest. As a matter of general principle 'where a man is not at mischief of corporal penance nor of a judgment to be given against him, he ought not appear if he has no day [in court] by the return of the sheriff'.[33]

INCONVENIENCE AND THE CONCEPT OF CONSISTENCY

The focal point of the usage of mischief is harm done to the individual. It is the individual who suffers the mischiefs of being without redress and procedural vexation. These wrongs the practitioners sought to prevent. In comparison, when they employ *inconvenience*, the common lawyers concentrate in the main not upon harm to the individual but harm to the law and established practice. In law French the word had a technical meaning (quite different from today's 'inconvenient' as 'awkward' or 'inopportune') and it was used time and time again to import an idea of consistency. The common lawyers eschewed inconvenient, unfitting or inconsistent results.

'Inconvenience', and its various forms, is used in this way in

[29] P&M, I, pp. 440, 441; Bracton, *De Legibus*, ff. 442b, 443.
[30] H 11 Ed. IV, 9, 1; Brooke, *GA*, 'Averment Conter Return', 21.
[31] Enever, *History of Distress*, p. 68; see also H 48 Ed. III, 1, 1 where D was allowed to appear to save himself from *capias*.
[32] '[E]t serra mischief al defendant s'il ne serra resceive d'apper', car icy *venire facias clericum* issera, par quel les profits de son esglise serront sequestres, etc., ce serra mischief a luy.'
[33] A delay without reasonable cause also constituted a mischief: M 10 Hen. VI, 17, 58 at 18 per Martin and Cottesmore; P 4 Ed. IV, 14, 25 at 15 per Srjts Brian and Littleton. Compare M 35 Hen. VI, 24, 31 at 25 where Prisot CJCP distinguishes mischief and delay.

162  *Fundamental authority in late medieval English law*

non-legal literature of the period. From the Latin *convenientia*,[34] 'convenience' signifies fitting or meeting together, agreement and conformity.[35] 'Inconvenience' means want of agreement, incongruity, inconsistency or contradiction.[36] In its adjectival form, 'inconvenient', it signifies simply not agreeing or unfitting, discordant or inconsistent, and sometimes unsuitable or inappropriate.[37] It is important to note, however, that in non-legal sources 'convenient' also meant morally suitable,[38] and 'inconvenience' moral unsuitableness or impropriety, and sometimes harm or trouble.[39] Occasionally 'inconvenient' meant morally improper.[40] It was not normal, though, for the word to have moral connotations for the legal practitioner.

Late medieval lawyers used *inconvenience* (and we shall adopt this same term, their technical term, throughout the chapter) mainly on two levels: to prohibit a judicial decision from being inconsistent with established practice and decisions in previous cases; and to prohibit

[34] *Convenio, convenire*, to come together; *inconveniens*, dissimilar. For a brief account of 'inconvenient' in law, see YB 12 Ed. II (81 Sel. Soc., London, 1964) p. cix, n. 2.
[35] *OED*; 'convenience', I. 'There is a manner of convenience between the thing that is seen in the mirror and that other that is seen without', *The Pylgremage of the Sowle* (c. 1400), IV, xxvi, 71. For Pecock, *Folower*, p. 140.
[36] *MED*: 'inconvenience' (d): 'If . . . there may be found . . . any contrariand thing or double rehearsal . . . that then it be taken . . . not after doublenesse, inconvenience, or repugnance', *Testamenta Eboracensia: A Selection of Wills from the Registry at York* (1458), 5 volumes (1836–84), volume II, edited by J. Raine, Surtees Society Publications, 30 (London, 1855) p. 229.
[37] *OED*: 'inconvenient', A.1, 2; *MED*: 'inconvenient' (d): 'What is so inconvenient and so far from man's reason as to say that Jesus should be the Son of God whom a virgin should conceive without knowledge of man?', *The Life and Martyrdom of St. Katherine* (1450), edited by A. G. H. Gibbs, Roxburghe Club Publications, 112 (London, 1884).
[38] *OED*: 'convenience', 5; *MED*: 'convenience', 4(a), (b): 'It is convenable and convenient that every man finds for trespass pain and for righteousness bliss', John de Trevisa, *Bartholomeus (de Glanvilla) de Proprietatibus Rerum* (1398) (MS. Tollemache; Add MS. (B.M.) 27944) 15b–b.
[39] *OED*: 'inconvenience', 2, 3; *MED* 'inconvenience' (a), (c): 'Against God if you have wrought any inconvenience', 'The Play of the Sacrament', (c. 1460), *The Non-Cycle Mystery Plays*, edited by O. Waterhouse, Early English Text Society, Extra Series, 104 (London, 1909) p. 83, line 819; 'In all these premises is found matter upon which might sue great inconveniences against the laws of God, of the Church, and of our said sovereign lord', *Declaration of Guilt: Coventry* (1446), photostat of MS. Cott. Cleopatra E. III in possession of *MED*.
[40] *OED*: 'inconvenient', A, 3, B.2; *MED*: 'inconvenience', noun, (b): 'It is open to every man . . . that neither in the king, my lord and fathers, nor in no other of our noble progenitor's days, so many inconveniences of right evil example have been attempted . . . against God and his church', *Letter Book of London*, K. 244 (1440), edited by R. R. Sharpe, Calendar of Letter-books preserved among the archives of the Corporation of the City of London at the Guildhall (1899–1912).

*Mischief and inconvenience* 163

decisions made in one case which are inconsistent with other decisions made in the same case. In short, inconvenience concerns inconsistency between cases as well as discordant results in one case. Being concerned with consistency, there is a point of contact with the practitioners' reason and its requirement that like be treated alike.[41] Often reason and inconvenience were used in the same argument or judgment.

### Inconsistency between cases

Though we can discern only the beginnings of the idea of precedent at this time, there is no doubt that established practice on a given matter did influence the making of succeeding decisions in the royal courts on the same matter. Sometimes the judges expressly turned to particular previous decisions on a point.[42] To depart from these, they tell us, would be inconvenient. As today, the medieval judge wanted consistency and certainty. Thirning CJCP made the point quite clearly in 1410.

The interest of a tenant-at-will was not one which the courts protected fully.[43] He was so called 'because he has no certain or sure estate, for the lessor may put him out at what time it pleased him'.[44] In 1410 the court declared the rule that a tenant-at-will, due to the poverty of his estate, could not pray in aid his freehold lessor.[45] Thirning CJCP described the practice as one well settled in law, and that to depart from it would create an inconvenience. Of the practice and of the inconvenience he explained: 'and one should not argue about an ancient principle of law, but judge it as other learned men have done, and if we do the contrary, now we could not know what inconvenience or damage could come from that'.[46] In 1454 when a reversioner prayed to be received (to show that he was seised and granted the land to the tenant with reversion to himself), the demandant was to challenge (traverse) the reversion and not the grant

[41] Above, ch 5, pp. 115–17.
[42] *IEHL*, p. 171; Allen, *Law in the Making*, pp. 190–203; see also above, chapter 1, pp. 22–6.
[43] Simpson, *History of the Land Law*, pp. 93–5.
[44] *Tenures*, Bk I, c. 8, s. 68.
[45] Brooke, *GA*, 'Aid', 53. In the case P sued D in trespass. D said at the time of the alleged trespass W had the freehold and granted a tenancy-at-will to D. P says it was his freehold. D seeks to pray in aid W.
[46] T 11 Hen. IV, 90, 46: 'et il n'est my a disputer sur auncient principle de ley, mes de luy ajudge sicome auters sages ont faits, et si nous faceomus le contrary, nous ore ne purromus scaver quel inconvenience ou damage purrent avenir d'icel'.

(which the reversioner alleged he made to the tenant).⁴⁷ This had been adjudged twelve times in the books 'and for the contrary there is no judgment'. Therefore, according to Prisot CJCP, it was inconvenient 'to try the cause in one case and not in another'.⁴⁸ In 1464 P sued debt *sur obligation*, D confessed the debt and pleaded a release. A date was set to try D's plea but D defaulted.⁴⁹ Judgment was given for P 'because diverse precedents as is said are in the court ... that the defendant will be condemned for this [default], this will not be changed, for it is inconvenient to change, and therefore it must be done according to the precedents'.⁵⁰

On these occasions the inconvenience at issue is that of producing a conclusion different from decisions upon the same matter in previous cases. An inconvenient result was one inconsistent with established practice. At this time, of course, established practice manifested in past usage was treated as *law*.⁵¹ Conceptually, because an inconvenient result might be one inconsistent with established practice, and as established practice itself constituted law, any result inconsistent with that practice was to be treated as inconsistent with law. The argument that a proposed result is 'against law and an inconvenience' or 'inconvenient and against law' is often repeated in the Year Books. These results the courts excluded. In 1413 Hankford JCP declared it 'against law and reason' for a plaintiff to sue two defendants separately and recover double damages, for one same trespass, in chancery and at common law. It was this result, one which was inconsistent with law and reason, that Hankford JCP described as an inconvenience.⁵² In 1424 the court declared as law the established rule that a stranger to a

⁴⁷ For receipt, see 13 Ed. I, Statute of Westminster II, c. 3; 13 Ric. II, St. I, c. 17; *CH*, p. 411.
⁴⁸ M 33 Hen. VI, 38, 17 at 41.
⁴⁹ For general discussion of default and the law's dislike of judgment when the defendant failed to appear, see P&M, II, pp. 594, 595, and *CH*, pp. 385, 386. For a curious use of mischief in this context, see M 5 Hen. VII, 2, 3 per Hussey CJKB: 'where the entry has been thus all times before these times, it will be great mischief to change the law in this point; for then all our precedents for this could be reversed by error'.
⁵⁰ M 5 Ed. IV, 86 (no plaint number) at 87 per Danby JCP: 'pur ceo que divers precedents come est dit sont en le court ... que le defendant serra condempne pur ceo, ce ne serra change, car est inconvenient a changer, et pur ceo il covient estre fait accordant as precedents'; Brooke, *GA*, 'Default and Appearance', 68.
⁵¹ M 34 Hen. VI, 22, 42 at 24 per Fortescue CJKB: 'usage makes law'. See generally above, chapter 1, n. 75.
⁵² H 14 Hen. IV, 21, 27. See also M 1 Ed. IV, 2, 7 for a similar use. The disruption to the law is well expressed in the phrase *inconvenience du ley*: H 22 Hen. VI, 39, 12 at 40 per Moile.

## Mischief and inconvenience

deed could not take advantage of that deed: to allow him to take advantage, the judges said, would be against law and an inconvenience.[53] In the same year Martin JCP expounded the rule that whenever an action is founded upon something which cannot commence without specialty, then 'it will be inconvenient and against law to maintain an action on a deed without showing the deed'.[54] In 1428, Hals JCP stated as a matter of principle that 'it would be inconvenient, when by law an action is given to the party, that we [the judges] by our act of a later time defeat the action of the party'.[55]

### Discordant results in one case

Inconvenience is also used to prohibit decisions made in one case which are inconsistent with other decisions made in the same case. When in 1420 P brought appeal against several defendants, three of whom were principals and the rest accessories, Cheyne JCP said a jury must decide first on the guilt of the principals before considering the accessories 'for the inconvenience which can come therefrom, for it may be that [the accessories] will be found guilty, and the principals acquitted'.[56] Likewise, in 1421, counsel argued that if a husband and wife and others had judgment against them in trespass and the husband and wife then successfully obtained a reversal of the judgment (by a writ of error), their co-defendants in the trespass action could benefit from the reversal, because otherwise 'an original [judgment] will be reversed, and also be in force, which will be inconvenient'.[57] There are many examples of this usage.[58] Let us concentrate upon one in some detail.

In 1454 P sued separate writs of debt against A and B naming each as from D in Leicestershire.[59] A and B were outlawed. Nevertheless, having later been apprehended, A obtained a reversal of his outlawry,

---

[53] M 3 Hen. VI, 18, 27; H 3 Hen. VI, 26, 8; see below, n. 99.
[54] T 2 Hen. VI, 14, 13: 'car il sera inconvenient et enconter ley de maintainer un accion sur un fait sans monstrer le fait'; Brooke, *GA*, 'Monstrance de Faits', 2 (cited by Neele JCP in H 15 Ed IV, 16, 4 at 17).
[55] P 7 Hen. VI, 28, 22 at 30: 'seroit inconvenient, quand par la ley action est done al party, que nous par nostre fait de puisne temps defeterons l'action le party'.
[56] H 8 Hen. V, 6, 26; Fitzherbert, *GA*, 'Corone', 463.
[57] M 9 Hen. V, 9, 5: Brooke, *GA*, 'Error', 54.
[58] T 11 Hen. IV, 90, 46 per Hill JCP; H 12 Hen. VI, 6, 5 at 7 per Strangeways JCP; T 14 Hen. VI, 18, 56 per Srjt Candish and Paston JCP.
[59] M 33 Hen. VI, 51, 37; Brooke, *GA*, 'Estoppel', 223.

as there was no such town as D.⁶⁰ B then sought reversal of his outlawry and the question was whether he could rely on the finding in A's case. It was held that he could: once it was settled that there was no such town as D, there would be no trial to prove this a second time, said the court, in case of the possibility that the tribunal found that there *was* such a town. Moile JCP explained that: 'this is the court of the king, and we in the name of the king have given judgment, and if this could be tried another time, and it was found that there be such a town, then we must give the contrary judgment, which is impertinent even if it was by attaint'.⁶¹ However, in the course of discussion, Prisot CJCP considered that it would be inconvenient for B to rely on the finding in A's case because, at some later date, P might successfully bring attaint against the finding in A's case: then B would remain acquitted on the finding in A's case when that finding had been shown to be wrong in attaint. He said: 'The plaintiff [P] can have attaint in your case on this verdict [in A's case]', and 'if the second defendant [B] would be acquitted by this first verdict and the jury was attainted, then it would be inconvenient to abate the writ against the other [B] when now the writ is affirmed by the attaint against the defendant who appeared first [A]'.⁶²

The essence of inconvenience in these cases is the contradiction of one decision by another. The last word might be given to Hals JCP when he said in 1428 that if a judgment is given 'which is absolutely against the first award, it would be inconvenient; for on this it would be that we give a judgment and in the same court an opposite where there is no error; which cannot be'.⁶³

### Inconvenience and reason

For the sake of completeness it is worth noting that 'inconvenient' and 'convenient' were also used in other contexts. Sometimes convenient

---

⁶⁰ For the questioning of a writ of debt when the town was alleged not to exist, see P 22 Hen. VI, 53, 28.
⁶¹ M 33 Hen. VI, 51, 37 at 52.
⁶² Ibid.: 'Le plaintiff puit aver atteint en votre cas sur ceo verdit, et si le second defendant serroit quite per ceo premier verdit et le jury fuit atteint, donques serroit inconvenient de abater le brefe envers l'auter quand or le brefe est affirme par l'attaint envers le defendant qui primes apperust'. For attaint, see above ch. 5, n. 68.
⁶³ P 7 Hen. VI, 28, 22 at 29: 'qui est mere contariant del premier agard, seroit inconvenient: car sur ceo ensueroit que nous donamus un jugement; et en meme le place le contrary, ou n'est errour; que ne peut estre'; Brooke, *GA*, 'Error', 16.

*Mischief and inconvenience* 167

was used to denote a suitable or fitting punishment or remedy.[64] Occasionally inconvenience was used to signify harm. This usage was found in non-legal sources,[65] but is never found in the Year Books: it only appears in legislation, as for example, in 1485 when riots, robberies and murders were described as inconveniences.[66] However, as we have seen, the predominant usage of inconvenience focussed immediately not upon the absorption of moral considerations into legal questions, but rather upon the objective of what might be described as legal symmetry. In this respect its use is close to that of reason when that word is used in the context of good sense and treating like alike.[67]

The courts used reason to exclude absurd results, and inconvenience is occasionally used in the same way. In 1422 Hankford CJKB said that to grant *audita querela*, by which a judgment would be re-considered,[68] when there will never be execution of judgment, was inconvenient.[69] In 1426 Martin JCP considered it inconvenient for a person to give another specific goods when the donor could not in law own those goods.[70] In 1441 Newton CJCP considered it inconvenient for a plaintiff to recover against someone who was not privy to a wrong.[71] And in 1458 Prisot CJCP decided that it was inconvenient for a person to recover on a false writ when he can have a good writ.[72]

Indeed, inconvenience and reason are often used by common lawyers in conjunction to attain the objectives of legal symmetry and good sense. As Prisot stated in the case of 1454 described earlier 'it would be inconvenient and against reason to try the cause in one case and not in another'.[73] The two words frequently appear together in this familiar type of setting: to justify preventing a plaintiff from recovering the value of a horse when he has retrieved and is actually seised of the animal;[74] to forbid the trial of a fact already determined

[64] 4 Hen. IV, c. 3 (*convenable*); 12 Ed. IV, c. 3 (*convenient et sure remedie*); 7 Hen. VII, c. 11.
[65] Above, n. 39.
[66] 1 Hen. VII, c. 7. See also 18 Hen. VI, cc. 13 (robberies and murders) and 19 (desertion from the king's service); 3 Hen. VII, c. 1 (murders, robberies, etc.); 3 Hen. VII, c. 14 (offences in the king's household).
[67] Above, chapter 5, pp. 113–17.
[68] Holdsworth, I, p. 224 and II, pp. 344, 593.
[69] P 9 Hen. V, 1, 2.
[70] T 4 Hen. VI, 31, 11.
[71] P 19 Hen. VI, 66, 10.
[72] M 37 Hen. VI, 9, 19. See also T 21 Hen. VI, 57, 14 per Newton CJCP.
[73] M 33 Hen. VI, 38, 17 at 41: 'seroit inconvenient, et enconter reason de trier la cause en un cas, et nemy en un auter'.
[74] M 21 Hen. VI, 14, 29 at 15 per Paston JCP.

once;[75] to condemn the vexation of a defendant twice upon one cause.[76] There are many similar examples.[77] An interesting occasion when the words were used in conjunction appears in a case of 1424, in which the issue of doing the impossible arose.[78]

In general, an action of replevin was available when a lord distrained his tenant to perform services.[79] The lord was obliged to return any goods taken by way of distress if the tenant offered to perform the services or find gage and pledge that he would contest the validity of the distraint in court.[80] Sometimes the tenant insisted that the lord pledges a return of the goods.[81] Then, the contest was founded on the tenant's claim that the distrainor's taking was wrongful. In turn, the lord either denied he took the goods or admitted the taking and disclose the reasons for it.[82] In 1424 P sued replevin against D for taking his cattle wrongfully, a taking which D admits but explains how he had granted the land on which they were taken to P for an annual rent. They agreed that for rent in arrears D could distrain. However, P alleges that D is still seised of the cattle and prays that D gage deliverance by putting in surety that he will return them. D argues that he need not gage deliverance because the cattle had died. Serjeant Paston says, therefore, that 'we must do a thing that cannot be done, this will be against reason and inconvenient'.[83] Though adjourned, on resumption the court found for D. He did not have to gage deliverance as he had shown the cattle were dead: 'and if this matter were true, it will be against reason and inconvenient to gage the deliverance, which is a judgment, where it appears by alleging this default [D's failure to feed the cattle] that this judgment can never be executed'.[84]

Throughout the period, the predominant usage of inconvenience,

[75] P 7 Ed. IV, 1, 3. Compare Srjts Catesby and Pigot with Srjts Jenney and Young.
[76] H 32 Hen. VI, 28, 23 at 29 per Prisot CJCP.
[77] M 4 Hen. IV, 4, 13 per Thirning; T 2 Hen. V, 8, 2 per Srjt Lodington; H 4 Hen. VI, 10, 4 per Martin JCP; H 32 Hen. VI, 25, 13 (compare Brown and Fortescue CJKB at 26); M 34 Hen. VI, 22, 42 per Danby JCP at 23.
[78] For the use of inconvenience in this context see M 33 Hen. VI, 45, 28 per Prisot CJCP; for inconvenience and logic, see above, n. 58. For Littleton, *Tenures*, Bk III, c. 5, s. 349; c. 12, s. 665; c. 13, s. 722.
[79] Enever, *History of Distress*, p. 156.
[80] *CH*, p. 368; P&M, II, p. 577.
[81] YB 5 Ed. II (63 Sel. Soc., London 1944), p. 218.
[82] Enever, *History of Distress*, p. 156.
[83] M 3 Hen. VI, 15, 20; Brooke, *GA*, 'Gage Deliverance', 1.
[84] H 4 Hen. VI, 13, 11; Brooke, *GA*, 'Gage Deliverance', 23. And for gage deliverance see also M 30 Hen. VI, 1, 6; M 21 Ed. IV, 63, 35; M 5 Hen. VII, 9, 21.

and its exclusion by the common lawyers, imports an idea of consistency in law. It is a usage which is peculiar to practice and which does not appear in legal theory. Inconvenience has nothing to do with morality, with conscience or natural law, or other more mundane forms of right and wrong, like reason or mischief. Its employment is specific, utilised simply as a means of prohibiting inconsistencies between judicial decisions and established practice, between case and case, as well as prohibiting dissonant results in one and the same case.

### MISCHIEF AND INCONVENIENCE

The respective usages of mischief and inconvenience reflect two fundamentally opposing concerns. Inconvenience seeks to eradicate repugnancy between cases, and the usage of mischief seeks the prevention of (particular forms of) wrong. When common lawyers employ mischief they participate directly in the treatment of wrongs: being without redress and procedural vexation. But these are wrongs more mundane than those prohibited by conscience or natural law. In contrast, the usage of inconvenience is divorced from conceptions of abstract right and wrong. Its usage merely emphasises legal symmetry, certainty and consistency, without recourse to claims based on large and explicitly moral ideas. Accordingly it is in cases where different arguments resting on mischief and inconvenience compete with each other, that we can see an immediate confrontation between the separate claims of preventing injustice to the individual, abstract wrong, and maintaining consistency in the application of law and established practice.

### *Typical arguments*

Two cases illustrate the divergence between the mischief argument and the argument from inconvenience. The first is dated 1430. P sued *quare impedit* against the patron and the incumbent of A. But the patron had died, so the incumbent sought abatement of the writ. The court was divided.[85] Babington CJCP said the writ would not abate, for if it were P would not be compensated and the disturbance would

---

[85] M 9 Hen. VI, 30, 1. Curiously, sometimes mischief and inconvenience are used to describe the same phenomenon: 1 Hen. IV, c. 14; 8 Hen. VI, c. 27; 20 Hen. VI, c. 3; 4 Hen. VII, c. 19; P 3 Hen. VI, 43, 20 (compare Martin JCP and Babington CJCP); P 9 Hen. VI, 1, 3 per Fulthorpe.

170  *Fundamental authority in late medieval English law*

go unpunished.[86] Martin JCP agreed that this would constitute a mischief to P.[87] Serjeant Paston and Hals and Cottesmore JJCP, though, said the writ would abate and that P must proceed afresh against the patron's successor. As Paston says, first if P recovers against the incumbent only, then he who has *droit* in the advowson (the successor) is out of possession: this would be a mischief to him.[88] Second, 'it is inconvenient to recover against him who has nothing [in the patronage], for the incumbent has nothing except by him who is dead'. The text ends inconclusively.[89]

A similar argument appears in a case from 1461 in which D brought *praecipe quod reddat* (in the king's court) against T, a tenant for life, who responded to the action.[90] The remainderman (R) prayed receipt to abate the writ saying it was land in ancient demesne and, therefore, the king's court could not try the matter. The ordinary real actions in the royal courts could not be used to recover land held in ancient demesne, so people had to use an action called 'the little writ of right close' in the local court.[91] For Moile and Danvers JJCP, as T had affirmed the jurisdiction of the royal court, by coming and answering, R should not abate the writ: 'it will be inconvenient that when the tenant of the land affirms the jurisdiction, and did all that was in him to answer for the land here in this court, that after this court will be ousted of jurisdiction'.[92] On the other hand Danby and Ashton JJCP think the writ abates. If it did not there would be a mischief to the remainderman and his heirs who are inherited to have their actions tried for all time in the court of ancient demesne. To allow R and his heirs to lose this benefit would be the mischief of being without the entitlement to redress. Once again, the report ends inconclusively.

---

[86] M 9 Hen. VI, 30 at 31: 'le disturbance serra dispuni'.
[87] Ibid.: 'Il y ad deux mischiefs: un, si le brefe abat', son disturbance ne serra punie ... et cestuy que fuit disturbe n'ad nul remedy de ceo disturbance, le quel est grand mischief.'
[88] Paston's use of *droit* here implies the idea of a right: see above, chapter 4, n. 56.
[89] For a similar problem and similar argument, see M 7 Hen. IV, 25, 3 at 26 per Gascoigne CJKB.
[90] M 2 Ed. IV, 27, 32; Brooke, *GA*, 'Resceit', 108; 'Ancient Demesne', 38.
[91] Simpson, *History of the Land Law*, pp. 165–6.
[92] M 2 Ed. IV, 27, 32 at 28: 'il serra enconvenient, que quant le tenant del terre affirme le jurisdiction, et fist tout ceo que en luy fuit de parder le terre icy en ceo court, que apres cest court serra ouste de jurisdiction' (per Danvers). Other cases where mischief and inconvenience appear together can be found at: M 8 Hen. IV, 16, 19; H 14 Hen. IV, 21, 27; M 7 Hen. VI, 9, 15; H 22 Hen. VI, 39, 12.

## The preference for consistency

We have already met the judicial preference in the fifteenth century to apply law strictly: in the usage of *rigor iuris*.[93] The parallel preference to prevent an inconvenient result, one offensive to legal consistency, and allow the party to bear the mischief consequent upon a strict application of law, was embodied in the idea that 'a mischief will be suffered sooner than an inconvenience'.[94] As expressed by Babington CJCP in a case dated 1425, the usual statement ran: 'And I say that where a mischief is, and an inconvenience, always the mischief will be suffered and the inconvenience will be driven out.'[95] In addition, as we have seen, when a statute created a mischief the judges applied it nevertheless: as Paston had said in 1443, 'we cannot take consideration of the mischief now: for when a statute is ... mischievous; yet this will be held for law until it be repealed'.[96]

The preference is to be found, in relation to a problem concerning privity of contract, in a case from 1424.[97] H and W, a husband and wife, brought a writ of debt *sur obligation* for twenty pounds against D. W had entered the agreement with D whilst single. However, D shows a deed made between W and J (made, again, whilst W was single), and claims that the obligation is no longer effective: D contends this because, by the deed, W had agreed that upon performance of certain conditions by J, the obligation between W and D would be at an end and thus D was released from liability to pay. Although D alleges that J had performed these, W maintains that D cannot take advantage of this deed made between W and J because he is a stranger to it. Stating the rule that strangers to a deed made between others

---

[93] Above, ch. 4, pp. 99–101.
[94] M 9 Hen. VI, 30, 1 at 31 per Srjt Paston; T 14 Hen. VI, 23, 67; M 37 Hen. VI, 1, 1 per Fortescue CJKB; M 6 Ed. IV, 4, 11 per Yelverton JKB. For a statement of the problem, see *CH*, p. 680; 94 Sel. Soc. (London, 1977) p. 38, n. 1.
[95] P 3 Hen. VI, 43, 20 at 44: 'Et jeo di que l'ou un mischief est, et un inconvenientise, tout le mischief sera suffre et l'inconvenientise sera oustre.' At H 12 Hen. VI, 6, 5 at 7 Strangeways JCP treated this as a principle of law: '*Nostre ley est*, plustost souffrer un mischief que un inconvenientise serra done.'
[96] T 21 Hen. VI, 56, 13; above, chapter 2, p. 58; see also *Tenures*, Bk II, c. 12, s. 231, and Co. Litt., p. 97b: 'An argument drawn from inconvenience is forcible in law, as has been observed before and shall be often hereafter. *Nihil quod est inconveniens est licitum*. And the law, that is the perfection of reason, cannot suffer any thing that is inconvenient. It is better, says the law, to suffer a mischief that is particular to one, than an inconvenience that may prejudice many.'
[97] M 3 Hen. VI, 18, 27; H 3 Hen. VI, 26, 8; Brooke, *GA*, 'Debt', 3; 'Estranger al Fait', 1.

cannot rely upon the deed, the court decides in favour of H and W: June JCP says there is 'a maxim, that a deed will not be put in trial except between those who are privy to that deed, or between strangers who claim by him who is privy'.[98] Moreover, Martin JCP, agreeing with June JCP, states that inasmuch as the deed is advantageous to D and as the conditions have been fulfilled by J, so bringing an end to the obligation, 'it seems reason, that he must have advantage, otherwise it will be a great mischief to him'; however, Martin then proceeds to reject this possible consequence of mischief by saying: 'And sir, I say yet that this mischief will be suffered: for . . . to the deed he is a total stranger, and is not to plead unless he was privy, or that he claims by him who was privy'; he continues: 'and to receive him to plead the deed as he has pleaded, will be against law and an inconvenience, and where an inconvenience and a mischief come together, the mischief will at all times be suffered and the inconvenience repelled'.[99] It is clear from this passage that Martin JCP prefers to apply the rule (or maxim, as June JCP describes it) which requires privity, rather than admit an exception to this, an exception which would itself prevent the consequential wrong to D to which he actually referred.

Occasionally the judges overtly justify their preference to exclude an inconvenience. The justification, indicated in a decision of 1440, for example, is purely utilitarian: a potential inconvenience will not be permitted for to do so would be to subvert the law, to cause uncertainty and trouble the courts.[100] The facts were these. P (the master of a convent) sued *scire facias* against B, a parson of A, to have execution of an annuity recovered by S (P's predecessor) against R (B's predecessor).[101] B urges against execution (i) because neither P nor his predecessors were in fact seised of the annuity, and (ii) because all the jurors in the annuity trial are dead and so he cannot have attaint against them when, as he alleges, they swore falsely to the

---

[98] H 3 Hen. VI, 26, 8 at 27 for June. For the principle see M 2 Hen VI, 1, 1 (misnumbered as 9, 1) at 2; M 10 Hen. VI, 7, 23 and P 28 Hen. VI, 6, 3; see also *HCLC*, pp. 153f. For other examples of strangers and inconvenience, see H 8 Hen. VI, 26, 16 at 27 per Srjt Chantrell; P 19 Hen. VI, 66, 10 per Newton CJCP; P 7 Ed. IV, 1, 3 per Srjts Jenney and Young.

[99] H 3 Hen. VI, 26, 8 at 27: 'et de luy recever pur pleder le fait come il ad plede, sera enconter ley et un inconvenientise, et ou un inconvenientise et un mischief vienent ensemble, le mischief sera tout temps suffre et l'inconvenientise rebote'.

[100] For similar ideas: T 21 Hen. VI, 57, 14 at 58 per Newton CJCP; in legislation, 4 Hen. IV, c. 3; 3 Hen. VI, c. 1; 15 Hen. VI, c. 4. See also *HCLC*, p. 100.

[101] M 19 Hen. VI, 39, 82; Brooke, *GA*, 'Aid', 78. And see T 12 Hen. IV, 26, 15 (misnumbered in YB as 14): 'we do not have power to give remedy'.

predecessor's seisin of the annuity. To allow execution in the light of this, argues Serjeant Fortescue, would constitute a mischief to B. On the other hand Serjeant Portington argues that B cannot have this plea: if the plea were allowed, effectively B would re-open the issue of the seisin of the annuity: 'for it is absolutely contrary to the issue found in the writ of annuity, in which case it would be inconvenient to try a thing again that was tried before on the same original process'. The judges agree with Portington and decide not to allow B's plea. As Ascough JCP stated: 'if a thing was tried and found, [and] it will be put in issue another time, the law will never have a final conclusion, and all the judgments and records of this court will be troubled if this will be allowed', and thus, he says, 'infinitely trial upon trial'. Newton JCP is equally clear: 'if a judgment was pronounced herein in such a way it would be void as they propose to avoid the other [the decision on the annuity], which will be a bad example, and the subversion of the law', as, furthermore, every plaintiff could be frustrated in this way. Accordingly, if the defendants were allowed to upset execution, says Newton JCP, 'thus from this so many inconveniences will arise'. Paston JCP is in agreement: B's plea based on the claimed inability to sue attaint will not be allowed 'because it is the greater inconvenience that can be, and the law sooner suffers a mischief, and the party to be without remedy, than an inconvenience'.[102]

CONCLUSION

The late medieval common lawyer's slogan that 'a mischief will be suffered sooner than an inconvenience' points the way directly to a fundamental element of the 'modern' positivist outlook. And it was directly opposed to the basic outlook of the chancery jurisdiction. Indeed, it is compelling to view the common law preference summed up in the slogan as part and parcel of the reason for the development of the chancery jurisdiction. The common law itself may have been founded on reason. The appeal to conscience may have been an important characteristic of reasoning in the common law, not to mention in legislation. But when it came to a direct clash, between the exclusion of mischief or the exclusion of inconvenience, it was the purely legal value of consistency that was to prevail. In the usages of

[102] M 19 Hen. VI, 39, 82 at 40: 'pur ceo que il est le plus inconvenience qui peut estre, et le ley plustost souffre mischief, et le party estre sans remedy que un inconvenientise'.

mischief and inconvenience we see the two basic authorities for individual legal decisions. With mischief the practitioner is concerned with the claims of abstract right and wrong, but of a more mundane type than those implied in the usage of conscience, reason or natural law. Yet, at the same time, with inconvenience the practitioner is concerned with making sense and coherence between decisions and established practice. And in the cases where the argument from mischief clashes with that seeking to exclude inconvenience, we see in clear relief the tension that plagues all systems of law. In the late medieval period the tension was beginning, with considerable regularity, to be resolved in favour of the positivist thesis.

CONCLUSION

Words such as consent, natural law, reason and conscience are employed extensively, during the late medieval period, by practising lawyers, in their disposing of ordinary cases and problems, and by the theorists, in their expositions of law. We shall never be able to re-construct with comprehensive certainty all the elements of the late medieval idea of law. Yet, the usage of these and similar words does reveal some fundamental ideas about law and sources of authority for law at this time. But it is not a straightforward and single concept of law and a single concept of authority that the materials disclose. The key words frequently represent different and sometimes opposing ideas of law and its authority. In broad terms, the materials suggest two sets of fundamental ideas. One stresses the connection between law and abstract right and wrong. The other separates law from these, emphasising instead the human will. Though they focus more upon the connection of law and abstract right and wrong, the theorists advance both ideas of law, ideas which appear to fight each other. The practising lawyers advance similar, though by no means identical, ideas. And often the theorists' ideas are far simpler and more exaggerated or extreme than the practitioners'. There is substantial correspondence between theory and practice. Also, there is often considerable dissonance.

Natural law, divine law and conscience signify a notion of morality. Through these the common law is married to the extraneous influence of abstract right and wrong. Legal theory postulates natural law, divine in origin, as a basic authority underlying human law. It has the quality of a higher law, one to which *all* human law is subordinate. If humanly created rules conflict with natural law they fail to obtain the status of law: an idea advanced by Fortescue and Saint German, but not by Pecock. And it is the purpose of human law to disclose justice and advance virtue. Yet, strict justice must be tempered by equity.

Apart from Fortescue's explicit equation of natural law and justice and Pecock's development from justice of the idea of a right based on claims, the connection of law to morality in legal theory was, on the whole, entirely orthodox in medieval jurisprudence.

In the practical sphere a slightly different picture emerges. Natural law is used infrequently in the Year Books and justice is (almost) never used. The practitioners did use, however, comparably moral ideas. The appeal to conscience and ideas of divine law were widespread, and this outside the chancery. Conscience and ideas of divine law were incorporated into legislation as sources of authority. Commonly, statutes were designed to duplicate the requirements of conscience or divine law. Likewise, the appeal to conscience was often used by the common lawyer: substantively, to justify judicial decisions, and in the administration of law, to regulate those participating in the process of law, judges, jurors and litigants. Through the pulpit and the confessional everybody knew that to offend conscience would imperil the soul: as an aid to the rule of law, the appeal to conscience was invaluable. Indeed, undoubtedly guided by Aquinas, D'Ailly, Gerson, the canonists and the chancery practice in his use of conscience, Saint German's connection of the common law and conscience was already anticipated, and perhaps influenced, by the fifteenth-century common lawyers' appeal to conscience.

The practitioners' usage of equity, mischief and reason, on the other hand, reflects more mundane ideas of abstract right and wrong than the overtly moral ideas of conscience or natural law. Practical equity rarely implies the moral idea in legal theory. It is used merely to enlarge the scope of existing legislative rules. Used to denote an earthly idea of wrong, mischief is employed in the common law courts to exclude the conditions of being without redress and procedural vexation. In legislation it merely represents general harm, sometimes with moral overtones, sometimes without. Reason, on the other hand, habitually appealed to by the common lawyers, implied an idea of abstract right. Signifying a conception of good sense, counsel and judges excluded absurd results as 'against reason'. Reason also forbad imbalanced results, imbalances between loss and recovery or between wrong-doing and punishment. In this respect there is a resemblance between the practitioners' reason, upon which the common law was founded, and the theorists' justice, which required that each be given his due. Whereas natural law in theory nullified all conflicting human law, in practice reason was used simply to invalidate local customary

## Conclusion 177

law. In short, like conscience, the common lawyers used reason to dispose of ordinary problems of litigation. And like conscience, in many ways, reason was a source of principle in the common law.

For these people the authority of morality (manifested in natural law, divine law, justice or conscience) and good sense and proportionality (manifested in reason) were of crucial importance for the existence and development of law. Theirs was a fundamentally heteronomist view of law. Law relied for its authority upon large ideas of abstract right and wrong. The justification for a decision was almost as important as the decision itself. The scope of morality as justification was widespread: to create new rules, to preserve, apply and extend existing rules, and to fill their gaps.

By way of contrast, consent, usage, inconvenience and *rigor iuris* are words central to that group of ideas separating law from the claims of abstract right and wrong. Law also derived from an act of the human will. In practice, the underlying authority of legislation was consent, the consent of the king and community. So too in legal theory. In his idea that legislation originates in the bilateral act of king and community Pecock anticipates Fortescue's *dominium politicum et regale* by around twenty years. And it would be pleasant to think that Fortescue was influenced by Pecock. It is not unlikely that the English lawyer knew the Welsh ecclesiastic. They moved in similar circles: the one was Chief Justice of the King's Bench (1442–61), the other Bishop of Saint Asaph (1444) and Chichester (1450). Both were triers of petitions in the parliaments of the 1450s, and Pecock was a member of the Privy Council in 1454 and also of Lincoln's Inn. Both antagonised and suffered under the Yorkist regime.

Consent also applied in practice to local custom. Yet, though the theorists expounded the idea of consent in relation to parliament's law, they failed to expound the same in relation to local custom or national custom, the common law. Only Saint German argued that the common law was approved by the community of the realm. Rather, and this was the predominant opinion of the practitioners, the common law originated in the judicial will: it was founded on established practice and the usage of the courts, ascertainable 'in the books'. Law was not conceived to be given by God. It was shaped by human usage or enactment. As such, composed of human commands, laws varied from place to place and from time to time, existing to serve mundane purposes, the common profit. The theorists' emphasis on virtue is distinctly absent from the Year Books.

This voluntarist view of law, issuing from consent and usage, prepared the way for the beginnings of a positivist idea of law. One of the accomplishments of Fortescue and Pecock was the idea that humanly created rules are still laws even when they depart from abstract right and wrong. In practice, too, legislation treated as against conscience or producing mischief had to be expressly repealed: it was not automatically void. It is the same with the judges: they do not decline to apply legislation if it is mischievous. The modern notion of sovereignty is clearly implicit in the incipient medieval positivist thesis. Moreover, it is common for the judges to reject the claims of conscience or reason in preference for those of established legal practice. They are shy of departing from the requirements of law, from the *rigor iuris*, for this, they tell us, would result in an 'inconvenience', inconsistency, and consequently uncertainty for the future. The common lawyers' idea that 'a mischief will be suffered sooner than an inconvenience' is thoroughly positivist. Within it may be contained one of the basic reasons for the growth of the chancery jurisdiction.

According to the heteronomist thesis, human law relies for its authority upon large moral ideas, such as natural law and conscience, and upon more earthly ideas of abstract right and wrong, such as reason and mischief. It is not the independent human will which shapes law. By accompanying or justifying their decisions with these flexible concepts, theorists and practitioners postulate an extraneous source of authority, absorbed into the actuality of the judicial and legislative process. The heteronomist thesis expresses itself in the usage of these words as a mode or practice of disposing of cases and problems. It is not that medieval lawyers take advantage of an absence of a comprehensive legal structure: along with the technical law embodied in usage and legislation, ideas like reason and conscience are themselves part and parcel of the legal structure. According to the voluntarist or autonomist thesis, on the other hand, separating law and morality, it is simply the human will that shapes law. It is from consent and usage that legal decisions originate. The one group of ideas indicates that authority is supplied by divine law, natural law, conscience and reason, supplied externally, from without. The other group suggests an authority supplied by purely human influences, by consent and usage.

On the face of it, to the modern lawyer, these appear to be two fundamentally opposing outlooks. The opposition or tension, in its most extreme form, is summed up in Fortescue's claims that 'law is that which is consented to by the king and people', and 'bad rules are still laws', and that, at the same time, 'law is that which is authorised by divinely created natural law', 'bad rules, if they offend natural law, are not laws at all', and 'law discloses (divinely created) justice'. The tension is also evident in the practical sphere. Arguments explicitly reliant upon reason, conscience or mischief are consciously rejected in favour of established practice. At other times, however, the requirements of the two ideas are designed to coincide. Not only does the authority of consent sit side by side with that of conscience or divine law in the *same* statute, but also there is agreement, in the *same* judicial decision, between the claims of conscience or reason and those of the common law.

# BIBLIOGRAPHY

PRIMARY SOURCES

Anonymous. *The Mirror of Justices* (thirteenth century), edited by W. J. Whittaker and F. W. Maitland, volume 7, Sel. Soc. (London, 1893).
Anonymous. *The Three Consideracions Right Necessarye to the Good Governance of a Prince*, edited by J-P. Genet, *Four English Political Tracts*, Camden Fourth Series, volume 18 (London, 1977) p. 174.
Anselm. *Monologium* and *Proslogium* (1077–8), translated by S. N. Deane (Chicago, 1939).
Aquinas, Thomas. *Summa Theologiae* (1265–73), 60 volumes (London, 1964–76).
Bracton, Henry. *De Legibus et Consuetudinibus Angliae* (*c*. 1220–40), translated by S. E. Thorne (Cambridge, Mass., 1968).
Brooke, Robert. *Graunde Abridgement* (In aedibus Richardi Tottell Vicesimo, 1573).
Coke, Sir Edward. *The Institutes of the Laws of England, The First Part*, A Commentary on Littleton's *Tenures*, 1628 and 1832 editions, 2 volumes (New York, 1979); *The Second Part*, 1832 edition, 1 volume (New York, 1979).
Fitzherbert, Anthony. *Le Graunde Abridgement* (In aedibus Richardi Tottell Vicesimo, 1577).
*Fleta* (early fourteenth century). Volume IV, edited by G. O. Sayles, volume 99, Sel. Soc. (London, 1983).
Fortescue, John. *De Natura Legis Nature* (*c*. 1463), *The Works of Sir John Fortescue*, collected and arranged by Thomas (Fortescue), Lord Clermont, 2 volumes (London, 1869).
  *De Laudibus Legum Angliae* (1468–71), edited and translated by S. B. Chrimes, Cambridge Studies in English Legal History (Cambridge, 1942).
  *The Governance of England* (*c*. 1471), edited by C. Plummer (Oxford, 1885).
Gratian. *Decretum* (*Concordance of Discordant Canons*, *c*. 1140), in *Corpus Iuris Canonici*, 2 volumes, edited by A. Friedburg (Leipzig, 1879, 1881, reprinted 1959).

# Bibliography

Hooker, Richard. *The Laws of Ecclesiastical Polity* (1594), BooksI–IV, edited by R. Bayne (New York, 1907); Book V, edited by F. Paget (Oxford, 1907).
Jacob, G. *New Law Dictionary* (5th edition, printed by H. Lintot, 1744).
Justinian. *Institutes*, translation and commentary by J. A. C. Thomas (Cape Town, 1975).
*Knight of La Tour-Landry, The Book of the*, (1450). edited by T. Wright, Early English Text Society, Original Series, 33 (London, 1868, revised, 1906).
Littleton, Thomas. *Tenures* (*c*. 1480), edited by E. Wambaugh (Washington, 1903).
Lyndwood, William. *Provinciale* (1430), edited by J. V. Bullard and H. C. Bell (London, 1929).
Major, John. *Historia Majoris Britanniae* (1521), translated by A. Constable, Publications of the Scottish History Society, volume 10 (Edinburgh, 1892).
Marsilius of Padua. *Defensor Pacis* (1324), edited by A. Gewirth, *Marsilius of Padua: The Defender of Peace*, 2 volumes (New York, 1951–6).
Paston. *Letters* (fifteenth century), edited by J. Gairdner, 6 volumes (Westminster, 1900).
Pecock, Reginald. *The Donet* (*c*. 1443–9), edited by E. V. Hitchcock, Early English Text Society, Original Series, 156 (London, 1921).
*The Reule of Crysten Religioun* (1443), edited by W. C. Greet, Early English Text Society, Original Series, 171 (London, 1927).
*The Repressor of Over Much Blaming of the Clergy* (1449–55), edited by Churchill Babington, 2 volumes, Chronicles and Memorials, number 19 (London, 1860).
*The Folower to the Donet* (*c*. 1453), edited by E. V. Hitchcock, Early English Text Society, Original Series, 164 (London, 1924).
*Book of Faith* (1456), edited by J. L. Morison (Glasgow, 1909).
Port, Sir John. *Notebook* (1493–1535), edited by J. H. Baker, volume 102, Sel. Soc. (London, 1986).
Saint German, Christopher. *Dialogue Between a Doctor of Divinity and a Student of the Common Law* (1528–31), edited by T. F. T. Plucknett and J. L. Barton, volume 91, Sel. Soc. (London, 1974).
Salisbury, John of. *Policraticus* (1159), edited by C. C. J. Webb (Oxford, 1909).
Smith, Thomas. *De Republica Anglorum* (1583), edited by L. Alston (Cambridge, 1906).
Statham, Nicholas. *Abridgement*, printed at Rouen (*c*. 1490), edited by M. C. Klingelsmith (1915).
*Statutes of the Realm*, Printed by Command of His Majesty King George III, volumes I and II (1816).
*Testamenta Eboracensia: A Selection of Wills from the Registry at York* (1458), edited by J. Raine, 5 volumes, Surtees Society Publications (London, 1836–84).
*The Epistle of Othea to Hector* (*c*. 1440), edited by G. F. Warner, Roxburghe Club Publications, 141 (London, 1904).

*Three Prose Versions of Secreta Secretorum* (1422), edited by R. Steele and T. Henderson, Early English Text Society, Extra Series, 74 (London, 1898).
Wyclif, John. *An Apology for Lollard Doctrines* (attributed to Wyclif, *c.* 1400), edited by J. H. Todd, Camden Society Publications (London, 1842).
  *The Lay Folks' Catechism* (*c.* 1400), edited by T. F. Simmons and H. E. Nolloth, Early English Text Society, Original Series, 118 (London, 1901).
*Year Book 6–11*, Henry IV, V, Edward V, Richard III, Henry VII, VIII (London, 1679); *Year Books Parts 7 and 8*, 1–39 Henry VI (London, 1679); *Year Book*, 1–22 Edward IV (1680) (printed by G. Sawbridge, W. Rawlins and S. Roycroft, Assigns of R. and E. Atkins).

SECONDARY SOURCES

Allen, C. K. *Law in the Making* (7th edition, Oxford, 1964).
Allen, J. W. *A History of Political Thought in the Sixteenth Century* (3rd edition, London, 1951).
Arnold, M. S., T. A. Green, S. A. Scully and S. D. White. *On the Laws and Customs of England: Essays in Honour of S. E. Thorne* (Chapel Hill, N. C., 1981).
Arnold, M. S. 'Statutes as judgments: the natural law theory of parliamentary activity in medieval England', 126 *University of Pennsylvania Law Review* (1977) p. 329.
Ault, W. O. 'Village by-laws by common consent', 29 *Speculum* (1954) p. 378.
Austin, J. *Lectures on Jurisprudence*, edited by R. Campbell (London, 1880).
Baildon, W. P. *Select Cases in the Chancery: 1364–1471*, volume 10, Sel. Soc. (London, 1896).
Baker, J. H. *The Reports of John Spelman*, volumes 93 and 94, Sel. Soc. (London, 1976, 1977).
  *Manual of Law French* (Avebury, 1979).
  'New light on *Slade's Case*', 29 *Cambridge Law Journal* (1971) pp. 51, 213.
  *An Introduction to English Legal History* (2nd edition, London, 1979).
  *The Legal Profession and the Common Law: Historical Essays* (London, 1986).
  *Doctor and Student: Christopher Saint Germain*, The Legal Classics Library (Birmingham, Ala., 1988).
  'Famous English canon lawyers: William Bateman, LL.D. (d. 1355), Bishop of Norwich', 3 *Ecclesiastical Law Journal* (1988) p. 3.
Baker, J. H. and S. F. C. Milsom, *Sources of English Legal History: Private Law to 1750* (London, 1986).
Bateson, M. *Borough Customs*, volumes 18 and 21, Sel. Soc. (London, 1904, 1906).
Baylor, M. G. *Conscience in Late Scholasticism and the Young Luther* (Leiden, 1977).

# Bibliography

Bentham, J. *Of Laws in General*, edited by H. L. A. Hart (London, 1970).
Berkowitz, D. S. *Humanist Scholarship and Public Order* (Washington, 1984).
Berman, H. J. *Law and Revolution: The Formation of the Western Legal Tradition* (Cambridge, Mass., 1983).
Black, A. J. *Monarchy and Community: Political Ideas in the Later Conciliar Controversy: 1430–1450* (Cambridge, 1970).
Blayney, M. S. 'Sir John Fortescue and Alain Chartier's *Traité de L'espérance*', 58 *Modern Language Review* (1953) p. 385.
Bolland, W. C. *The Eyre of Kent: 6 & 7 Ed. II*, volume 24, Sel. Soc. (London, 1909).
Borthwick, A. and H. MacQueen. 'Three fifteenth-century cases' [Scottish], *Juridical Review* (1986) p. 123.
Burns, J. H. 'Fortescue and the political theory of *dominium*', 28 *Historical Journal* (1985) p. 777.
Cam, H. M. *Law-Finders and Law-Makers in Medieval England: Collected Essays in Legal and Constitutional History* (London, 1962).
Canning, J. P. *The Political Thought of Baldus de Ubaldis* (Cambridge, 1987).
Carlyle, R. W. and A. J. Carlyle. *A History of Mediaeval Political Theory in the West*, 6 volumes (Edinburgh, 1903–36).
Chambers, R. W. and M. Daunt. *A Book of London English: 1384–1425* (Oxford, 1931).
Chrimes, S. B. *English Constitutional Ideas in the Fifteenth Century* (Cambridge, 1936).
Collas, J. P. *The Year Books of Edward II*, volume 81, Sel. Soc. (London, 1964).
Copleston, F. C. *Aquinas* (Harmondsworth, reprinted 1970).
Cross, R. *Precedent in English Law* (Oxford, 1977).
Cutts, E. *Parish Priests and Their People in the Middle Ages in England* (London, 1898).
Daly, L. J. *The Political Theory of John Wyclif*, Jesuit Studies (Chicago, 1962).
Davies, E. T. *The Political Ideas of Richard Hooker* (New York, reprinted 1972).
de Haas, E. and G. D. G. Hall. *Early Registers of Writs*, volume 87, Sel. Soc. (London, 1970).
del Vecchio, G. *Justice: An Historical and Philosophical Essay*, edited by A. H. Campbell (Edinburgh, 1952).
Dias, R. W. M. *Jurisprudence* (5th edition, London, 1985).
Doe, N. 'Fifteenth-century concepts of law: Fortescue and Pecock', 10 *History of Political Thought* (1989) p. 257.
  'The problem of abhorrent law and the judicial idea of legislative supremacy', 10 *Liverpool Law Review* (1988) p. 113.
  'The positivist thesis in fifteenth-century legal theory and practice', 11 *JLH* (1990) p. 31.
Dworkin, R. M. 'Is law a system of rules', *Essays in Legal Philosophy*, edited by R. S. Summers (Oxford, 1970) p. 25.

## Bibliography

Elton, G. R. *The Tudor Constitution* (2nd edition, Cambridge, 1982).
Enever, F. A. *History of the Law of Distress for Rent and Damage Feasant* (London, 1931).
d'Entreves, A. P. *Natural Law: An Introduction to Legal Philosophy* (2nd edition, London, 1970).
Esmein, A. *History of Continental Criminal Procedure*, translated by J. Simpson, volume 5, The Continental Legal History Series (New York, 1968).
Farr, W. E. *John Wyclif as Legal Reformer* (Leiden, 1974).
Ferguson, A. B. 'Reginald Pecock and the renaissance sense of history', 13 *Studies in the Renaissance* (1966) p. 147.
Fifoot, C. H. S. *History and Sources of the Common Law: Tort and Contract* (London, 1949, 6th Impression, 1969).
Flower, C. T. *Introduction to the Curia Regis Rolls: 1199–1230*, vol. 62, Sel. Soc. (London, 1943).
Fox, J. C. 'Process of imprisonment at common law', 39 *LQR* (1923) p. 46.
Friedrich, C. J. *The Philosophy of Law in Historical Perspective* (2nd edition, Chicago, 1963).
Ganshof, F. L. *Qu'est-ce que La Féodalité?* (2nd edition, Brussels, 1944).
Gaudemet, J. 'Equité et droit chez Gratien et les premiers décrétistes', *La Formation du droit canonique médiéval* (London, 1980) chapter 10.
Genet, J-P. *Four English Political Tracts*, Camden Fourth Series, volume 18 (London, 1977).
Gibbs, A. G. H. (ed.). *The Life and Martyrdom of St. Katherine* (1450), Roxburghe Club Publications, 112 (London, 1884).
Gilbert, F. 'Fortescue's *dominium regale et politicum*', 2 *Medievalia et Humanistica* (1944) p. 88.
Gill, P. E. 'Politics and propaganda in fifteenth-century England: the polemical writings of Sir John Fortescue', 46 *Speculum* (1971) p. 333.
Gillespie, J. L. 'Sir John Fortescue's concept of royal will', 23 *Nottingham Medieval Studies* (1979) p. 47.
Green, V. H. *Bishop Reginald Pecock: A Study in Ecclesiastical History and Thought* (Cambridge, 1945).
Guy, J. A. *The Public Career of Sir Thomas More* (Brighton, 1980).
 *Christopher Saint German on Chancery and Statute*, vol. 6, Sel. Soc., Supplementary Series (London, 1985).
Hamelius, P. (ed.). *Mandeville's Travels*, Early English Text Society, Original Series, 153, 154, 2 volumes (London, 1919, 1923).
Harding, A. *The Law Courts of Medieval England* (London, 1973).
Hart, H. L. A. *The Concept of Law* (Oxford, 1961).
Hazlitt, W. C. *Remains of Early Popular Poetry in England* (1864).
Helmholz, R. H. *Marriage Litigation in Medieval England* (Cambridge, 1974).
 *Canon Law and the Law of England* (London, 1987).
Hinton, R. W. K. 'English constitutional theories from Sir John Fortescue to Sir John Eliot', 75 *English Historical Review* (1960) p. 410.
Holdsworth, W. S. *A History of English Law*, 16 volumes (London, 1922–66).

Holt, J. C. *Magna Carta* (Cambridge, 1965).
Hyams, P. R. 'Trial by ordeal: the key to proof in the early common law', *On the Laws and Customs of England: Essays in Honour of S. E. Thorne*, edited by M. S. Arnold, T. A. Green, S. A. Scully and S. D. White (Chapel Hill, N. C., 1981) p. 90.
Jacob, E. F. *Essays in the Conciliar Epoch* (3rd edition, Manchester, 1963).
  'Reynold Pecock, Bishop of Chichester', 37 *Proceedings of the British Academy* (1951) p. 121.
Jefferson, R. L. 'The uses of natural law in the royal courts of fifteenth-century England', unpublished Ph.D. thesis (University of Utah, 1972).
Jones, G. H. *'Per quod servitium amisit'*, 74 *LQR* (1958) p. 39.
Jurow, K. 'Untimely thoughts: a re-consideration of the origins of due process of law', *AJLH* (1975) p. 265.
Keir, D. K., and F. H. Lawson, *Cases in Constitutional Law*, edited by F. H. Lawson and D. J. Bentley (6th edition, Oxford, 1979).
Kelly, J. M. *'Audi alteram partem'*, 9 *Natural Law Forum* (1964) p. 103.
Kiralfy, A. K. R. *The Action on the Case* (London, 1951).
  'Law and right in legal history', 6 *JLH* (1985) p. 49.
  'Custom in mediaeval English law', 9 *JLH* (1988) p. 26.
Knafla, L. A. 'Conscience in the English common law tradition', 26 *University of Toronto Law Journal* (1976) p. 1.
Kretzmann, N., A. Kenny, and J. Pinborg, (eds.). *The Cambridge History of Later Medieval Philosophy* (Cambridge, 1982).
Kunkel, W. *An Introduction to Roman Legal and Constitutional History*, translated by J. M. Kelly (2nd edition, Oxford, 1973).
Lefebvre, C. 'Natural equity and canonical equity', 8 *Natural Law Forum* (1963) p. 122.
Levi, E. 'Natural law in Roman thought', 15 *Studia et Documenta Historiae et Iuris* (1949) p. 1.
Lewis, E. *Medieval Political Ideas*, 2 volumes (London, 1954).
  'The positivism of Marsiglio of Padua', 38 *Speculum* (1963) p. 541.
Lewis, T. E. 'The history of judicial precedent', 46 *LQR* (1930–2) pp. 207, 341; 47 *LQR* p. 411; 48 *LQR* p. 230.
Lloyd, W. H. 'The equity of a statute', 58 *University of Pennsylvania Law Review* (1910) p. 76.
McGrade, A. S. *The Political Thought of William of Ockham* (Cambridge, 1974).
  'Ockham and the birth of individual rights', *Authority and Power*, Studies on Medieval Law and Government Presented to Walter Ullmann on His Seventieth Birthday, edited by B. Tierney and P. Linehan (Cambridge, 1980) p. 149.
McIlwain, C. H. *The Growth of Political Thought in the West* (New York, 1932).
  'Due process of law in *Magna Carta*', 14 *Columbia Law Review* (1914) p. 27.
  *The High Court of Parliament and Its Supremacy* (New Haven, Conn., 1934).
  *Constitutionalism and the Changing World* (Cambridge, 1939).

Maine, H. S. *Ancient Law* (1861), with an introduction by J. H. Morgan (London, 1917, reprinted 1977).
Maitland, F. W. *Select Passages from the Works of Bracton and Azo*, volume 8, Sel. Soc. (London, 1895).
  *Roman Canon Law in the Church of England* (London, 1898).
  *Forms of Action at Common Law* (Cambridge, 1936).
  'The history of the register of original writs', *Collected Papers*, volume II, edited by H. A. L. Fisher (Cambridge, 1911) p. 110.
Martos, J. *Doors to the Sacred: A Historical Introduction to Sacraments in the Christian Church* (London, 1981).
Meynial, E. 'Notes sur la formation de la théorie du domaine divisé', *Mélanges Fitting*, II (Montpellier, 1908).
Milsom, S. F. C. 'Trespass from Henry III to Edward III', 74 *LQR* (1958) pp. 195, 407, 561.
  'The sale of goods in the fifteenth century', 77 *LQR* (1961) p. 257.
  'Law and fact in legal development', 17 *University of Toronto Law Journal* (1967) p. 1.
  *The Legal Framework of English Feudalism*, Cambridge Studies in English Legal History (Cambridge, 1976).
  *Historical Foundations of the Common Law* (2nd edition, London, 1981).
Moore, E. G., and T. Briden. *Introduction to English Canon Law* (2nd edition, Oxford, 1985).
Nicholas, B. *An Introduction to Roman Law* (Oxford, 1982).
Oakley, F. *The Political Thought of Pierre D'Ailly: The Voluntarist Tradition* (New Haven, Conn., 1964).
Owst, G. R. *Literature and Pulpit in Medieval England* (Oxford, 1961).
Pascoe, L. B. *Jean Gerson: Principles of Church Reform*, Studies in Medieval and Reformation Thought (Leiden, 1973).
Pike, L. O. 'Common law and conscience in the ancient court of chancery', volume II, *Select Essays in Anglo-American Legal History* (Boston, 1908) p. 722.
Plucknett, T. F. T. *Statutes and Their Interpretation in the First Half of the Fourteenth Century*, Cambridge Studies in English Legal History (Cambridge, 1922).
  *The Legislation of Edward I* (Oxford, 1949).
  *A Concise History of the Common Law* (5th edition, London, 1956).
Pollock, F. *A First Book of Jurisprudence* (6th edition, London, 1929).
Pollock, F. and F. W. Maitland. *The History of English Law Before the Time of Edward I*, 2 volumes (2nd edition, Cambridge, 1898, re-issued 1968).
Post, G. *Studies in Medieval Legal Thought: Public Law and the State, 1100–1322* (Princeton, 1964).
Potter, H. *An Historical Introduction to English Law and its Institutions*, edited by A. K. R. Kiralfy (4th edition, London, 1958).
Potts, T. C. *Conscience in Medieval Philosophy* (Cambridge, 1980).
  'Conscience', *The Cambridge History of Later Medieval Philosophy*, edited by N. Kretzmann, A. Kenny and J. Pinborg (Cambridge, 1982) p. 687.
Quillet, J. *Le Défenseur de la paix* (Paris, 1968).
Radin, M. 'The conscience of the court', 48 *LQR* (1932) p. 506.

# Bibliography 187

Raz, J. *The Concept of a Legal System* (Oxford, 1970).
Richardson, H. G. and G. O. Sayles. 'The early statutes', 50 *LQR* (1934) pp. 201, 540.
*Select Cases of Procedure Without Writ under Henry III*, volume 60, Sel. Soc. (London, 1941).
Riess, L. *The History of the English Electoral Law in the Middle Ages*, translated by K. L. Wood-Legh (first published, 1940, New York; reprinted 1973).
Robinson, F. N. (ed.). *The Works of Geoffrey Chaucer*, 2nd edition (Oxford, 1957).
Rueger, Z. 'Gerson's concept of equity and Christopher St. German', 3 *History of Political Thought* (1982) p. 1.
Salmond, W. G. *Jurisprudence*, edited by P. J. FitzGerald (12th edition, London, 1966).
Sayles, G. O. *Select Cases in the Court of King's Bench under Edward I*, volume 57, Sel. Soc. (London, 1938).
Schramm, P. E. *The History of the English Coronation* (Oxford, 1937).
Schoeck, R. J. 'Strategies of rhetoric in St. German's *Doctor and Student*', *The Political Context of Law*, Proceedings of the Seventh British Legal History Conference (London, 1987) p. 77.
Sigmund, P. E. *Nicholas of Cusa and Medieval Political Thought* (Cambridge, Mass., 1963).
Simpson, A. W. B. *A History of the Common Law of Contract: The Rise of the Action of Assumpsit* (Oxford, 1975).
*An Introduction to the History of the Land Law* (2nd edition, Oxford, 1986).
Stein, P. *Regulae Iuris: From Juristic Rules to Legal Maxims* (Edinburgh, 1966).
Stubbs, W. *The Constitutional History of England* (1874-8), abridged by J. Cornford (Chicago, 1979).
Suk, O. 'The connection of the virtues according to Ockham', *Franciscan Studies* (1950) pp. 9, 91.
Thayer, J. B. *A Preliminary Treatise on Evidence at the Common Law* (Boston, 1898).
Thompson, F. *Magna Carta, Its Role in the Making of the English Constitution, 1300–1629* (Minneapolis, Minn. 1948).
Tierney, B. '*Natura id est Deus*: a case of juristic pantheism?', 24 *Journal of the History of Ideas* (1963) p. 307.
Tuck, R. *Natural Rights Theories: Their Origin and Development* (Cambridge, 1979).
Ullmann, W. 'Bartolus on customary law', 52 *Juridical Review* (1940) p. 265.
'Baldus' conception of law', 58 *LQR* (1942) p. 386.
*The Medieval Idea of Law as Represented by Lucas de Penna: A Study in Fourteenth-Century Legal Scholarship* (London, 1946).
*Medieval Papalism: The Political Theories of the Medieval Canonists* (London, 1949).
*Principles of Government and Politics in the Middle Ages* (London, 1961).

*Law and Politics in the Middle Ages: An Introduction to the Sources of Medieval Political Ideas* (London, 1975).
*Medieval Political Thought* (Harmondsworth, 1975).
*Medieval Foundations of Renaissance Humanism* (London, 1977).
Vinaver, E. (ed.). *The Works of Sir Thomas Malory*, 3 volumes (Oxford, 1967).
Wade, E. C. S. and A. W. Bradley. *Constitutional and Administrative Law* (10th edition, London, 1985).
Washington, G. T. 'Damages in contract at common law', 47 *LQR*, (1931) p. 354.
Waterhouse, O. (ed.). *The Non-Cycle Mystery Plays*, Early English Text Society, Extra Series, 104 (London, 1909).
Watkin, T. G. *'Honeste vivere'*, 5 *JLH* (1984) p. 117.
Wilkinson, B. *Constitutional History of England in the Fifteenth Century: 1399–1485* (London, 1964).
*The Later Middle Ages in England: 1216–1485* (London, 1969).
Woolf, P. H. *Bartolus of Sassoferrato* (Cambridge, 1913).
Yale, D. E. C. *'Iudex in propria causa*: an historical excursus', 33 *CLJ* (1974) p. 80.

# INDEX

accessories, 165
account, action of, 113, 122–3
Accursius (*Glossa Ordinaria*, *c*.1240), 35, 49
action on the case, 121, 122, 126
adultery, 73
advowsons, 95 n.56, 113, 115–16, 126, 170
*aequitas*, *see* equity
aid prayer, 24, 118–19
ancient demesne, 17 n.47, 170
annuity, writ of, 114, 147, 161, 172–3
Anselm (1033–1109), 90
appeal of robbery, 114–15, 118
Aquinas, Thomas (1225?–1274), 8 n.5, 154
  conscience and, 133–4
  consent, 13 n.27
  divine law and, 61
  election, 12 n.24
  equality, 106 n.106
  equity, 102
  justice and, 85 n.8, 86, 87, 88, 90 n.36, 91, 95 n.58, 97 n.66, 106 n.106, 120
  law and virtue, 49, 99 n.76
  law as commands, 35
  natural law, 61, 62, 63 n.16, 64 nn.19, 22
  obligatory nature of law, 37 n.21
  promulgation, 38
  reason, 61–2, 64 n.22, 113 n.23
  Saint German and, 135, 176
  teleological view of law, 47
  unjust law, 53, 54–5, 78, 135 n.20
  variability of law, 43 n.65, 44 n.71
arbitration, 71
Aristotle, 8 n.5, 102
arrest, 13, 27, 67, 141, 160, 161
Ascough, Srjt, JCP, 99, 113, 173

Ashton, Nicholas (d.1466), JCP, 23 n.76, 25, 28 n.99, 151 n.89, 170
assault, 73
*assumpsit*, action of, 4, 126
  *see also* contract
attaint, 124–5, 166
*audi alteram partem*, 89 n.28
*audita querela*, 105, 167
Augustine (354–430), 78
authority, for law, *see* autonomist thesis, heteronomist thesis, populist thesis, positivist thesis, voluntarist thesis
autonomist thesis, 4, 5, 51–2, 60, 155, 175–9
avowry, 23
Azo (d.1220), 35, 49 n.103, 94

Babington, William (d.1454), CJCP, 24 n.77, 80 n.85, 100, 118 n.43, 149, 169, 171
Baldus de Ubaldis (1327–1400)
  equity and, 102 n.92
  law and virtue, 49 n.100
  natural law, 62 n.8, 63 n.16, 64 n.20
Bartolus, of Sassoferrato (d.1357)
  customary law, 19, 40, 42 n.60
  natural law, 63 n.16
  representative legislature, 12
  species of law, 40
  statute, 19
Bateman, William (Bishop) (d.1355), 2 n.5
benefit of clergy, 68, 157 n.7
Bereford, William de (d.1326), CJCP, 23, 28 n.97, 104 n.99
Biel, Gabriel (d.1495), 91 n.43, 134
bill of deceit, 2, 142
  *see also* deceit
Billing, Thomas (d.1481), Srjt, CJKB, 85, 89

## Index

borough english, 41
Bracton, Henry (1200?–1268?), 7, 25
  conscience, 146
  distress, 88 n.26
  equity, 106
  essoins, 116–17
  *ius*, three precepts of, 98 n.74
  jury, 146
  justice, 85 nn.1, 8, 87 n.17, 90 n.35, 91 n.38, 95
  law and justice, 97 nn.68, 71
  law and virtue, 49
  law as commands, 35
  law-making and, 11, 12
  natural law, 64 n.20, 69 n.48, 95
  positivism in, 55 n.121
  species of law, 40
  supremacy of law, 27
  theocratic kingship, 10
  variability of law, 43
  *venire facias clericum*, writ of, 161 n.29
Brian (Bryan), Sir Thomas (d.1500), Srjt, CJCP (1471–1500), 10 n.15, 22 n.70, 23 n.72, 29 n.105, 30, 42 n.60, 80 n.88, 81, 101, 104 n.99, 125 n.74, 150 n.84, 152, 161
Brutus, legend of, 9 n.8
Butler, Srjt, 16 n.46

Candish, Srjt, 165 n.58
canon law
  canonists, 4, 7, 18 n.50, 61, 76 n.71, 85 n.1, 88 n.25, 154
  church courts, 2, 136, 158
  conscience, 134 n.15, 136, 144, 152 n.99
  divine law and, 61
  divorce, 140
  equity in, 102 n.92
  jurisprudence in, 2, 144
  natural law and, 61, 65
  Roman Law and, 2
  Saint German and, 136, 176
  system of rules, 2
*capias*, writ of, 24, 127–8, 141, 145, 160
Carletus, Angelus, 136 n.23
casuistry, 5, 136, 151, 154
Catesby, John (d.1487), Srjt, JCP, 19 n.57, 20 n.60, 23 n.72, 41, 74 n.63, 82 n.92, 112 n.22, 147, 151 n.89, 168 n.75
chancery, 72, 124, 132, 135 n.21, 136, 144, 153–4, 164, 173, 176

Chantrell, William (d.1438), Srjt, 172 n.98
Chaucer, Geoffrey, 133 n.3, 156 n.2
Cheyne, JCP, 165
Choke, Richard (d.1483), Srjt, JCP, 24 n.78, 28, 35 n.13, 42 n.58, 71, 79 n.81, 82, 103 n.94, 140, 160, 160 n.28, 161
classical positivism, 33, 34 n.5
  *see also* positive law, positivist thesis
Cockayne, John (d.1428/29?), JCP, 104, 113
*comen droit*, 28, 79–82, 89, 99, 101 n.87
common law
  authority of reason and, 108–31
  common erudition and, 23 n.72
  conscience and, 132–54
  custom of the realm as, 2, 41–2, 80 n.88, 82, 127
  early, 1
  judges as legislators of, 22–4
  judicial consent and, 22–4, 33, 177
  maxims of, 36, 172
  morality and, *see* heteronomist thesis
  natural law and, 70–74
  popular consent and, 7, 19, 22–6
  principles of, 36
  promulgation, 39
  *see also* law, precedent, substantive law
*common weal*, 14, 48–9, 71, 86, 102
*communitas regni*, 11
conciliarist thought, 8, 13 n.31
confessions, 132, 136, 146, 176
Coningsby, Humphrey (d.1535), Srjt, JKB, 112 n.21
conscience, 132–54, 175–9
  administration of law and, 137, 144–53
  chancery and, 132, 144
  common law and, 58, 132–54
  confessions and, 132, 136, 146, 176
  *droit* and, 138–9
  judicial conscience, 144–6
  jurors and, 137, 138–9, 144, 146–8
  litigants, of, 137, 144, 148–53
  positivist thesis and, 56–7
  preaching and, 132
  theory and, 133–7
  reason and, 46 n.86, 137, 138, 142–3, 145
  substantive law and, 5, 56–7, 103, 104, 137–44, 153–4
*synderesis*, 133, 134

# Index

wager of law, and, 150–3
  *see also* Saint German
consent, 4, 5, 7–26, 33, 59, 80, 83, 88, 93, 131, 175–9
  *see also* populist thesis
conspiracy, 145
continual claim, 157–8
contract, 1, 47
  corporations and, 101
  involuntary, 2, 138
  privity, 171–2
  *see also* assumpsit, debt
Cottesmore, John (d.1439), Srjt, JCP, 28 n.96, 79 n.81, 161 n.33, 170
covenant, 47, 93, 121, 142
Culpeper (Colepeper), John (d.1414), Srjt, JCP, 116 n.35
custom, *see* common law, local custom
custumals, 20–2, 72, 88 n.25
  *see also* local custom
Cynus of Pistoia (early fourteenth century), 97

D'Ailly, Pierre (1350–1420)
  abhorrent law, status of, 78
  conscience and, 134 n.14
  divine law and, 62, 66 n.34
  election and, 9 n.6
  equity and, 102 n.92
  justice and, 90 n.36, 96 n.64
  law as commands, 35
  natural law and, 62, 66 n.34
  rights, idea of, 9 n.6, 94
  Saint German and, 135, 154, 176
  secular authority and, 8
  species of law, 34 n.3, 41 n.50
  supremacy of law, 26
damages, 2, 114, 123, 124–5, 129, 145, 164
*damnum absque injuria*, 50, 123
Danby, Robert (d.1471?), Srjt, JCP, CJCP, 24, 25, 30 n.109, 48, 71, 117, 128, 130, 141 n.42, 147, 170
Danvers, Robert (d.1467), JCP, 25, 140 n.34, 170
debt, 4, 21, 23, 24, 25, 29, 30, 72, 100, 104–5, 114, 122–3, 126–7, 139–40, 141, 143, 149, 158–9, 160, 164, 165, 171–2
  *see also* contract, *assumpsit*
debtors, 29, 141
deceit, 23, 25, 100, 122, 127
  *see also* bill of deceit
defamation, 21

demurrer, 2 n.7, 23, 25, 142
detinue, 130, 150, 151–2
Dillon, Peter, 121, 122
distraint, 30, 130, 168
  damage feasant, 88
distress, process of, 58, 148, 160, 161
divine law, 5 n.16, 50, 60–70, 73, 83, 108, 110, 131, 132, 134, 135, 157, 175–9
  legislation and, 66–70
  *see also* natural law
Donington, William (d.1485), 125
*droit*, as a right, 94–5, 170
  *see also comen droit*
due process of law, 27–31
duty, idea of, 68, 95, 99, 138

Elderkar (Ellerker), John (d.1438/9?), Srjt, 89 n.28, 125 n.74
election, 8–9, 18 n.50, 57
embracery, 69
entry, writ of, 105, 157–8
equity, 84, 101–6
  as fairness, 103–4
  canonical, 102 n.92
  equal mischief and, 105, 106 n.105
  equity of a statute, 104–6, 107, 176
  practice and, 100, 103–6, 115, 117, 131, 176
  similarity, idea of, 105–6
  theory and, 101–3, 115, 176
essoins, 21, 116–17
estoppel, 17
eternal law, *see* Natural Law
excommunication, 126

Fairfax, Guy (d.1495), Srjt, JKB, 38, 74 n.63, 82, 117 n.41
fairs, 28, 67, 103
false imprisonment, 29, 73, 81, 128
felony, 29, 68, 81, 99, 148
feudalism
  law-making and, 7, 10–14, 19
  nature, 10–11
Fineux (Fyneux), Sir John (d.1526), CJKB (1495–1526) 15, 23 n.76, 24, 30 n.106, 47, 48, 49 n.98, 73–4, 112 n.19, 122 n.56, 140
fire, liability for, 2, 127
Fitzherbert, Sir Anthony (d.1538), JCP (1522–38) 99
*Fleta*, 159 n.22
Fortescue, Sir John (1394?–1476?), Srjt, CJKB (1442–61)

# Index

abhorrent law, status of, 53–4, 75–8, 79, 175
canon law, 65, 79
common law, 19, 22, 26, 32, 41
conscience in, 133, 134, 146 n.63
custom, 40–1, 79
deterrence, 37 n.26
divine law and, 61, 75
election and, 8–9
equity and, 102–3
eternal law and, 61
in practice, 15, 19, 23, 35 n.14, 38, 42 nn.63, 64, 57–8, 74 n.63, 105 n.103, 112 n.19, 115 n.31, 118, 123 n.64, 129 n.96, 133, 141, 142, 157, 168 n.77, 171 n.94
*ius* and *lex*, 40, 41, 94
jurors, 43, 76–7, 146
justice and, 85, 86, 87, 88, 90–2, 94, 97–8, 120 n.50
justice and natural law, 95–7, 106, 176
justification for populist theory, 18–9
law and justice, 97–8, 99
law and virtue, 35, 49–50, 59, 98
law as commands, 34, 35
law as sacrosanct, 69–70
law-making in, 7–8, 12–13, 16, 23, 164 n.51
law, obligatory nature, 37
life, 3, 177
local custom, 26, 41
maxims, 36 n.19
natural law and, 40, 54, 60–1, 63–5, 75–8
politics and, 9 n.8
populist theory and, 7–10, 12–13, 16, 19, 21, 136, 177
positivist thesis, 53–4, 177
promulgation, 38
purpose of law, 47–8, 49–50, 98
reason and, 64, 96, 110
rights, idea of, 94
species of law, 39, 40, 41
supremacy of law, 27
tensions in, 83, 179
theocratic kingship and, 9–10, 16 n.44
variability of law, 43–4
works, 3 n.13, 7
franchises, 89
Fray, John (d.1458/61?), CB, 15 n.43, 27

Frowicke (Frowyk), Sir Thomas (d.1506), Srjt, CJCP (1502–6) 116 n.32, 126–7, 147 n.68
Fulthorpe, Thomas (d.1456/7?), JCP, 3 n.10, 36 n.16, 119, 169 n.85

gage deliverance, 168
Gascoigne, Sir William (d.1419), CJKB (1400–13) 15, 16 n.44, 145, 170 n.89
gavelkind, 20, 41, 79
Gerson, Jean (1363–1429)
abhorrent law, status of, 78
divine law and, 62, 66
election and, 9 n.6
equity and, 102 n.92
justice and, 85, 90 n.36
law as commands, 35 n.12
law, obligatory nature, 37
natural law and, 62, 66
promulgation, 38 n.29
purpose of law, 47
rights, idea of, 94
Saint German and, 35 n.12, 62 n.9, 66, 135, 154, 176
secular authority and, 8–9
supremacy of law, 26 n.89
variability of law, 44 n.71
Giraldus Cambrensis (1145–1223), 144
Godrede (Godered), William (d.1443–7?), Srjt, 124
Gratian (*Decretum*, c.1140), 34 n.3, 65 n.23, 78, 95
Gray's Inn, 121
Grosseteste, Robert (1168–1253), 11 n.23

Hals, John (d.1434?) Srjt, JCP, 104 n.100, 112, 149, 165, 166, 170
Hankford, William (d.1423), JCP, 42 n.64, 50, 57 n.128, 81 n.91, 89, 100 n.84, 101, 106 n.105, 124, 126, 129, 150, 158 n.13, 164, 167
hats, 137–8, 143
Heidon, counsel, 158 n.17
Hengham, 23
heteronomist thesis, 5–6, 74–83, 178
*see also* morality
Hill, Robert (d.1425?) JCP, 14, 20, 50, 79 n.81, 89, 95 n.56, 127
Hody, CJKB, 17, 23 n.76, 57
Hooker, Richard (1553–1600) 62 n.7, 70 n.50
Horton, Roger (d.1423), Srjt, 104 n.100, 125 n.74

# Index

Hostiensis (Henricus de Segusia) (d.1271), 144 n.56
human law, 4, 33–59, 83, 84, 97–9, 175–9
Hussey (Huse), William (d.1495), CJKB (1481–95) 10 n.15, 23 n.72, 24, 36 n.17, 82, 114–15, 116, 140 n.34, 164 n.49
Hyndestone, Srjt, 28

Illingworth, CB, 71, 140
imparlance, 117
inconvenience, 90, 129
  concept of consistency and, 155, 161–6
  inconsistency between cases and, 162, 163–5
  mischief and, 6, 155, 169–74, 178
  positivism and, 6, 155
  reason and, 166–8
  substantive wrongs and, 167
Inner Temple, 122
innkeepers, 2, 42, 82
*ius*, three precepts of, 98–9
*iustitia*, see Justice

Jenney, William (d.1483), Srjt, 168 n.75, 172 n.98
John of Salisbury (*Policraticus*, 1159), 78
judges, 13, 14, 50, 95, 111
  abhorrent law, status of, 57–9, 78–83
  as legislators, *see* common law
  conscience of, 137, 144–6, 176
  impartiality of, 88–90
  natural law and, 70–4, 78–83, 95, 108
  positivist thesis and, 57–9, 100
June (Juyn), John (d.1440), JCP, 158, 172
jury, 16, 18 n.50, 25, 58, 79–80, 89 n.28, 90, 118, 124–5, 137, 145, 150, 166
  conscience of, 138–9, 146–8, 176
justice, 84–107, 132, 175–7
  and rights, 84, 92–5
  as virtue, 86–7
  consideration of others and, 87–90
  equity and, 101, 102–3
  giving each his due, 90–2, 106, 111, 121, 131, 176
  law and, 97–9, 106, 175
  moral texture, 5 n.16, 84, 92
  natural law and, 92, 95–7, 120
  practice and, 99, 111, 120–1
  reason and, 79, 84, 110–11, 120–1, 126, 130–1, 176

substance of, 85–92
theocratic idea of, 85, 86
justifications, 5, 89, 136, 139, 143, 172, 176–8

Keble (Kebell), Thomas (d.1500), Srjt, 23 n.72, 30 n.109, 74 n.63, 79 n.81, 102 n.92, 112 n.22, 116 n.32
king, 2, 3 n.10, 7–19, 21, 26–9, 39, 55, 57, 67, 74, 85, 99, 100, 102, 118, 138, 145, 160, 170, 177
  *see also* legislation, theocratic government
Kingsmill, John (d.1509), JCP, 46 n.86, 49

law
  abhorrent, status of, 51–9
  as an entity, 4
  as made, 34, 35
  autonomy of, 4, 33, 178
  commands, 4, 33, 34–8
  deterrence and, 37–8
  development of, and pleading, 22–3
  due process of, 27–31
  French, 43, 53
  maxims of, 36, 172
  obedience to, 17–18
  obligatory nature, 36–8
  principle of, 36
  promulgation, 38–9, 132, 139
  public utility and, 48–9
  purpose of, 4, 5, 33, 47–51, 98
  reason and, 111–3, 114, 124, 126, 137, 164, 173, 179
  rules and, 1–3, 4, 6, 23, 36
  social control and, 3
  species of, 39–42
  supremacy of, 26–31
  variability, 33, 43–6
  virtue and, 49–51, 98
  *see also* canon law, common law, custom, divine law, human law, legislation, local custom, natural law, populist thesis, positivist thesis, Roman Law
legislation
  as a judgment, 15, 25
  conscience and, 56, 57, 58, 137–9, 153
  consent and, 7–19, 48, 59
  equity of a statute, 104–6, 115
  fixed term and perpetual, 44–6
  justification for consent, 17–19

local custom and, 22, 42, 81
mischief and, 156–7, 171, 178
positivist thesis and, 55–9, 74
theocratic, 66–70
types of, 39, 40–1
literature, non-legal, 50 n.108, 51 n.110, 62 n.5, 67 n.37, 90 n.33, 108–110, 113, 119, 130, 132, 156, 161–2, 167
Littleton, Richard, 122
Littleton, Sir Thomas (1422–1481), JCP (1466–81)
  abhorrent custom and, 79, 80–1, 82
  common law, 19, 42
  continual claim, 157–8
  equity, 104 n.100
  inconvenience, 168 n.78, 171 n.96
  life, 4
  local custom, 19, 41
  maxims and, 36
  mischief, 157–8, 161
  *nemo iudex in sua causa*, 88, 89, 92
  reason, 79, 88, 89, 112 n.22, 121–2
  works, 4 n.15
livery, 2, 48
local custom
  against reason, 42 n.61, 79–83, 108, 176
  as law, 41–2
  consent and, 20–2, 33, 59, 80
  natural law and, 72
  parliamentary legislation and, 22, 42, 81
  prescription and, 28, 80
  village customs, 20 n.59
Lodington, counsel, 168 n.77
Lollards, 3 n.12, 37, 51 n.108, 67–8
  *see also* Wyclif
Lucas de Penna (d.c.1390), 85 nn.1, 3, 90 n.36, 97, 99
Lynwood, William (d.1446)
  rejection of conciliarism, 13 n.31
  theocratic government and, 10 n.15
  variability of law, 43 n.67

Magna Carta, 31, 46, 117 n.40
maintenance, 69, 123
Major, John (1469–1550), 9 n.6
majoritarianism, 18
Malory, Thomas, 109 n.8
*malum, prohibitum* and *in se*, 73–4
Mandeville, *Travels*, 62 n.5
Markham, John (d.1479), Srjt, 29, 36 n.18, 42, 72, 118 n.43, 119, 123, 128 n.88, 129, 141 n.40, 145, 151 n.89, 152 n.93
married women, 30
Marsilius of Padua (d.1343?)
  justice in, 85 n.3, 91 n.39, 99
  law as commands, 35
  law, obligatory nature, 37 n.21, 39 n.36
  natural law and, 65 n.23, 75 n.64
  populist theory of law-making, 11–12, 18 n.50
  positivist thesis and, 55 n.121
  rights, 95 n.56
  variability of law, 43 n.65
Martin, John (d.1436), JCP, 23 n.76, 30, 37 n.25, 79 n.81, 90, 95 n.56, 105, 114, 146 n.63, 157 n.6, 158 n.17, 161 n.33, 165, 167, 168 n.77, 169 n.85, 170, 172
*Mirror of Justices*, 26, 39, 42 n.58, 43, 46 n.86
mischief
  inconvenience and, 6, 155, 169–74
  moral wrong and, 5 n.16, 156–7
  legislation and, 156–7
  positivist thesis and, 55–7, 58–9, 74
  procedural vexation and, 159–61, 176
  substantive wrongs and, 156–7, 159–60
  without redress, as, 157–9, 176
Moile (Moyle), Walter (d.1480), JCP, 16 n.44, 23 n.76, 25, 27 n.95, 28, 35 n.14, 36 n.17, 41, 80, 117, 119 n.47, 123, 149–50, 157 n.5, 166, 170
morality, 4, 5, 33, 51–2, 59, 60, 62–4, 65 n.27, 75, 83, 84, 97, 104, 106, 110–11, 132, 136, 139, 155, 175–9
  *see also* heteronomist thesis, natural law
Mordant (Mordaunt), John (d.1504), Srjt, 16 n.44, 28, 142 n.46
More, Thomas, 134 n.15, 135 n.18, 136 n.24
murder, 38, 42 n.64, 51 n.110, 68, 69, 157, 160, 167

natural law, 60–83, 84, 85, 131, 132, 175–9
  access to, 64–6, 83
  commands of, 62–3
  divine law and, 60–2
  divine origin, 61–3
  eternal law and, 61

*Index*

higher law, as, 74–83, 175
immutability, 63
instinct and, 64, 70
interstitial use of, 71–2, 83, 102
judges and, 70–4, 83, 108
justice and, 92, 95–7, 106, 120
public utility and, 71
purpose of, 63–4
reason and, 61–2, 63, 65, 110–11
scripture and, 65
substance of, 62–4
theocratic legislation, 66–70, 176
Nedham (Nedeham), John (d.1480), JCP, JKB, 72, 112 n.22, 151 n.89, 158 n.17, 160
Neele, Richard (d.1486), JCP, 3 n.10, 16, 24 n.78, 36, 165 n.54
*nemo iudex in sua causa*, 88–90
*see also* justice
Newton, Richard (d.1448), CJCP, 3 n.10, 17, 36, 89 n.28, 100, 113, 119 n.47, 142, 152, 157 n.6, 167, 172 nn.98, 100, 173
Nicholas of Cusa (d.1464)
election and, 9 n.6
law, obligatory nature, 18, 37
natural law, 62 n.7
obedience to law, 18
purpose of law, 47 n.89
*quod omnes tangit*, 18
secular authority and, 8
supremacy of law, 26
theocratic kingship and, 10
Norton, Richard (d.1420), Srjt, 158

Ockham, William of (1280–1349), 7
anointing, 10
consent, 12 n.24
justice and, 86 n.9
purpose of law, 49 n.102
*quod omnes tangit*, 18 n.51
rights, idea of, 94

Parliament, 8, 9, 13, 27, 35, 39, 44–6, 55, 57, 67, 70, 74, 82, 117, 137, 138, 156, 157, 177
binding its successors, 46, 138
intention of, 44, 102, 103, 143 n.50
positivist thesis and, 55–7
whole community present, 8, 13, 15, 16 n.46, 34
*see also* legislation
*Paston Letters*, 148
Paston, William (d.1444), Srjt, JCP, 37 n.25, 58, 95 n.56, 105 n.103, 119 n.47, 160, 165 n.58, 167 n.74, 168, 170, 171, 173
Pecock, Reginald (1395?–1460?), Bishop
abhorrent law, status of, 52–3, 75, 77–8
anticipates Fortescue, 3 n.13, 13, 32, 176
common law, 19 n.57, 26, 113 n.23
conciliarist thought and, 13 n.31
conscience in, 102, 134, 150 n.86
deterrence, 37 n.26
divine law and, 34, 37, 50, 62, 134
election and, 9
equity, 101–2
inconvenience, 162 n.35
justice and, 85, 87, 88, 89, 90–1, 92–3, 95, 96, 101, 120
justification for populist theory, 17–8
law as commands, 13, 34
law as made, 34, 39
law, obligatory nature, 17–18, 34, 37
life, 3 n.12, 177
local custom, 19, 22, 41
mischief and, 156 n.2
natural law and, 50, 52, 60–3, 71 n.54, 77–8, 95, 102
obedience to law, 17–18
populist theory of law, 13–14, 17–18, 19, 88, 177
positive law, 34
positivist thesis and, 52–3, 54
purpose of law, 47, 50
reason and, 52, 61–2, 63, 65, 89, 93, 95, 102, 110, 113 n.23, 134
rights, idea of, 18, 84, 92–3, 94, 106, 176
rules and, 36 n.17
species of law, 39
supremacy of law, 27
usury, 97 n.67
variability of law, 44, 52
works, 3 n.12, 7
perjury, 147, 148, 151
*per quod servitium amisit*, 129
*persona mixta*, 10 n.15
Philip the Chancellor (d.1236), 133
piepowder courts, 103
Pigot, Richard (d.1483), Srjt, 82 n.92, 112 n.21, 168 n.75
Pope, the, 9 n.7, 74 n.63
populist thesis, 4–6, 7–32, 51, 60, 88, 177–8

## Index

Port, John (1472?–1540), JKB, *Notebook*, 9 n.8, 30 n.109, 47 n.91, 49 n.98, 74 n.63, 95 n.56, 100 n.82, 102 n.92, 104 n.100, 122 n.56, 157 n.6
Portington, John (d.1454?). Srjt, 127 n.83, 173
positive law, 23, 25, 34–5, 71
positivist thesis, 4, 5, 6, 33–59, 60, 74–5, 83, 155, 171, 173–4, 178
  see also classical positivism
*praecipe quod reddat*, 24, 116, 117, 149, 159, 170
*praemunire*, 39, 126
preaching, 132, 176
precedent, 22–5, 108, 115, 116, 130, 160, 163, 164
  see also common law
prescription, 28, 80–1
  see also local custom
principals, 165
Prisot (Prysot), John (d.1461), Srjt, CJCP, 25, 28, 35, 37 n.25, 42 n.60, 80, 95 n.56, 116, 125 n.74, 128 n.90, 130, 147, 149, 157 n.6, 160, 161 n.33, 164, 166, 167, 168 nn.76, 78
procedural vexation, 130, 159–61, 176
prohibition, 158

*quare clausum fregit*, 24
*quare impedit*, 113, 169
*quod omnes tangit*, 18–19
*quod principi placuit*, 19, 53

reason
  appeal to, 5, 56, 67, 88, 106, 113–15, 119–20, 153
  as authority, 108–131, 132, 177–9
  as foundation of common law, 112–13
  as good sense, 79, 111, 113–20, 128, 131, 153, 167, 176
  as justice, 79, 111, 120–30, 131, 153, 176
  custom and, 79–83
  delays and, 117–19, 131
  double liability and, 121, 129–30
  double recompense and, 121, 124–5
  imbalances and, 111, 120–1, 176
  inconvenience and, 166–8
  law and, 111–13, 114, 124, 126, 164, 173, 179
  practice and, 110–31
  punishment and, 111, 121, 125–8
  recompense for loss and, 111, 120–3, 157
  theory and practice, 110–11
  theory's justice and, 84, 95, 120–1, 126, 131, 176

treating like alike and, 106, 115–17, 131, 167
  see also natural law, Fortescue, Pecock
receipt, 36, 116, 117, 163, 170
Rede, Robert (d.1519) JKB, CJCP, 3 n.10, 128
*res publica*, 11
Rickhill, William (d.1407), JCP, 114 n.26, 118
rights, idea of, 84, 92–5, 106, 176
  practice and, 94, 95 n.56
  see also *droit*, justice
*rigor iuris*, 84, 99–101, 106, 143, 155, 171, 178
  rejection of, 100–1
robbery, 69, 157, 160, 167
  see also appeal of robbery
Rolf, Thomas (d.1440), Srjt, 36 n.18, 41, 157 n.5
Roman Law, 12, 18, 19, 35, 36 n.19, 40, 69 n.48, 76 n.71, 79 n.82, 85 n.1, 90
  canon law and, 2, 7
  civilians and, 4, 84, 94
  gifts and, 141 n.40
  *ius*, three precepts of, 98
  natural law and, 64 n.21
  *ratio legis*, 112
Rufinus (writing c.1157), 64 n.21

Saint German, Christopher (1460?–1540)
  abhorrent law, status of, 76, 77, 82, 175
  common law, 19, 26, 42, 135–6, 177
  conscience and, 134–6, 146
  consent, 26
  influences on, 35 n.12, 62 n.9, 66, 134, 135–6, 154, 176
  justice and, 95 n.58
  law and virtue, 50 n.104
  law as commands, 35 n.12, 37 n.22
  life, 3, 137
  local custom, 19, 41
  maxims, 36 n.19
  natural law and, 62 n.7, 63 n.15, 64 n.19, 76, 82
  reason, 112–3
  rules, 36 n.17
  theocratic government, 10 n.13
  variability of law, 43 n.67
  works, 3 n.14

## Index

Saunders, Sir Edward (d.1576), Srjt, 144
*scire facias*, 114, 172
sheriffs, 29, 58, 128, 137, 142, 149, 159, 160, 161
Smith, Thomas (1514?–77), 16, 34 n.1, 70 n.50
souls, 67, 68 n.42, 72–3, 132, 140, 146, 148, 150, 151, 176
Stanton, Hervey de (d.1327), JCP, 23
Statham, Nicholas (d.1472), 133 n.4
Stillington, Robert, Bishop, LC, 34 n.2, 85
Stonore, John de (d.1354), JCP, CJCP, 105 n.102, 112 n.18
Strangeways, James (d.1443?), Srjt, JCP, 171 n.95
*subpoena*, 72
substantive law
 absence of, 1–2
 conscience and, 137–44
 emergent, 1–6
 implicit, 1, 5
 judges and, 2, 5
 legislation and, 2
 meaning, 2
 *see also* common law, law
Sulyard, John (d.1488), Srjt, 37 n.25
*supersedeas*, 124, 141
supremacy of law, see Law
*synderesis*, 133, 134
 *see also* conscience

taxation, 12, 13, 14, 16 n.44, 17, 27, 34
theocratic government, 9–10
theocratic law, 66–70
Thirning, William (d.1413), JCP, CJCP, 42 n.64, 50, 57 n.128, 89, 112 n.22, 146 n.63, 158 n.13, 163, 168 n.77
Thomism, 4, 62, 84, 87, 113 n.23
 *see also* Aquinas
Thorpe, Robert de (d.1372) Srjt, CJCP, 23 n.73, 39
*Three Considerations*, 86–7, 98–99
Tirwit (Tyrwhit), Robert (d.1428), Srjt, 15 n.43, 57, 89 n.28, 101 n.87
torture, 53
Townsend (Townshend), Roger (d.1493), JCP (1485–93) 73, 95 n.56, 101
treason, 31, 138
Tremaile (Tremayle), Thomas (d.1508), Srjt, JKB, 49 n.99, 95 n.56, 105 n.103, 142 n.46

trespass, 4, 21, 25, 29, 30, 48, 73, 80, 82, 90, 99, 122, 124, 125, 129, 140, 143, 145, 149, 158, 159, 163 n.45, 164, 165
trial by battle, 114–15
Trovomara (Trovamala), Baptista, 136 n.23
trusts, *see* uses

*ultra vires*, 29
usage, 4, 5, 7, 19–26, 41, 42, 100 n.84, 142, 177
 *see also* common law, judges, local custom
uses, 58, 140
usury, 97, 143

Vampage, John, counsel, 112 n.18
Vavasour, John (d.1506) JCP, 15, 16, 36 n.17, 147 n.68
*venire facias clericum*, 160–1
vice, 49–51, 86
view, 117
virtue, 49–51, 86–7, 92, 98
*volenti non fit injuria*, 36, 88
voluntarist thesis, 14, 33, 34, 35, 60, 74, 84, 91–2, 97, 155, 175–9
 *see also* autonomist thesis
voucher to warranty, 118–19

wager of law, 21, 23, 25, 117, 148
 conscience and, 150–3
Wangford, Srjt, 159
waste, writ of, 58
weirs, 67, 156
wills, 68, 140–1
 administrators, 104–5, 114
 executors, 21, 23, 30, 72–3, 100, 104–5, 114, 139–40, 143
 married women, and, 30
 testators, 21, 23, 139–40
writs, 29, 114, 116, 159, 170
 abatement of, 130, 158, 160, 169, 170
 inconsistent, 114
 procedure without, 1
 Register of, 1, 2 n.4
 return of, 24, 128, 149, 160, 161
 system of, 1–2
Wyclif, John (d.1384), 49 n.100, 51 n.108, 63 n.11, 65, 109 n.6, 144, 156 n.1
 *see also* Lollards

Yaxley, counsel, 125 n.74, 127
Yelverton, William (d.1476), JKB, 23, 35, 36, 71, 74 n.63, 112 n.22, 171 n.94
Young (Yonge), Thomas (d.1477), Srjt, 123, 158, 168 n.75, 172 n.98